MANUAL OF OREGON
TREES AND SHRUBS

WARREN R. RANDALL

ROBERT F. KENISTON

DALE N. BEVER

EDWARD C. JENSEN*

**Dendrologists, Past and Present
Oregon State University**

D1775171

Reprinted by
O.S.U. Book Stores, Inc.
Corvallis, Oregon
1994

Litho—U.S.A.

*1958 Edition by Warren R. Randall
1968 Revision by Robert F. Keniston
1974 Revision by Dale N. Bever
1981 Revision by Dale N. Bever and Edward C. Jensen
1988 and 1990 Revision by Edward C. Jensen

0-88246-019-6

PREFACE TO FIRST EDITION

This manual has been prepared to aid student forest-ers and game managers in the identification of major tree and shrub species to be found in Oregon. Emphasis is placed on Oregon species. They are also almost all species of importance in other Pacific Northwest states. No attempt has been made to include all native woody plants.

Although the botanical description of each species is by no means comprehensive, sufficient detail has been included for identification. As an aid to identification several keys are included. In addition to the two large keys for the conifers and broadleaf species, there are separate keys for each genus that has more than one species.

The scientific names used in this manual follow the U.S. Forest Service "Check List of Native and Natural-ized Trees of the United States," issued in 1953. Scien-tific names for shrubs are in accord with those found in "Standardized Plant Names," 2nd edition, published in 1942.

The cover and all illustrations in the Introduction are the work of Robert R. Kinkead, Jr.

W. R. Randall

Corvallis, Oregon
April 1, 1957

PREFACE TO THE 1968 EDITION

For over 18 years Warren R. (Casey) Randall served with vigor and enthusiasm as dendrologist and professor of forest management at Oregon State University's School of Forestry. At the time of his decease in 1966 he had intended to revise the first edition of this book. He wished to correct two systematic errors and various mechanical and random errors, and generally to improve the accuracy and usefulness of his book. He believed that the addition of illustrations to the descriptions of the trees and shrubs would be particularly helpful. He also wished to add descriptions of a few species, such as white manzanita *(Arctostaphylos viscida)*.

In order to carry out Casey Randall's intentions as nearly as possible, the second author, a long-time friend and colleague, has undertaken the revision. Seventy-four illustrations have been added. These are line drawings prepared under the direction of Charles R. Ross, Oregon State University Extension Forester for extension circulars entitled "Oregon Tree Quiz," "Western Oregon Shrub Quiz," and "Eastern Oregon Shrub Quiz." W.R. Randall had provided advice and suggestions in the preparation of these circulars. These 74 pictures have been reproduced here through the courtesy of the Federal Cooperative Extension Service.

In the revised edition, descriptions of four species were added; descriptions of several varieties and minor species were condensed, and most keys have been revised. An attempt was made to correct errors and to improve the accuracy and clarity wherever possible. A guiding principle was to minimize the enlargement of the book so that it would remain a truly pocket-size manual.

Robert F. Keniston
March 1, 1968

PREFACE TO THE 1981 EDITION

Plant taxonomy is not static to the dismay of foresters and forestry students alike. Every year new information is discovered, and opinions changed, regarding the classification of plants. To keep this field manual up-to-date, we felt that a new edition was required. The structure of the manual remains unaltered, although individual entries may differ from previous editions.

The intent of this manual is, as always, to aid users in identifying the primary trees and shrubs native or naturalized to Oregon. Therefore, several species included in previous editions but not meeting these qualifications were dropped (e.g. the true cedars, blue spruce and Monterey pine). Scientific names used in the manual follow those of Hitchcock and Cronquist in **Flora of the Pacific Northwest**, 1973, which is the most commonly used flora in the Northwest; whenever possible, common names do the same. In several cases names used by Hitchcock do not agree with those of the latest U.S.F.S. checklist, **Checklist of United States Trees** by Little, 1979 (most notably *Calocedrus - Libocedrus);* in those instances we have followed Hitchcock, but made note of the discrepency.

Dale N. Bever & Edward C. Jensen
August 18, 1980

PREFACE TO THE 1990 EDITION

Differences between the 1988 and 1990 editions are minor. If you find any errors, or have ideas for improvements, please let me know and I'll incorporate them in subsequent editions.

Edward C. Jensen
July 30, 1990

CONTENTS

INTRODUCTION

All species included in this manual are woody plants. Such plants are characterized by the following features:

1. **Perennial:** The plant lives for many years. The life span for some species may be measured in terms of decades and for others in terms of centuries.

2. **Persistent Stems:** The aerial portion of the plant remains alive indefinitely, i.e., the stems do not die back to the ground each winter as do many herbaceous plants.

3. **Cambial Tissue:** The cambium is the layer of meristematic tissue located between the youngest layer of wood and the inner bark. Cambial cells are capable of repeated division and enable the plant to increase in diameter. Each year the cambium produces new xylem (see next characteristic) and new phloem (inner bark).

4. **Vascular Tissue:** The phloem and xylem are the vascular or conductive tissues. The phloem is the principal tissue involved in the translocation of manufactured foods. The xylem, or wood, imparts strengh to the stem, and is the tissue involved in conducting water and minerals upward from the roots.

The distinction between trees and shrubs, and shrubs and vines is not always definite. The form and size of a species is influenced by its age and environmental factors. A species may normally be classified as a tree, but at the extremities of its range or near timberline may be shrubby in appearance. A clump of young sprouts arising from a low tree stump, and in which no single stem has gained dominance over the others, may resemble a shrub. Likewise an immature shrub may initially exhibit the habit of a trailing vine but later become erect. Poisonoak is most commonly a shrub, but when growing adjacent to a tree may develop into a climbing vine.

In determining the habit of a woody plant one might be guided by the following differentiations: A **tree** generally attains a height of 20' or more at maturity, has a single erect stem, and a well-defined crown. **Shrubs** are shorter, have several erect stems arising from a common base, and lack a well-defined crown, i.e., they are bushy. Woody **vines** are prostrate creeping plants, or climbers dependent on other plants or objects for support.

Plant Classification

Within the plant kingdom there are five broad groups or divisions: *Pteridophyta, Spermatophyta, Sphenophyta, Lycophyta,* and *Psilophyta* (Benson, 1959).

All species included in this manual belong to the division Spermatophyta. The spermatophytes are the most complex of the plant divisions. They possess true roots, stems and leaves, and reproduce by means of seeds. Included in this group are the conifers, palms, broadleaf trees and shrubs, cycads, ginkgo, grasses and other herbaceous plants.

Present plant classification systems are based on presumed natural relationship, i.e., the origin and evolution of plant species. As there is not total agreement amongst botanists as to the order of these relationships, there is more than one system of classification.

The following example serves to illustrate one system of plant classification:

Kingdom:	Plant	Plant
Division:	Spermatophyta	Spermatophyta
Class:	Conopsida	Angiospermae
Order:	Coniferales	Fagales
Family:	Pinaceae	Betulaceae
Genus:	Pseudotsuga	Corylus
Species:	Pseudotsuga menziesii (Mirb.) Franko	Corylus cornuta Marsh

Variety:	Pseudotsuga menziesii var. glauca (Beissn.) Franko	Corylus cornuta var. californica (A. DC.) Sharp

The **species** (the term is both singular and plural) is the basic unit in plant classification; that is, the level to which we most often identify plants. In its simplest sense it is a group or collection of plants so similar structurally as to suggest a common parent. Unfortunately, species is a biological concept, imposed on plants by man, rather than a biological fact. As a result, the lines drawn between species are artificial and somewhat arbitrary. Although in natural situations members of two different species within the same genus are generally prohibited from interbreeding due to spatial, temporal, or physiological difference, many species are capable of interbreeding when brought together. For example, *Abies procera* and *Abies magnifica* sometimes interbreed in the shared portions of their ranges, resulting in offspring that share characteristics of both species. Some authors call these offspring a separate variety, *Abies magnifica* var. *shastensis,* but it's becoming increasingly common to simply refer to them as hybrids, designated *Abies magnifica* x *procera,* or vice versa; the important thing is to realize that in nature the two species are not as clearly divided as they may seem on paper. It's important for the novice dendrologist to realize that species is a dynamic, rather than static, concept and that not all trees and shrubs encountered will fit neatly into pre-specified categories.

Varieties arise in other fashions in addition to the crossing of species, however. Sometimes it's as simple as one segment of the population being isolated by a natural barrier. The isolated population, through natural selection, may develop some minor but constant feature that distinguishes it from the larger population. In the example of plant classification given above, *Pseudotsuga menziesii* var. *glauca* is a variety of *P. menziesii* that differs in several minor respects such as cone size and bract display. In normal usage the concept of variety is often used interchangeably with that of subspecies.

The word "species" is abbreviated "sp." when it means **one** species, but "spp." when it means **two or more** species.

A **genus** (plural **genera**) is a group of closely related species, and a **family** a group of closely related genera. Each of the higher categories is a collection of closely related groups in the next lower group.

When a group the size of a genus or larger contains but one smaller unit, it is termed **monotypic** or a **monotype**.

Nomenclature

Rules of botanical nomenclature aim to establish uniform and stable names for the plants found throughout the world. The objective has been fairly well attained with respect to scientific names. With respect to common names the aim has not been so well achieved. Language obstacles and regional preference or use has often resulted in a specific plant being known by a great number of names.

Common Names: Common names of plants are frequently reflections of characteristics or situations that people associate with the species. Following are some examples of ways in which some common names have originated. (1) **Distinctive feature**—bigleaf maple, whitebark pine, sugar pine, knobcone pine, incense-cedar, bitter cherry. (2) **Habitat**—mountain hemlock, subalpine fir, creek dogwood, bog birch. (3) **Locality**—western hemlock, Sierra juniper, Pacific yew, California-laurel, Oregon ash. (4) **Use**—tanoak, lodgepole pine, Labrador-tea. (5) **Commemoration**—Engelmann spruce, Douglas-fir, Brewer spruce, Jeffrey pine. (6) **Adaptation from foreign name**—chinkapin, arborvitae.

Different species often have the same common name. Red fir is a common name for immature, rapidly growing

Douglas-fir, as well as for California red fir. Yellow pine is a commonly used name for several two and three needle pines. Larch is a *Larix* species, but many loggers and lumbermen in western Oregon apply the name to noble fir, a species in the genus *Abies*. Cedar is a common name applied to species in the genera *Thuja, Calocedrus, Juniperus* and *Chamaecyparis;* however, the true cedars belong to the genus Cedrus.

Common names that would be misleading as to the true character of the plant are hyphenated or written as one word. Thus Douglas-fir is hyphenated because it is not a true fir, and redcedar is one word since it is not a true cedar. Additional examples will be found in the main text of the manual.

Scientific Names: In order to reduce the confusion that is often associated with common names systematic botanists have adopted the "International Code of Botanical Nomenclature" which sets forth a detailed set of rules governing the naming of plants. A binomial system of nomenclature is used. Scientific names are composed of two words, the genus (generic name) which is always capitalized, and the species (specific name), which is not capitalized. In technical publications it is common practice to record the name of the author (the botanist who named the plant), usually in abbreviated form, immediately after the specific name.

A trinomial name results when a variety of a species is recognized, i.e., the components of the name include the genus, species, and variety.

Aids to Identification

There are numerous ways in which one can go about identifying trees and shrubs. In this manual dichotomous keys have been provided for this purpose, one for the conifers and one for the broadleaf species. For each genus where there is more than one species, a key to the species will be found following the generic description.

When using a dichotomous key the user is given choices between two alternatives, at each step, i.e., for example, the choice between alternate or opposite leaves. The figures on the right hand side of the key refer to subsequent numbers on the left hand side of the key. When sufficient features have been described, the scientific name of the species is given. To the beginner the keys may appear to be quite complicated but with practice he will soon find that he can use the keys with relative ease. In some instances the user may find that the description does not fit the plant he is attempting to identify. If this appears to be so he can assume one of two conclusions (1) he has erred in his selection of features, or (2) the tree or shrub is not included in the manual.

Before attempting to identify a plant become acquainted with the terms discussed in the following sections.

A. Leaves

1. **Leaf parts:**
   a. Blade—the expanded portion of the leaf.
   b. Petiole—the stem of a leaf or leaflet. Leaves lacking a stem or petiole are termed **sessile**.
   c. Rachis—the stem of a compound leaf.
   d. Margin—the edge of a leaf or leaflet.
   e. Stipule—leafy appendage at the base of the leaf stem.
   f. Stomata—pores in the epidermis of the leaf blade.

2. **Leaf composition:**
   a. Simple—there is but one leaf blade on the petiole.
   b. Compound—more than one leaf blade shares a common stem. The individual blades are termed leaflets.
      (1) Palmately compound—all leaflets have a common point of attachment on the rachis.
      (2) Pinnately compound—each leaflet has a separate point of attachment on the rachis.

3. **Leaf arrangement:**
   a. Alternate—single leaves alternate along the length of the twig.
   b. Opposite—single leaves are borne at the same height on the twig, but are attached on opposite sides.
   c. Whorled—three or more leaves arise from the same level on the twig.

Alternate leaf arrangement is further divided into 2-ranked, 3-ranked, 5-ranked, etc., according to how many rows of leaves may be seen while looking down a twig from the tip. These arrangements are expressed by fractions in a system of numerical **phyllotaxy** (leaf arrangement), where the fraction indicates the portion of the circumference of the twig that must be traversed in going from one leaf or bud to the next (just higher or lower) on the twig. Thus 1/2 phyllotaxy means 2-ranked; 1/3 means 3-ranked, and 2/5 means 5-ranked. More complex leaf arrangements are difficult to recognize and may be called "indeterminate" for most purposes.

Leaf arrangement of conifers is usually either **spiral** (one leaf per node) or **decussate** (two leaves per node, with successive paris in alternating perpendicular planes). Some junipers have a **ternate** leaf arrangement (3 leaves per node).

The leaf arrangement on spur shoots cannot be readily distinguished because of the absence of definite internodes. In determining leaf arrangement it is best to determine the position of the leaves on the twig growth of the present growing season.

4. **Leaf shapes:**
   a. Acicular—long, slender and pointed; needle-like.
   b. Linear—very narrow, sides nearly parallel, several times longer than broad.
   c. Scalelike—very small, usually less than 1/4" long, closely appressed to the twig and overlapping.

LEAF COMPOSITION

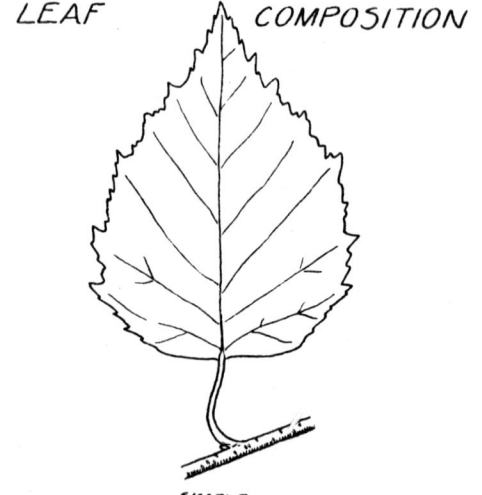

SIMPLE

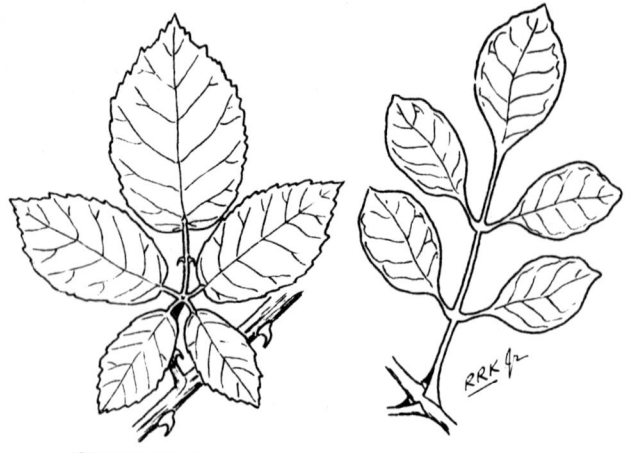

PALMATELY COMPOUND   PINNATELY COMPOUND

LEAF ARRANGEMENT

ALTERNATE

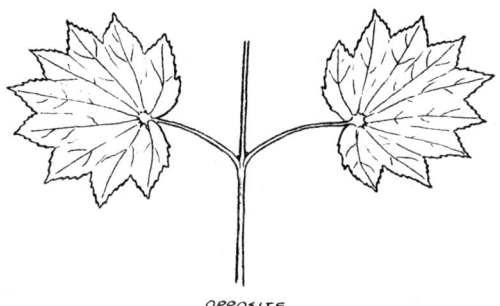

OPPOSITE

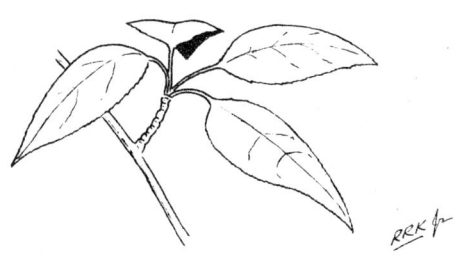

WHORLED ON SPUR SHOOT

RRK Jr

LEAF SHAPES

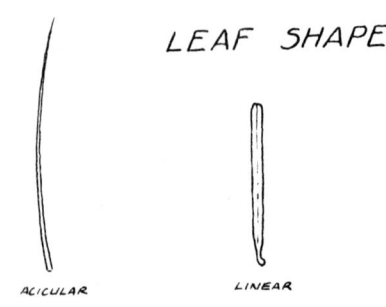

ACICULAR   LINEAR   AWL - SHAPED

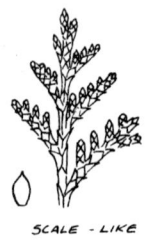

SCALE - LIKE   ORBICULAR   OVAL

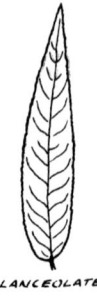

RRK

OVATE   OBOVATE   LANCEOLATE

LEAF SHAPES

OBLANCEOLATE

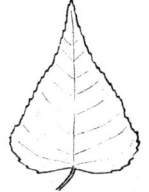

DELTOID

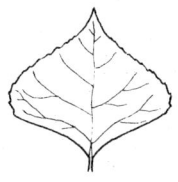

RHOMBOID

CUNEATE

SPATULATE

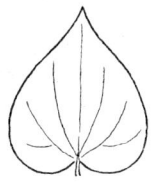

CORDATE

OBLONG

ELLIPTICAL

RRK Jr

    d. Awl-shaped—very narrow and tapered, several times longer than broad, the apex is long and sharp.

The above leaf shapes are most commonly found on coniferous species. The following are characteristic of the broadleaf species.

    e. Ovate—egg-shaped; the broadest point is below the center of the leaf.
    f. Obovate—inverted egg-shaped.
    g. Lanceolate—lance-shaped, several times longer than broad, the broadest point is about 1/3 of the distance up from the base, the upper portion of the leaf is long and tapered.
    h. Oblanceolate—inverted lance-shaped.
    i. Oblong—at least twice as long as broad, the sides are nearly parallel
    j. Elliptical—broadest in the center and tapering evenly toward each end, i.e., shaped like an ellipse or slender football.
    k. Orbicular—round or circular in outline.
    l. Oval—nearly circular in outline, but with the sides slightly compressed.
    m. Deltoid—triangular.
    n. Rhomboid—diamond-shaped.
    o. Cordate—heart-shaped, broadest near the base.
    p. Spatulate—narrow obovate.
    q. Cuneate—wedge-shaped.

5. **Leaf texture:**
    a. Coriaceous—leathery, thick or tough.
    b. Membranous—thin and somewhat translucent.

6. **Leaf surfaces:**
    a. Glabrous—smooth, lacking hairs.
    b. Glaucous—having a white powdery or waxy coating.
    c. Hirsute—short, stiff hairs.
    d. Pubescent—soft short hairs.
    e. Tomentose—woolly hairs, usually curled and matted, felt-like or velvety.

    f. Rugose—wrinkled, i.e., sunken veins.
    g. Scabrous—sandpapery.

7. **Leaf margins:**
    a. Entire—smooth, lacking teeth or lobes.
    b. Repand—wavy or undulating.
    c. Serrate—having sharp teeth or serrations which point upward.
    d. Doubly serrate—small teeth on the larger teeth.
    e. Crenate—having rounded teeth.
    f. Doubly crenate—smaller crenations on the larger teeth.
    g. Dentate—sharp teeth pointing outward.
    h. Revolute—the very edge of the margin is rolled down and under.
    i. Lobed—indentations (sinuses) in the margins extended from 1/3 to 1/2 the distance from the margin to the midrib, and dividing the margin into lobes.
    j. Cleft—marginal lobes resulting from sinuses extending more than half the distance to the midrib.
    k. Parted—unattached lobes resulting from sinuses extending from the margin to the midrib; lobes may appear to be leaflets.

8. **Leaf apex:**
    a. Round—almost semi-circular or with a sweeping arc.
    b. Obtuse—bluntly pointed; apex forms angle greater than $90°$.
    c. Acute—forms an angle of less than $90°$, tip not attenuated.
    d. Accuminate—narrowly acute with a long attenuate point.
    e. Emarginate—shallowly notched.
    f. Mucronate—abruptly bristle-tipped.
    g. Cuspidate—terminating abruptly with a sharp, rigid point.

9. **Leaf base:**
   a. Round—almost semi-circular or with a sweeping curve.
   b. Obtuse—blunt, the sides form an angle greater than 90°.
   c. Acute—the sides form an angle less than 90°, but not attenuated.
   d. Cuneate—wedge-shaped.
   e. Cordate—heart-shaped.
   f. Truncate—abruptly horizontal, i.e., nearly straight across.
   g. Inequilateral—lop-sided or asymmetrical.

10. **Leaf persistence:**
   a. Deciduous—the leaves fall from the tree or shrub in the autumn, and the plant is bare of living foliage during the winter.
   b. Persistent—green, living foliage is present on the tree or shrub the entire year.
   c. Evergreen · refers to plants with persistent leaves. The leaves are persistent, but the plant is evergreen.

B. Flowers

Flowers contain the reproductive organs of the plant. In most woody plants the flowers are small, not particularly conspicuous and are short-lived. All natural classification systems of seed plants are based upon flower structure.

1. **Flower parts:**
   a. Pistil—the ovary or seed-bearing organ.
   b. Stamen—the pollen-bearing organ.
   c. Sepal—the leafy appendage beneath the petal, usually green, but occasionally they may be some other color. Collectively, all the sepals in a flower are termed the **calyx.**
   d. Petal—the most colorful appendage of the flower. Collectively, the petals form the **corolla.**
   e. Receptacle—the expanded portion of the flower on which the pistils, stamens, petals and sepals are borne.
   f. Peduncle—the supporting stem or stalk of a flower.

LEAF MARGINS

ENTIRE

SLIGHTLY WAVY

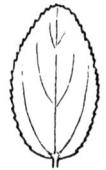

SERRATE

DOUBLY SERRATE

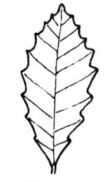

DENTATE

CRENATE

DOUBLY CRENATE

PALMATELY LOBED

PINNATELY LOBED

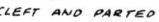

CLEFT AND PARTED

REVOLUTE

RRK Jr.

16

LEAF APEX

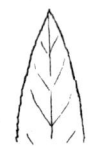
ACUTE

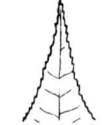
ACCUMINATE

ROUND

MUCRONATE

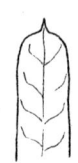
CUSPIDATE

OBTUSE

EMARGINATE

LEAF BASE

ACUTE

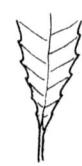
CUNEATE

OBTUSE

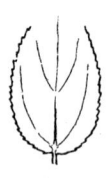
ROUND

CORDATE

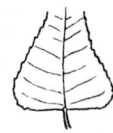
TRUNCATE

INEQUILATERAL

LEAF VENATION

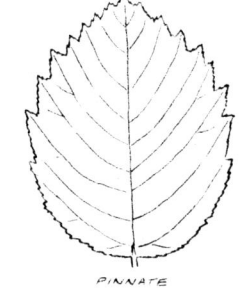

PINNATE

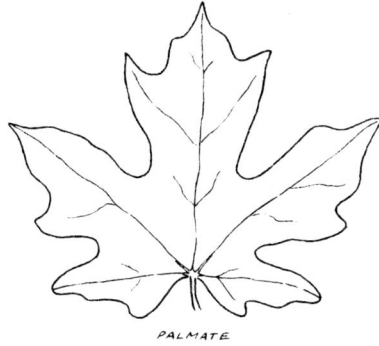

PALMATE

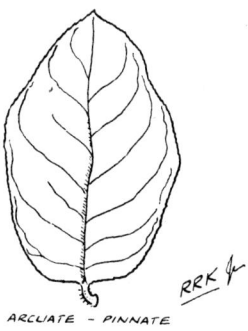

RRK Jr

ARCUATE - PINNATE

FLOWERS

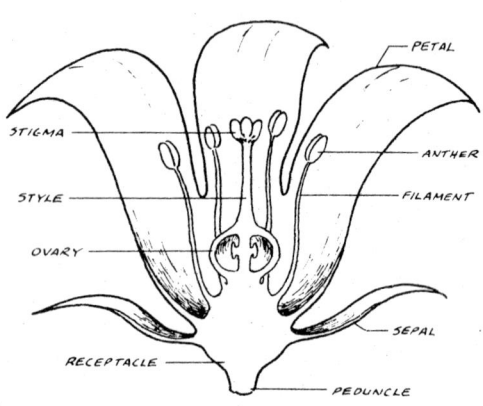

STIGMA

STYLE

OVARY

RECEPTACLE

PETAL

ANTHER

FILAMENT

SEPAL

PEDUNCLE

FLOWER PARTS

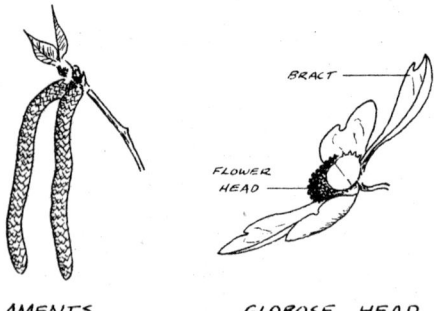

BRACT

FLOWER HEAD

AMENTS

GLOBOSE HEAD

2. **Flowers:**
   a. Complete—individual flowers that possess stamens, one or more pistils, petals and sepals.
   b. Incomplete—individual flowers in which one or more of the aforementioned parts are missing.
   c. Perfect (bisexual)—a flower having both functioning pistil(s) and functioning stamens; either or both of the petals and sepals may be present or absent.
   d. Imperfect (unisexual)—a flower having only a pistil or stamens, but not both; either or both the petals and sepals may be present or absent.
   e. Staminate—an imperfect flower possessing only stamens, i.e., a male flower.
   f. Pistillate—an imperfect flower possessing only a pistil, i.e., a female flower.

A single plant that bears only unisexual flowers of both sexes is termed **monoecious**. If only pistillate flowers are borne on one plant and only staminate flowers on another plant, the species is said to be **dioecious.**

3. **Inflorescence:** i.e., floral arrangement.
   a. Ament (catkin)—a pendent spike of unisexual flowers; the individual flowers lack petals.
   b. Head—a compact cluster of sessile flowers borne on a common receptacle.
   c. Raceme—an inflorescence with a long central axis bearing flowers on short pedicels of equal length. The flowers usually have petals and/or sepals.

Inflorescences other than the three described above will be referred to hereafter as clusters and the shape described.

C. Fruits

A fruit is the seed-bearing organ of a plant.

1. **Gymnospermous Fruits:** bear naked seeds.
    a. Types.
        (1) Cone—woody, leathery or semi-fleshy scales spirally arranged, or alternating in pairs at right angles, and inserted on a central axis. Each fertile scale bears one or more seeds.
        (2) Aril—a fleshy appendage partially or wholly surrounding a single seed.
    b. Cone scale features.
        (1) Apophysis—the portion of the cone scale exposed when the cone is closed.
        (2) Umbo—a small terminal or dorsal scar on the apophysis of a pine cone.
        (3) Imbricate(d) scales—overlapping scales; characteristic of some cones in which the scales are spirally arranged on a central axis.
        (4) Peltate scales—shield-shaped, umbrella-shaped, or mushroom-shaped scales.
        (5) Boss—a raised, usually pointed, projection on the apophysis of a peltate scale.
        (6) Armed scale or umbo—a scale or umbo bearing a spine, prickle or claw.
        (7) Valvate scales—meet at the base or edges without overlapping.

2. **Angiospermous Fruits:** a ripened ovary (part of the pistil containing the ovule), and frequently including other accessory parts of the flower, such as the receptacle, bracts, calyx and style.

3. **Simple Fruits:**
    a. Dry, indehiscent fruits.
        (1) Achene—one-seeded, unwinged fruits; may or may not have hairy or feathery appendages.
        (2) Samara—a one-seeded, winged fruit, two samaras may be united as in the maples.

FRUITS

CONE - IMBRICATED
SCALES

CONE - PELTATE
SCALES

NUT

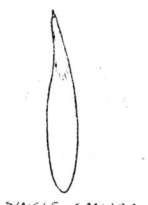

SINGLE SAMARA

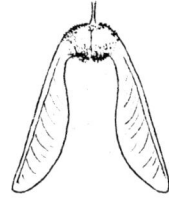

DOUBLE SAMARA

ACHENE

NUT - ACORN

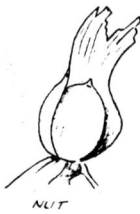

NUT

RRK Jr

FRUITS

CAPSULE

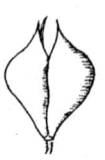

FOLLICLE

LEGUME

POME

DRUPE

DRUPE

BERRY

AGGREGATE FRUIT

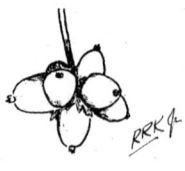

MULTIPLE FRUIT

RRK 9

      (3) Nut—a one-celled, one-seeded fruit with a woody or leathery wall, and partially or wholly surrounded by a husk.

  b. Dry, dehiscent fruits.

      (1) Legume—product of a simple pistil splitting down two sides.

      (2) Follicle—product of a simple pistil splitting down one side only.

      (3) Capsule—product of a compound pistil splitting down two or more sides.

  c. Fleshy fruits.

      (1) Pome—product of a compound pistil, the inner wall surrounding the seeds is papery or cartilaginous, the outer wall, which develops from the enlarged receptacle, is thick and fleshy. These are applelike fruits.

      (2) Berry—a many-seeded fruit in which the seeds are imbedded within a pulpy body.

      (3) Drupe—product of a simple pistil, usually one-seeded, with a hard inner wall and a fleshy outer wall. A cherrylike fruit.

4. Compound Fruits:

  a. Aggregate fruit—a tight cluster of simple fruits borne on a common receptacle (or **one** flower).

  b. Multiple fruit—a cluster of simple fruits which are products of pistils of separate flowers, and which are borne in a tight, compact cluster.

D. Twigs

Twig characteristics are good features to use for identification when the flowers and leaves are absent, and other plant characteristics are inadequate.

1. Buds—small axillary or terminal structures on the stem or branch, consisting of rudimentary foliage or floral leaves.

  a. Position.

      (1) Lateral—the buds borne along the side of the twig, in the axil between the leaf stem and the twig, or in the leaf scar.

TWIGS

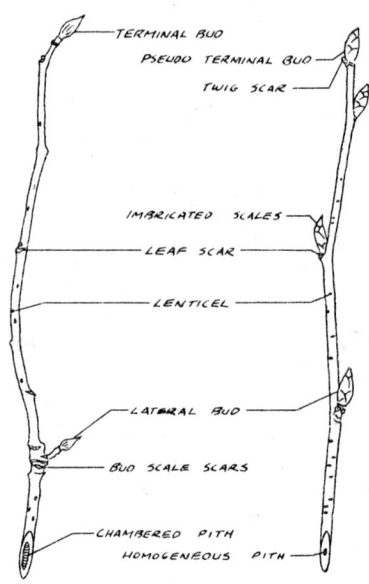

TERMINAL BUD
PSEUDO TERMINAL BUD
TWIG SCAR
IMBRICATED SCALES
LEAF SCAR
LENTICEL
LATERAL BUD
BUD SCALE SCARS
CHAMBERED PITH
HOMOGENEOUS PITH

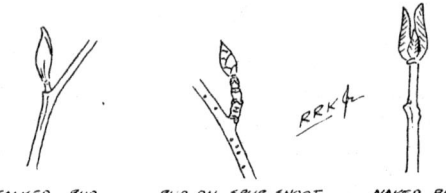

STALKED BUD   BUD ON SPUR SHOOT   NAKED BUD

    (2) Terminal—buds borne at the tip of the twig.
    (3) Pseudoterminal—buds which appear to be terminal but which are actually lateral buds; a twig scar is evident at the end of the twig.
    (4) Submerged buds—buds which are buried in the leaf scar.
  b. Kinds of buds.
    (1) Flower—the bud contains only floral parts; flower buds are usually larger than leaf buds.
    (2) Leaf—buds containing only embryonic leaves.
    (3) Mixed—buds containing both flowers and leaves.
  c. Bud scales.
    (1) Imbricated—scales overlap like shingles.
    (2) Valvate—scales meet along their margins but do not overlap.
    (3) Naked—scales are absent; if the bud is exposed the embryonic leaves are visible.

2. **Bud scale scar**—scar left on the twig when the scales of the terminal bud drop off.

3. **Leaf scar**—the scar found on the twig at the point where a fallen leaf was attached.

4. **Node**—that position on the twig where the leaf is attached. The **internode** is that portion of the twig between two nodes.

5. **Lenticels**—round, oval or slitlike pores on the twigs, branches and stems of a plant which are concerned with aeration.

6. **Spur shoots**—short, lateral, scarred twigs which lack internodal development.

7. **Lammas shoots**—a twig bearing leaves which developed in the late summer from the current season's bud, and which arises immediately above a leaf.

8. **Spines, thorns, and prickles:**
  a. Foliar spines—leaves are modified into spines and carry on the function of leaves. Best example is gorse.

    b. Prickles (cortical spines)—spines modified cork (bark) tissue. Examples: *Rosa* spp. and *Rubus* spp.

    c. Stipular spines—the stipules have been modified into spines. Example: *Robinia*.

    d. Woody thorns—are modified twigs, the tissue is wood. Example: *Crataegus* spp.

9. **Pith**—the center or core of the twig, branch or stem.

    a. Shapes.

        (1) Terete—round.

        (2) Stellate—star-shaped.

        (3) Triangular—three-sided.

    b. Types.

        (1) Solid—continuous and unbroken throughout.

        (2) Spongy—soft and porous, large in cross section when compared to the dimension of the twig.

        (3) Chambered—in longitudinal section it resembles a slender, hollow pipe with disks inserted at regular intervals.

        (4) Hollow—pipelike, i.e., the center is open.

E. Bark

On larger plants the color, thickness, texture, configuration and other prominent features frequently are definite aids to the identification of some species. Familiarity with distinctive features of outer and inner bark is best acquired by close observation of the plant in the field rather than committing to memory written or verbal descriptions.

STUDY HINTS

1. Look for characteristics that are different or distinctive (**opposite** branching, **chambered** pith, **stalked** buds, **1/2** phyllotaxy, etc.). Learn these characteristics and ignore the commonplace.

2. Learn thoroughly the characteristics of each genus; then you won't have to learn them separately for each species in that genus.

3. Spend much of your allotted study time for this course in the field observing and examining the

species. You will find it much more effective than staying in your room memorizing facts.

4. Get together with others in the course and review the species together. You will find it mutually beneficial.

5. The instructor will put special emphasis on outstanding characteristics and pertinent facts for each of the species. Underline these points in your manual.

6. All plants of the same species were not cast from the same mold. Become familiar with the **variation** in features that exist within a given species. Don't guess, but weigh the evidence when confronted with a particular specimen that is not an exact duplicate of one of the same species you have previously examined.

7. See summary lists on pages 259 to 262 of common and distinctive features. These lists include: opposite leaves, compound leaves, persistent leaves, aromatic foliage, revolute margins, flowers borne in aments, preformed staminate flowers, fruit a pome, fruit an achene. Notice in each of these categories the genera that have the feature. There will be species within some of the genera that are exceptions and these should be noted.

8. You won't become familiar and adept at plant identification by overnight "cramming." Allot as much time as you can to studying the material. Be guided by the above suggestions and try to develop other study habits that are of aid to you. The course instructor will be glad to assist you with any difficulties or problems.

9. Always keep in mind that while there are aids to learning there are no short-cuts.

10. When you **read** about a tree or shrub, **visualize.**

11. When you "know" a tree, you have a clear mental image of that tree. Work toward improving that image.

CHECKLIST OF COMMON WOODY PLANTS NATIVE OR NATURALIZED TO OREGON*

GYMNOSPERMAE (Conifers and Yews)

Taxaceae

Taxus brevifolia Nutt. — Pacific yew

Pinaceae

Abies amabilis (Dougl.) Forbes	Pacific silver fir
" concolor (Gord. & Glend.) Lindl.	white fir
" grandis (Dougl.) Lindl.	grand fir
" lasiocarpa (Hook.) Nutt.	subalpine fir
" magnifica A. Murr.	California red fir
" procera Rehd.	noble fir
Larix lyallii Parl.	subalpine or alpine larch
" occidentalis Nutt.	western larch
Picea brewerana S. Wats.	Brewer spruce
" engelmannii Parry	Engelmann spruce
" sitchensis (Bong.) Carr.	Sitka spruce
Pinus albicaulis Engelm.	whitebark pine
" attenuata Lemm.	knobcone pine
" contorta Dougl.	lodgepole pine
" flexilis James	limber pine
" jeffreyi Grev. & Balf.	Jeffrey pine

" lambertiana Dougl. — sugar pine
" monticola Dougl. — western white pine
" ponderosa Laws. — ponderosa pine
Pseudotsuga menziesii (Mirb.) Franco — Douglas-fir
Tsuga heterophylla (Ref.) Sarg. — western hemlock
" mertensiana (Borg.) Carr. — mountain hemlock

Taxodiaceae
Sequoiadendron giganteum (Lindl.) Buchho — bigtree
Sequoia sempervirens (D. Don) Endl. — redwood

Cupressaceae
Chamaecyparis lawsoniana (A. Murr.) Parl. — Port-Orford-cedar
" nootkatensis (D. Don) Spach — Alaska yellow-cedar
Cupressus bakeri Jeps. — Baker cypress
Juniperus californica Carr. — California juniper
" communis L. — common juniper
" occidentalis Hook. — western juniper
" scopulorum Sarg. — Rocky Mountain juniper
Calocedrus decurrens (Torr.) Florin. — incense-cedar
Thuja plicata Donn — western redcedar

30

ANGIOSPERMAE (Broadleaf Trees and Shrubs)

Salicaceae

Populus angustifolia James	narrowleaf cottonwood
" tremuloides Michx.	quaking aspen
" trichocarpa Torr. & Gray	black cottonwood
Salix spp. L.	willow

Myricaceae

Myrica californica Cham.	Pacific bayberry
" gale L.	sweetgale

Betulaceae

Alnus rhombifolia Nutt.	white alder
" rubra Bong.	red alder
" sinuata (Reg.) Rydb.	Sitka alder
" incana (L.) Moench	thinleaf alder
Betula glandulosa Michx.	bog or scrub birch
" occidentalis Hook.	water birch
" papyrifera Marsh.	paper birch
Corylus cornuta var. californica (A. DC.) Sharp	California hazel

Fagaceae

Castanopsis chrysophylla (Dougl.) A.DC.	golden chinkapin
Lithocarpus densiflorus (Hook. & Arn.) Rohn.	tanoak

Quercus chrysolepis Liebm. — canyon live oak
  " garryana Dougl. — Oregon white oak
  " kelloggii Newb. — California black oak

Ulmaceae
Celtis reticulata Torr. — netleaf hackberry

Berberidaceae
Berberis aquifolium (Pursh) Nutt. — tall Oregon-grape
  " nervosa (Pursh) Nutt. — dwarf Oregon-grape
  " repens (Lindl.) G. Don — creeping Oregon-grape

Laureaceae
Umbellularia californica (Hook. & Arn.) Nutt. — California-laurel

Hydrangeaceae
Philadelphus lewisii Pursh — mockorange

Grossulariaceae
Ribes sanguineum Pursh — red-flowering currant
  " lacustre (Pers.) Poir. — swamp currant; prickly currant
  " cereum Dougl. — wax currant

Rosaceae
Amelanchier alnifolia Nutt. — Pacific serviceberry
Cercocarpus betuloides Nutt. — birchleaf mountain-mahogany

Rosaceae (cont.)

Cercocarpus ledifolius Nutt.	curlleaf mountain-mahogany
Crataegus douglasii Lindl.	black hawthorn
" columbiana Howell	Columbia hawthorn
Holodiscus discolor (Pursh) Maxim.	ocean spray
Oemleria cerasiformis (H. & A.) Landon	Indian-plum
Physocarpus capitatus (Pursh) Ktze.	ninebark
" malvaceus (Greene) Ktze.	mallow ninebark
Prunus emarginata Dougl.	bitter cherry
" subcordata Benth.	Klamath plum
" virginiana L.	common chokecherry
Purshia tridentata (Pursh) DC.	bitterbrush
Pyrus fusa Raf.	western crab apple
Rosa gymnocarpa Nutt.	little wood rose
" multiflora Thumb.	multiflora rose
" eglanteria L.	sweetbriar rose
Rubus laciniatus Willd.	evergreen blackberry
" leucodermis Dougl.	blackcap
" parviflorus Nutt.	thimbleberry
" spectabilis Pursh	salmonberry
" discolor Weihe & Nees	Himalaya berry
" ursinus Cham & Schlecht.	wild blackberry
Sorbus scopulina Greene	Cascade mountain-ash

Sorbus sitchensis Roem. — Sitka mountain-ash
Spiraea douglasii Hook — western spiraea
   "   betulifolia Pall. — shiny-leaf spiraea

Leguminosae
Cytisus scoparius L. — Scotch broom
Robinia pseudoacacia L. — black locust
Ulex europaeus L. — gorse

Anacardiaceae
Rhus diversiloba T. & G. — poisonoak
   "   glabra L. — smooth sumac
   "   trilobata Nutt. — skunkbush

Celastraceae
Pachistima myrsinites (Pursh) Raf. — Oregon boxwood

Aceraceae
Acer circinatum Pursh — vine maple
   "   glabrum Torr. — Rocky Mountain maple
   "   glabrum var. douglasii (Hook.) Dipp. — Douglas maple
   "   macrophyllum Pursh — bigleaf maple

Rhamnaceae
Ceanothus cuneatus Nutt. — narrowleaf, buckbrush
" integerrimus H. & A. — deerbrush
" prostratus Benth. — squawcarpet
" sanguineus Pursh — redstem ceanothus
" thyrsiflorus Esch. — blueblossom
" velutinus Dougl. — snowbrush
Rhamnus californica Esch. — California coffeeberry
" purshiana DC. — cascara buckthorn

Elaeagnaceae
Shepherdia canadensis Nutt. — russett buffaloberry
" argentea (Pursh) Nutt. — silver buffaloberry

Araliaceae
Oplopanax horridum (Sm.) Miq. — devilsclub

Cornaceae
Cornus nuttallii Aud. — Pacific dogwood
" stolonifera var. occidentalis (T. & G.) Hitchc. — western dogwood

Garryaceae
Garrya elliptica Dougl. — tree silktassel
" fremontii Torr. — Fremont silktassel

Ericaceae

Arbutus menziesii Pursh	Pacific madrone
Arctostaphylos columbiana Piper	hairy manzanita
" patula Greene	green manzanita
" uva-ursi Spreng.	bearberry or kinnikinnick
Gaultheria shallon Pursh	salal
Rhododendron macrophyllum D. Don	Pacific rhododendron
" occidentale (T. & G.) Gray	western azalea
Ledum glandulosum Nutt.	Pacific Labrador-tea
Vaccinium membranaceum Dougl.	big whortleberry
" ovatum Pursh	evergreen huckleberry
" parvifolium Smith	red huckleberry
Menziesia ferruginea Hook.	rusty menziesia

Oleaceae

Fraxinus latifolia Benth.	Oregon ash

Caprifoliaceae

Lonicera involucrata Banks	black twinberry
Sambucus racemosa L.	red elder
" cerulea Raf.	blue elder
Symphoricarpos albus (L.) Blake.	snowberry
" mollis Nutt.	spreading snowberry
Viburnum ellipticum Hook.	western viburnum

Caprifoliaceae (cont.)
Viburnum edule (Michx.) Raf.   moosewood viburnum
Linnaea borealis L.   twin-flower

Compositae
Artemisia tridentata Nutt.   big sagebrush
Baccharis pilularis DC.   kidneywort baccharis
Chrysothamnus nauseosus (Pall.) Britt.   gray rabbitbrush
      ʺ   viscidiflorus (Hook.) Nutt. green rabbitbrush

*Although this list contains most important species in Oregon it is by no means comprehensive.

KEY TO NATIVE AND INTRODUCED CONIFERS
(AND OTHER GYMNOSPERMS)

1. Leaves and cone scales, or bundles or clusters of leaves, **spirally** arranged on twig. Leaves needle-like or linear; awl-like in one species.   2

1. Leaves and cone scales **decussate** (opposite in alternating perpendicular planes) or ternate (3 per node). Leaves scalelike or awl-like.   10

   2.   Leaves borne in bundles, or in clusters on spur shoots. Leaves needle-like or linear.   3

   2.   Leaves occur singly, the leaf bases spirally arranged on twig. Leaves linear or awl-like.   4

3. Leaves acicular (needle-like) in bundles of 2 to 5. Bundle sheath deciduous or persistent. Cones pendent.   **Pinus** p. 48

3. Leaves linear, borne in clusters of 12 or more on spirally arranged spur shoots; borne singly on new shoots. Cones erect.   **Larix** p. 61

   4.   Leaves have distinct petioles.   5

   4.   Leaves sessile (lack a petiole).   7

5. Base of leaf parallels and adheres to twig. Leaves pointed, often 2-ranked. No white bloom on underside. Fruit fleshy, one-seeded.   **Taxus** p. 107

5. Base of leaf does not parallel or adhere to twig. White stomatal bloom on underside of leaf. Leaves blunt or inconspicuously pointed; 2-ranked or scattered all around twig. Ultimate twigs slender. Fruit a cone.   6

6. Leaf scar small, oval, half-raised. Leader erect. Buds about 1/4" long. Cone bracts longer than scales. Leaves at least 3/4" long.   **Pseudotsuga** p. 68

6. Leaf scar slender, diagonally-raised, peg-like. Leader droops. Buds about 1/16" long. Cone bracts shorter than scales. Leaves 1/4" to 3/4" long.   **Tsuga** p. 71

7. Leaves borne on conspicuously-raised, peg-like projections; leaves often very sharp, never 2-ranked. Cones pendent, with imbricate scales.
                                                          Picea p. 64

7. Leaves not borne on raised projections from twig; leaves blunt or pointed, often 2-ranked. Cones pendent with peltate scales, or erect with deciduous, imbricate scales.   8

8. Leaf scars large, round, flat. Leaves linear, blunt; 2-ranked or upswept (concentrated on upper side of twig). Cones erect, with deciduous, imbricate scales. Dead leaves fall singly.   **Abies** p. 75

8. Leaf scars non-existent; twig scars ellipti-cal, elongated laterally; leaves pointed, and either (1) linear, flat, 2-ranked, or (2) awl-like to lanceolate and scattered spirally around twig. Cone scales peltate. Leaves fall in sprays (small twig plus leaves), not singly.   9

9. Leaves linear, flat, 2-ranked.   **Sequoia** p. 85

9. Leaves awl-like to lanceolate. **Sequoiadendron** p. 85

10. Leaves scalelike.   11

10. Leaves awl-like or lanceolate.   17

11. Leaves in flat sprays. 12

11. Smallest sprays square or hexagonal in cross-section. 14

    12. Internodes and scales much longer than broad; scales elongated, decurrent (adhering to twig with only tip of scale sticking out). Cone semi-woody, 3/4" to 1" long, with only 3 main scales evident. Overlapping of lateral leaf scales on facial scales, produces a "wine-glass" effect.
        Calocedrus p. 94

    12. Internodes and scales about as long as broad. Cones less than 1/2" long. 13

13. Ultimate sprays about 1/8" wide; white butterfly or bow-tie pattern on underside. Cone scales in valvate pairs in an overlapping-decussate arrangement. **Thuja** p. 92

13. Ultimate sprays about 1/16" wide. White "X" pattern or no white bloom on underside. Cones have peltate scales. **Chamaecyparis** p. 96

    14. Leaves ternate (3 per node); may also be some decussate leaves; some leaves may be awl-shaped or lanceolate. Cones about 1/4", fleshy, berrylike. **Juniperus** p. 100

    14. Leaves and cone scales decussate (opposite in alternating perpendicular planes); some leaves may be awl-shaped; some cones may be fleshy. 15

15. Cone diameter 1/2" or larger; leaves scalelike, with awl-like leaves on young shoots.
        Cupressus p. 106

15. Cone diameter 1/4" to 1/3". 16

16. Leaves consistently scale-like and decussate. Cones have 4 to 6 convex scales, each with a conspicuous point. **Chamaecyparis** p. 96

16. Leaves mostly scale-like, but awl-like on new shoots. Cones fleshy, berry-like, with decussate, peltate scales fused together.
Juniperus p. 100

17. Cones 1/2'' or larger in diameter, woody. Leaves awl-like on new shoots; otherwise scale-like. **Cupressus** p. 106

17. Cones 1/6'' to 1/3'' in diameter, fleshy, berry-like, with soft peltate scales fused together. Leaves may be chiefly awl-like but some scale-like leaves usually present. **Juniperus** p. 100

GYMNOSPERMS

Generic Characteristics

Genus	Characteristics
Abies (fir)	Leaves spirally arranged, sessile, linear; flat or thickened in cross-section; round, flat leaf scars on twigs; buds more or less resinous; erect cones mature in one season, borne in the top of the crown and disintegrate when ripe.
Calocedrus (incense-cedar)	Scalelike, decussate leaves, 1/8'' to 1/2'' long, in flat sprays; overlapping of the lateral scales on the facial scales results in a wine-glass outline. Cones valvate, semi-woody; resemble a duck's bill when closed; there appear to be 3 cone scales, although the center scale consists of 2 scales fused together; 2 large outer scales cover the seeds; an additional 2 basal scales are aborted. Cones mature in one growing season. Leader droops. Wood durable.
Chamaecyparis (white-cedar)	Scale-like, decussate leaves arranged in flat or 4-angled sprays; cones small, 1/4'' or 1/3'', and round, with peltate, decussate scales; mature in one or two growing seasons; leader droops; wood durable.
Cupressus (cypress)	Decussate, scalelike leaves (awl-like on juvenile or vigorous growth), resin-dotted in some species; youngest branchlets 4-angled in cross-section in many species. Cones 1/2'' or larger, round or nearly so, with woody or leathery peltate, decussate

scales each scale with a central projection (boss); cones mature in two years; wood durable.

Juniperus
(juniper)

Leaves decussate or ternate, scale-like and/or awl-like (on all species the leaves are awl-like on juvenile growth and frequently on vigorous shoots; some species have only awl-like leaves); leaves resin-dotted in a few species; dioecious; cones fleshy, small and round, coated with a white bloom, mature in one, two, or three years; wood durable.

Larix
(larch)

Leaves deciduous, linear; borne singly, and spirally on current year's twigs, thereafter clustered on spur shoots; cones erect, with spirally arranged, imbricate scales; bracts longer than cone scales on western species; cones mature in one season, but often persist several years on the tree.

Picea
(spruce)

Sessile, spirally arranged, stiff, usually pointed, linear leaves borne on peglike projections on the twigs; leaves flat or 3- to 4-angled in cross-section; cones pendent, with spirally arranged, imbricate scales, maturing in one growing season; cones scales woody or semi-papery.

Pinus
(pine)

Acicular (needlelike) leaves borne in spirally arranged bundles of 2 to 5 (1 in *P. monophylla*). Bundle sheath persistent in the 2- and 3-needle pines; deciduous in the 5-needle pines. Cones pendent and with spirally arranged, imbricate, woody scales. In the 2- and 3-needle pines the umbo on the cone scale is dorsal and armed; in the 5-needle pines it is terminal and unarmed. Cones mature in 2 years.

Pseudotsuga
(Dougas-fir)

Linear, flat, petiolate leaves, spirally arranged on the twig; leaf scars small round, half-raised. Cones pendent, with spirally arranged, imbricate scales, and 3-pointed bracts longer than the cone scales; cones woody or semi-woody, maturing in one season. Buds reddish-brown, sharp-pointed, with imbricate scales which persist during the growing season.

Sequoia
(sequoia)

Leaves sessile, with bases spirally arranged on twig; leaves linear, flat, and superficially 2-ranked. Cones pendent, with woody, spirally arranged, peltate scales; mature in one year. Wood durable.

Sequoiadendron
(giant sequoia)

Leaves sessile, with bases spirally arranged on twig; leaves awl-like to lanceolate, scattered around twig. Cones pendent, with woody, spirally arranged, peltate scales; mature in two years. Wood durable.

Taxus
(yew)

Leaves linear, petiolate, pointed, with bases spirally arranged on twig; superficially 2-ranked in native species. Dioecious. Fruit fleshy, one-seeded, red (an aril). Wood durable, hard.

Thuja
(thuja)

Scale-like, decussate leaves, in flat sprays. Cones about 1/2" long, with several overlapping, decussate pairs of valvate scales, each of which is minutely spine-tipped; mature in one growing season. Leader droops. Wood durable.

Tsuga
(hemlock)

Leaves spirally arranged, petiolate, linear; flat or thickened in cross-section, 2-ranked in some species. Cones pendent, with thin, spirally arranged, imbricate scales, woody or semi-woody; mature in one season. Twigs roughened with ridges terminating in a slender diagonally raised peg to which a leaf is attached. Leader droops.

SUMMARY OF DISTINCTIVE AND COMMON CHARACTERISTICS OF NORTHWEST GYMNOSPERMS

LEAVES

Deciduous Leaves
Larix spp.

Leaves Borne in Bundles
Pinus spp.

  a. **Two per Bundle:**
    P. contorta

  b. **Three per Bundle:**
    P. attenuata
    P. jeffreyi
    P. ponderosa

  c. **Five per Bundle:**
    P. albicaulis
    P. flexilis
    P. lambertiana
    P. monticola

Leaves Clustered on Spur Shoots
Larix spp.

Leaves 2-Ranked
Abies grandis
Abies concolor
Sequoia sempervirens
Taxus brevifolia
Tsuga heterophylla

Linear Leaves
Abies spp.
Larix spp.
Picea spp.

Awl-like or Lanceolate Leaves
Juniperus spp.
Sequoiadendron giganteum
Cupressus spp.

Scalelike Leaves

  a. **Arranged in Flattened Sprays**
    Chamaecyparis spp.
    Calocedrus decurrens
    Thuja plicata

  b. **Not Arranged in Flattened Sprays**
    Cupressus spp.
    Juniperus spp. (not J. communis)

Petiolate Leaves
Pseudotsuga menziesii
Taxus brevifolia
Tsuga spp.

Leader Droops
Chamaecyparis spp.
Calocedrus decurrens
Thuja plicata
Tsuga spp.

Pseudotsuga menziesii
Tsuga spp.
Sequoia sempervirens

FLOWERS

All the Northwest species are monoecious, except the *Juniperus* spp. and *Taxus brevifolia,* which are *dioecious.*

The flowers of all gymnosperm species are unisexual.

The stamens and pistils are borne in conelike bodies termed strobili (singular is strobile). A given strobile is unisexual, i.e., it has only stamens or only pistils, not both.

FRUITS

The fruiting structure of the conifers is a cone, and that of the yews is an aril. Most coniferous fruits mature in one growing season.

Cones Mature in 2 Growing Seasons
Chamaecyparis nootkatensis   Pinus spp.
Cupressus spp.   Sequoiadendron
Juniperus spp.   giganteum

Cones Borne Erect
Abies spp.   Chamaecyparis spp.   Thuja plicata
Larix spp.

Bracts Longer Than the Cone Scales
Abies procera   Pseudotsuga menziesii
Larix spp.

Cones Disintegrate on the Tree When Mature
Abies spp.

Peltate Cone Scales
Chamaecyparis spp.
Cupressus spp.
Sequoia
Sequoiadendron

WOOD

Durable Heartwood

Chamaecyparis spp.
Cupressus spp.
Juniperus spp.
Calocedrus decurrens

Sequoia sempervirens
Sequoiadendron giganteum
Taxus brevifolia
Thuja plicata

PINACEAE   Pine Family

Pinus L.

pine

Habit: Evergreen, cone-bearing trees with needlelike leaves borne in bundles or fascicles.

Leaves: Persistent, acicular (needle-like), triangular or semi-circular in cross section, and borne in fascicles (bundles) of 2 to 5[*]; a membranous persistent or deciduous sheath initially encloses the base of each fascicle of needles. Each bundle is borne in the axil of a scalelike leaf. These scale-leaves are spirally arranged on the twig. Bundle scars are round and half raised.

Flowers: Monoecious; borne in a strobile (conelike flower cluster in which the floral parts are spirally arranged on an elongated axis). The red or yellow staminate (male) flowers are borne in cylindrical strobili which are clustered at the base of the twig growth of the current season. The pistillate flower cluster resembling an embryonic cone, often reddish in color, is borne terminally or subterminally on the twig of the current season.

Cones: Persistent, woody; mature in 2 (rarely 3) growing seasons; umbo dorsal and armed, or terminal and unarmed; each fertile scale bears 2 winged or wingless seeds. In some species the cones may fall from the tree shortly after maturing; other species may retain their cones for several months after the seeds are released. In a few species the cones are serotinous, i.e., the mature cones remain on the tree unopened for several seasons before releasing their seeds.

Buds: Size and shape variable; bud scales imbricated; resinous or nonresinous.

_____

[*]*P. monophylla* (in southwestern U.S.) has but a single needle.

Remarks: The pines are found worldwide in the Northern Hemisphere. (Two species extend below the equator in the East Indies.) If any group of trees is to be labelled as being the most important, it would be the pines. There are over 80 species of pine, 41 of which are native to the United States. Eight species are indigenous to Oregon, four to Washington, and 18 to California.

Uses: A list of the commercial uses of the pines would run to several hundred items. Some principal uses include: lumber for general construction, boxes and crates, pattern stock; wood fiber for pulp and paper manufacture; poles, piling, mine timbers, crossties; distillation of the resins and wood for turpentine, rosin, wood tar, and oil; and pine-leaf oil for medicinal and pharmaceutical uses. The seeds of several species are edible and are sold commercially.

Natural Enemies: Numerous natural enemies attack the pines. Here in the West considerable loss is incurred each year from bark beetles and diseases. Among the most important beetles are *Dendroctonus monticolae,* the mountain pine beetle; and *Ips* spp., the pine engravers. Among the diseases having the pines as hosts are *Arceuthobium* spp., the dwarf mistletoes; and a large variety of heart rots. *Elytroderma deformans,* needle blight, is an enemy of ponderosa and lodgepole pines; and *Cronartium ribicola,* white-pine blister rust, is a devastating enemy of all white (5-needle) pines.

SUBGENERA OF PINES

yellow pines	white pines
Cones: dorsal umbos; armed.	Cones: terminal umbos; unarmed.
Leaves: 2 or 3 per bundle; usually long and/or thick; bundle sheaths persistent.	Leaves: 5 per bundle; usually short, slender; bundle sheaths deciduous.

yellow pines	white pines
Twigs: scaly (scale-leaves persistent).	Twigs: smooth (scale-leaves deciduous).
Intolerant (rarely intermediate).	Intermediate tolerance.
Wood: abrupt transition from springwood to summerwood.	Wood: gradual transition from springwood to summerwood.

KEY TO NORTHWESTERN PINES

1. Needles 5 per fascicle. Cones have terminal umbos. (white pines)   2

1. Needles 2 or 3 per fascicle. Cones have dorsal umbos. (yellow pines)   5

   2. White lines of bloom on all needle surfaces; cone scales thick.   3

   2. White lines of bloom on ventral (inner) surfaces only. Cone scales thin, flexible. *P. monticola*

3. Needles 2-1/2" to 4" long, flexible, apex pointed; bark rough, scaly, reddish. Cones over 9" long. *P. lambertiana*

3. Needles 1-1/2" to 3" long, stout, clustered near the ends of the branches; bark not red. Cones less than 8" long.   4

   4. Cones stay closed, egg-shaped, 1-1/2" to 3" long; purplish to brown; scales thick and with spurlike apex; bark thin, brownish-white to grayish-white, scaly. *P. albicaulis*

   4. Cones open when mature, elongated, 3-1/2" to 7" long, yellowish to yellowish-brown; scale tips thick, often reflexed; bark dark and blocky on mature trees. *P. flexilis*

5. Needles 1-1/2" to 3" long, 2 per fascicle, dark green to yellow-green, often twisted; cones small, recurved on branch, persist. *P. contorta*

5. Needles 3" to 11" long, 3 or 2 and 3 per fascicle; cones 3" long or longer. 6

    6. Cones with knoblike apophyses, asymmetrical, recurved on branches, in clusters, persist unopened. Needles 3" to 7" long, in 3's, yellow-green, flexible. *P. attenuata*

    6. Cone apophyses flat. Needles yellow-green to blue-green, 5" to 11" long, thick, mostly in 3's. 7

7. Cones 5" to 9" long, broad; needles blue-green to green; purplish-white to bluish-white bloom on new twigs. *P. jefferyi*

7. Cones 3" to 5" long; needles yellow-green; new twigs olive-brown. *P. ponderosa*

Pinus monticola Dougl.

western white pine

Habit: Tree 120' to 180' tall and 2' to 4' in diameter, with a long cylindrical bole that is commonly free of branches for 1/3 to 1/2 its length. The state tree of Idaho.

Needles: 5 per fascicle, 2" to 4" long, blue-green, slender and flexible, with white line of stomatal bloom on the 2 ventral (inner) surfaces only; apex blunt; sheath deciduous; leaves persist 3 to 4 years.

Cones: 5" to 12" long, cylindrical, thin-scaled, usually curved; apophyses yellowish-brown to brown; inner surface dark brown; umbo terminal and unarmed.

Twigs: Moderately stout, brown to gray; buds 1/4'' to 1/3'' long, apex acute, with yellowish-brown imbricate scales, loose at the tips.

Bark: Grayish-green, thin and smooth on young trees; resin blisters evident. On older trees the bark is dark gray to purplish-gray, broken into square or rectangular blocks, seldom over 1-1/2'' thick.

Habitat & Range: Found in the mountains on a variety of soils; but does best where soil is moist and well-drained. Ranges from southern British Columbia south to central California and western Nevada, also northeastern Oregon and the Inland Empire. Elevational range is 2,000 to 10,000 feet.

sugar pine   western white pine

Uses: Building construction, matches, boxes, millwork, pattern stock.

Remarks: The largest and finest stands composed predominantly of western white pine are found in northern Idaho. Elsewhere it occurs in mixture with other conifers. Attacked by white pine blister rust. Distinguished from *Pinus lambertiana* by grayer bark, blunter needles, erect appearance of the foliage, and smaller cones.

Pinus lambertiana Dougl.

sugar pine

Habit: Largest of the pines. 150' to over 200' tall, and 2' to 7' in diameter. Distinguishing characters include red, ridged bark; cylindrical bole free of branches for much of its length, and topped by an open crown composed of a few long, nearly horizontal, branches, with long cones, mostly solitary, hanging from the ends of these branches.

Needles: 5 per fascicle, 2″ to 4″ long, blue-green sharp-pointed; white lines of stomatal bloom on all surfaces; sheath deciduous; needles frequently tend to droop; persist 2 to 3 years.

Cones: 10″ to 18″, sometimes longer, cylindrical, thick-scaled, stalked; apophyses yellowish-brown; inner surface brown; umbo terminal, unarmed, commonly pitchy. Seeds 1/2″ to 5/8″ long.

Twigs: Moderately stout, grayish-yellowish-brown and minutely hairy; buds about 1/4″ long, round at the tip, scales yellowish-brown.

Bark: Thin, grayish-green and smooth on young trees; but begins to break up and roughen while the tree is still small. On old trees the bark is 1-1/2″ to 3″ thick, with reddish, narrow, broken, scaly ridges separated by deep furrows.

Habitat & Range: Occurs on a wide variety of soils in the mountains, usually a mixture with ponderosa pine, Douglas-fir, white fir, incense-cedar, and other conifers, never in pure stands. Ranges from Santiam Pass in the north-central Cascade Mountains in Oregon, southward through the Sierra Nevada Mountains in California and western Nevada, and into northern Baja California. Elevational range: 2,000 to 9,000 feet.

Uses: Building construction, boxes and crates, sash, doors, blinds, interior and exterior trim, siding, panels, matches, and pattern stock.

Remarks: Attacked by white pine blister rust. Tree wounds secrete a sweet and sugary exudate which has cathartic properties. Seeds of sugar pine were formerly carried by Indians as emergency rations. Intermediate tolerance.

Pinus flexilis James

limber pine

Habit: A high-altitude Rocky Mountain white pine. Usually a short, much-branched tree 25' to 50' tall, and 1' to 2-1/2' in diameter. The branches are tough and flexible with the needles clustered near the ends.

Needles: 5 per fascicle, 2" to 3" long, stout, dark green to yellow-green, with white lines of stomatal bloom on all surfaces (not always distinct); apex blunt; persist 4 to 6 years. Sheath deciduous.

Cones: 3-1/2" to 7" long, ovoid-cylindrical, bright green, but becoming yellowish-brown at maturity; scale tips thickened and often slightly reflexed; umbo terminal, unarmed; cones stalked.

Bark: Thin, greenish-gray to light brown on smaller trees; dark grayish-brown on old trees, furrowed and broken into rectangular blocks, 1-1/2" to 2" thick.

Habitat & Range: Occurs on dry, rocky soils; but does best on moist, well-drained sites, on subalpine slopes and ridges. Ranges from southeastern British Columbia and southern Alberta, southward through the Rocky Mountains, the Southwest, central and southern Sierra Nevada Mountains, and northeastern Oregon and the Black Hills; also northern Mexico. Elevational range: 7,000 to 10,500 feet.

Uses: None, except locally for mine timbers and railroad ties.

Remarks: Small branches very flexible. Occurs singly or in small pure stands; but more commonly found associated with lodgepole pine and mountain hemlock. Attacked by white pine blister rust.

Pinus albicaulis Engelm.

whitebark pine

Habit: A high-altitude white pine of the Pacific states; 20' to 50' tall, and 1' to 2' in diameter, often with a distorted bole, especially near timberline. Bark grayish white; needles clustered near tips of branches.

Needles: 1-1/2" to 3" long, somewhat stiff, green to yellow-green, with indistinct lines of white stomatal bloom on all surfaces; in fascicles of 5; sheath deciduous; leaves persist 4 to 8 years.

Cones: 1-1/2" to 3" long, broadly ovoid, purplish-brown when mature; scales thick; umbo terminal, pointed but unarmed. The cones fall from the tree unopened, and the seeds germinate in the disintegrating cone.

Bark: Usually less than 1/2" thick, grayish-white to brownish-white or grayish-brown; scaly; inner bark reddish-brown.

Habitat & Range: Found on subalpine slopes and ridges, usually on rocky soils. Ranges from central British Columbia to southwestern Alberta, southward through the Cascade Mountains of Washington and Oregon, and the Sierra Nevada Mountains to central California and western Nevada; also in the Rocky Mountains in Montana and Wyoming. Elevational range: 5,000 to 11,000 feet.

Uses: No commercial uses. Seeds large, eaten by humans and rodents.

Remarks: Susceptible to white pine blister rust.

Pinus jeffreyi Grev. & Balf.

Jeffrey pine

Habit: 80' to 140' tall and 3' to 4' in diameter; thick, straight, cylindrical bole; orange-brown or reddish-brown scaly bark; superficially very similar to ponderosa pine, but has larger cones, redder bark, and pitch with a fruity odor.

Needles: 3 (occasionally 2) per fascicle, 5" to 11" long, dark blue-green, often twisted, persisting 5 to 8 years; sheath persistent.

Cones: 5" to 9" long, occasionally longer, ovoid, broad, sessile; apophyses purplish-red, becoming dark reddish-brown; umbo dorsal, armed with a recurved prickle.

Twigs: New twigs covered with a purplish-white bloom. Cut or bruised twigs emit a sweet fruity odor.

Bark: Young bark similar to that of ponderosa pine; brown to nearly black, ridged and furrowed. Mature bark in broad, flat, scaly plates, orange-red to cinnamon-red in color.

Habitat & Range: Occurs on a wide variety of soils, including serpentine soils. Does best on gravelly to sandy, moist, well-drained sites, either in pure stands or mixed with ponderosa pine, lodgepole pine, sugar pine, white and red firs, and incense-cedar. Ranges from south-central Cascade Mountains in Oregon, southward through the Sierra Nevada Mountains of California and extreme western Nevada, occurs also in northern Baja California. Elevational Range: 3,000 to 9,500 feet.

Uses: Sold along with and as ponderosa pine.

Remarks: Wood contains the hydrocarbon "heptane," which is not found in ponderosa pine. Will endure greater extremes of climate than ponderosa pine. The bark beetle *Dendroctonus jeffreyi* commonly attacks this species but avoids ponderosa pine.

Pinus ponderosa Laws.

ponderosa pine

Habit: Very important large timber tree 125' to 180' tall and 3' to 6' in diameter. Open crown of green to yellow-green foliage clustered out near the branch ends. Yellow-brown bark in scaly plates. State tree of Montana.

Needles: 3, sometimes 2, per fascicle, 5" to 10" long, green to yellow-green, flexible; persist about 3 years. Sheath persistent.

Cones: 3" to 5" long (mostly 3" to 4"), ovoid, green to purplish-brown just before maturity, but turning brown; sessile; umbo dorsal, armed with a straight prickle.

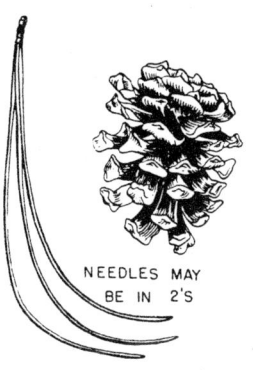

NEEDLES MAY BE IN 2'S

ponderosa pine

Twigs: Stout; new twigs olive-drab, yellowish, or tannish-green. Cut twigs emit odor of turpentine.

Bark: Young bark brown to nearly black, ridged and furrowed, eventually turning yellowish-brown in the furrows near the base of the tree, and gradually spreading over the ridges and up the bole. On old trees the bark is yellowish-brown in broad, flat, scaly plates and deep furrows. The scales look like jigsaw puzzle parts.

Habitat & Range: Grows on a wide variety of soils, and under varying moisture conditions, but most commonly found on dry, sandy, or gravelly soils. Ponderosa pine occurs in every state from the Rocky Mountains to the Pacific Coast, also in the Black Hills of South Dakota, and from southern British Columbia to northern Mexico. Elevational range: as low as 200 feet on the floor of the Willamette Valley, and up to 9,000 feet in the San Jacinto Mountains in California. Intolerant.

Uses: Millwork, boxes and crates, furniture, piling, poles, mine timbers, and general construction. It is probably the most important millwork and general-use species because of the large volume available and its versatility.

Remarks: Ponderosa pine has one of the most extensive ranges of any western conifer and is second only to Douglas-fir in the volume of sawtimber produced. It is the most important timber species in the vast region lying west of the Great Plains and east of the summit of the Cascades and east of the Coast Range of California. It forms extensive pure stands on drier sites, and also occurs in mixture with western larch, Douglas-fir, white fir, lodgepole pine, sugar pine, Jeffrey pine, incense-cedar, and other conifers.

Bark beetles that attack ponderosa pine include *Dendroctonus brevicomis* that attacks mature pines, and *Dendroctonus monticolae* that kills younger pines. Porcupines deform pines by girdling. Dwarf mistletoe weakens trees. Heart rots, however, are not a serious problem with ponderosa pine.

Pinus contorta Dougl.

lodgepole pine   **shore pine**

Habit: A tree 30' to 100' tall and 1' to 2' in diameter. Near the Pacific Ocean this species is often malformed, twisted, and contorted by the winds, and at times is no more than a large, bushy shrub. In the mountains it is often found in pure stands and has a straight, clear, cylindrical bole free of branches for much of its length.

Needles: 2 per fascicle, 1-1/2" to 3" long, green to yellow-green, stiff and commonly twisted; persist 4 to 8 years; sheath persistent. Other than Bishop pine, *P. muricata,* found in the Coast Range of California, it is the only 2-needle pine native to western United States.

Cones: 1" to 2" long, egg-shaped; base asymmetrical; apophyses yellowish-brown to brown, often slightly raised on one side near the base; umbo dorsal, armed with a deciduous prickle.
Cones are often recurved on the twig. Some cones will release seeds shortly after maturing; others may remain unopened several years; varies by location and specimen. Many trees have closed and open cones on them at all times.

Bark: Thin, dark, scaly (flaky), usually under 1" thick.

LITTLE CONES

lodgepole pine

Habitat & Range: Found on moist sandy and gravelly soils, in the dunes near the coast, coastal swamps, and northern bogs, and in the mountains at middle and higher elevations. Ranges from the Rocky Mountains to the Pacific Coast, and from the Yukon and southeastern Alaska southward into northern Baja California; also in the Black Hills. Elevational range: sea level to 11,500 feet. This pine occurs in the greatest range of altitudes and latitudes of any North American conifer.

Uses: Lumber, mine timbers, railroad ties, poles, boxes and crates, log building construction, corral poles, and pulpwood.

Remarks: Two varieties of this species are generally recognized. Shore pine (var. contorta) grows along the Pacific coast in association with Sitka spruce, rarely surpasses 45′ in height and generally has a rounded or windblown crown. Lodgepole pine (var. latifolia) inhabits the mountains throughout western North America, grows to 110′ tall and has a columnar growth form; associated species include ponderosa, Jeffrey and western white pines, mountain hemlock, red fir, subalpine fir and western larch. Both varieties are intolerant of shade.

NOTE: Little's 1979 **Checklist of United States Trees** recognizes a 3rd variety, *P. contorta* var. *murrayana,* Sierra lodgepole pine.

Pinus attenuata Lemm.

knobcone pine

Habit: Tree 40′ to 80′ tall, and up to 2′ in diameter; usually of poor form.

Needles: 3 per fascicle, 3″ to 7″ long, green or yellow-green, slender and flexible; sometimes twisted.

Cones: 4″ to 6″ long, ovoid-conic, yellowish-brown, asymmetrical at base; apophyses near the base and on one side of the cone raised and knoblike; umbos dorsal and initially armed with a minute prickle. The cones are recurved on the twigs, 3 to 6 in a cluster; they persist indefinitely on the tree unopened. Will open following a fire.

Bark: On the upper bole and larger branches thin, gray-orange-brown or gray-reddish-brown, with small, flaky scales; on the base of old trees gray-reddish-brown, furrowed, with superficially scaly, flattened ridges.

Habitat & Range: Usually on dry, rocky, sandy, or gravelly soils in the sun. Ranges from the Umpqua-

Willamette Divide in southwestern Oregon southward to northwestern Baja California. Will occupy drier sites than any other native Oregon pine.

Uses: Used locally for fuel.

Remarks: Aggressive on burns. It usually takes a fire to open the cones. Older trees are commonly forked.

Larix Mill.

larch

Habit: Moist-site, intolerant coniferous trees with deciduous leaves borne in clusters on spur shoots.

Leaves: Deciduous, soft, linear; borne singly and spirally on the current year's twigs, thereafter in dense clusters of 12 to 40 or more on spur shoots; leaves flat, or ridged on one or both surfaces.

Flowers: Monoecious. Staminate strobiles (cones) round to oblong, yellow to yellow-green; pistillate cones erect, bright red when young.

Cones: 1/2" to 2" long, oblong to subglobose, erect, stalked; scales thin and stiff; bracts longer or shorter than the scales; mature in one season, but persist indefinitely on the tree.

Twigs: Scaly. New twigs ridged or grooved; raised leaf scars on youngest twigs; spur shoots abundant on older branches.

Remarks: *Larix* is one of the few genera of conifers that have deciduous foliage. The arrangement and appearance of the leaves is very much like that of *Cedrus* (cedar), which is evergreen. All larches are found in the cooler regions of the Northern Hemisphere.

KEY TO NORTHWESTERN LARCHES

Leaves flattened-triangular in cross section, yellow-green; cones 1'' to 1-1/2'' long, with bracts slightly longer than cone scales. Young twigs smooth or with a few hairs.   *L. occidentalis*

Leaves 4-angled in cross section, yellow-green to blue-green; cones 1-1/2'' to 2'' long, with bracts much longer than cone scales. Young twigs densely woolly.   *L. lyallii*

Larix occidentalis Nutt.

western larch

Habit: A large tree 100'-180' tall, and 3'-4' in diameter; with soft, feathery foliage borne in clusters on spur shoots.

Needles: Deciduous, 1''-1-3/4'' long, linear; yellow-green, turning golden yellow in the fall; flattened-triangular in cross section.

Twigs: New twigs light colored, may be slightly hairy, but becoming smooth by the second year; yellowish-brown; bud scales slightly hairy.

Cones: Ovoid-oblong, 1''-1-1/2'' long, light brown; scales reflexed, with the apex finely toothed; shouldered bracts with central spines are longer than the cone scales.

Bark: Grayish-brown, thin and scaly on young trees; on mature trees yellowish-brown to cinnamon-brown, 3'' to 6'' thick, with flattened ridges separated by deep furrows. Sometimes resembles mature bark of ponderosa pine.

Habitat & Range: Found on moist mountain slopes, flats and near streams. Ranges from southeastern British Columbia southward through eastern washington to northern and northeastern Oregon, eastward to western Montana.

Uses: Lumber for general construction, interior trim, boxes and crates, poles, posts, ties, mine timbers, and general millwork.

Remarks: Western larch, the largest species in the genus *Larix,* attains its largest size in western Montana and northern Idaho. The thick bark at the base of the large trees makes it resistant to ground fires. It is one of the first species to seed-in an area following a fire. Occurs both in pure stands and in mixture with other intolerant conifers. It is very intolerant and moisture demanding. Logs are often defective because of "ring shake."

BARE IN WINTER.

western larch

Larix lyallii **Parl.**

subalpine larch   **alpine larch**

Habitat & Range: A timberline tree often growing on rocky soils. Found at high elevations in southern Alberta, southeastern British Columbia, eastern Washington, and northern and western Idaho. Not known to occur in Oregon.

Distinguishing Characteristics: Similar to *L. occidentalis* in most respects, but is a smaller tree, 30' to 40' tall, often stunted or distorted; also its leaves are 4-angled in cross section, sometimes blue-green, and its cones are longer, 1-1/2" to 2", with very long bracts. New twigs are covered with dense, white "wool"; so the tree is sometimes called "woolly larch"; this hair disappears after two years. Bark at first smooth, ashy-gray, becoming brown and separated into scaly ridges.

Remarks: Thought to be long-lived. Found in small, pure stands, as a scattered tree, or in mixture with mountain hemlock, subalpine fir, Engelmann spruce, and whitebark pine.

Picea A. Dietr.

spruce

Habit: Tolerant, evergreen coniferous trees 50' to 180' tall, with pointed, pyramidal crowns, and flaky (scaly) bark. The spirally arranged, linear leaves are often sharp.

Leaves: Persistent, spirally arranged, linear or acicular; 4-angled, semi-circular, or flatly triangular in cross section; sessile (lack a petiole), but borne on peg-like projections which are part of the twigs; apex pointed; one or all surfaces may be covered with a white stomatal bloom.

Flowers: Monoecious. Staminate cones erect or pendent; immature pistillate cones greenish to purple, borne in and near the top of the tree.

Cones: Pendent, borne predominantly in the top of the tree; ripen in one growing season; scales spirally arranged, imbricate, papery or semi-woody. Bracts much shorter than cone scales.

Twigs: Moderately slender, roughened with narrow, platelike scales ending in peglike projections (leaf scars); buds nonresinous or resinous; bud scales imbricated.

spruce

Remarks: Spruces are found in the temperate and cooler regions of the Northern Hemisphere. There are three spruces native to Oregon, and one or two others that are commonly planted. Each of the native species occupies a different type of habitat, and their ranges do not intermingle.

KEY TO NORTHWESTERN SPRUCES

1. Leaf apex round or blunt, leaves semi-circular in cross section; crown sparse; lateral branchlets very pendulous and flexible. Cones 2-1/2" to 6" long, with rounded scale-tips.   *P. brewerana*

1. Leaves slender, apex sharp. Cones 1-1/2" to 3-1/2" long, scales with erose margins.   2

    2. Leaves about 1" long, tend to be perpendicular to the twig; apex with a long callus tip; flat or flattened-diamond shape in cross section. Cone bracts slender-pointed, at least 1/3 as long as cone scale.   *P. sitchensis*

    2. Leaves about 1" long; tend to point forward; 4-angled in cross section; emit a rank odor when bruised. Cone bracts blunt-pointed, not over 1/3 as long as cone scales.   *P. engelmannii*

Picea sitchensis (Bong.) Carr.

Sitka spruce

Habit: Largest of the spruces. 125' to 180' tall, and 3' to 5' in diameter, with an open crown of somewhat pendulous branchlets; bases of very large trees frequently buttressed.

Leaves: 1/2" to 1-1/8" long, linear, flat to flattened-diamond shape in cross section; yellowish-green with white stomatal bloom on one side; apex with an attenuate callus tip; leaves tend to be perpendicular to the twig. A Sitka spruce leaf does **not** roll easily between the fingers (test for flatness).

Cone: 1-1/2" to 3-1/2" long, oblong shape; scales yellowish-tan, papery but somewhat stiff, margins erose.

Twigs: Current year's twigs moderately slender, smooth, yellowish-brown to orange-brown.

Bark: Thin and scaly on young trees; on larger trees usually less than 1'' thick, gray (or brown) and scaly.

Habitat & Range: Moist, well-drained sites along the coast, seldom more than 50 miles from the Pacific Ocean and usually much less. Ranges from southern and southeastern Alaska southward along the coast to northern California. Elevational range: sea level to 4,000 feet in the north, seldom above 1,800 feet in the Pacific Northwest.

Uses: Lumber for light construction, aircraft and boats; food containers; general millwork; ladder rails, piano sounding boards; dairy, poultry and apiary supplies. It is the second most important pulpwood species in the Pacific Northwest.

Remarks: A tidewater, fogbelt species. Sitka spruce and western hemlock are the principal species in the coastal forests of Alaska. A mixed stand of these two species has the greatest growth rate of any of our timber species.

Picea engelmannii Parry

Engelmann spruce

Habit: An inhabitant of the mountains, 80' to 120' tall, and 1-1/2' to 3' in diameter, with a dense crown of blue-green foliage.

Leaves: About 1" long, slender, pointed, linear, 4-angled in cross section, sharp to the touch; tend to point forward emit a rank odor when crushed. A leaf rolls easily between the fingers.

Cones: 1'' to 2-1/2'' long, oblong, yellowish-tan in color; scales thin and papery; scale margins erose; bract blunt-pointed, usually not over 1/3 as long as the scale.

Twigs: New twigs minutely hairy the first season, moderately slender, grayish-brown.

Habitat & Range: Does best on moist, well-drained soils, but can grow on thin soils of mountain slopes or the wet margins of swamps, streams and lakes. Ranges from central British Columbia and southwestern Alberta, southward thorugh the Cascades of Washington and Oregon into extreme northern California, eastward into the Rocky Mountains from central Montana to southern New Mexico. Elevational range: 1,500 to 6,000 feet in Canada; 3,500 to 10,000 feet in the Cascades; and up to 12,500 feet in the southern Rocky Mountains.

Bark: Thin, purplish to reddish-brown, with loosely attached scales.

Uses: Principally for lumber and pulp; limited uses for mine timbers, railroad ties and poles; also subflooring, sheathing and studding.

Remarks: Found only in the inland mountains, not in the Coast Range. It is essentially a species of the higher altitudes and is found growing in the timberline zones. It forms extensive pure stands; or is often found in mixture with lodgepole pine, mountain hemlock, subalpine fir, Alaska yellow-cedar, silver and noble firs, and occasionally with Douglas-fir. Very tolerant in its younger years, but becomes less so as it ages. Usually a heavy seed producer. Prostrate branches which become covered with soil or humus may root.

Picea brewerana S. Wats.

Brewer spruce   weeping spruce

Habit: A little-known tree distinguished by its sparse, open crown, and long pendulous middle and lower branches. 50' to 80' tall, and 1-1/2' to 2-1/2' in diameter.

Leaves: 3/4" to 1" long, flat to rounded-triangular; white stomatal bloom on lower surface; apex round to blunt; leaves tend to point forward on the twig.

Cones: 2-1/2" to 6" long, oblong-cylindrical, with rounded scale-tips; purplish-red, but becoming reddish-brown at maturity; scales semi-woody in texture. Similar in appearance to mountain hemlock but usually longer.

Twigs: Pendulous, slender, flexible, and whip-like, 4' to 8' long; grayish brown; at first slightly hairy, but becoming smooth.

Bark: Usually less than 1" thick, reddish-brown, and with long, firmly attached scales.

Habitat & Range: Found on steep mountain slopes and ridges, on dry to moist rocky soils, in the Siskiyou Mountains of southwestern Oregon and northern California.

Remarks: The rarest and least know American spruce. Difficult to propagate. Species name sometimes spelled "breweriana."

Pseudotsuga **Carr.**

Douglas-fir

Habit: Coniferous trees with dense, pyramidal crowns; sharp-pointed buds; cones with 3-pronged bracts that are longer than the cone scales.

Leaves: Spirally arranged, linear, slender, flat, with two broad, white bands of stomatal bloom on the underside; apex blunt to pointed; base of leaf constricted into a petiole; leaf scar small, nearly round, half-raised.

Flowers: Monoecious. Both sexes borne throughout the crown; staminate cones cylindrical; immature pistillate cones erect, reddish or green, with 3-pronged bracts longer than the floral scales.

Cones: Pendent, ovoid-cylindrical; semi-woody scales, subtended by 3-pronged bracts; mature in one season.

Buds: Spindle-shaped, sharp pointed; with shiny, reddish-brown imbricated scales, which persist during the first growing season.

Twigs: Slender; leaf scar small, oval, half-raised. Knobby nodes.

Remarks: There are two species of *Pseudotsuga* native to the Pacific Coast region of the United States and British Columbia, three other species are found in Formosa, Japan, and southwestern China. The lesser species native to the United States is *Pseudotsuga macrocarpa* (Vasey) Mayr, bigcone Douglas-fir, native to the mountains of southern California.

Pseudotsuga menziesii (Mirb.) Franco.

Douglas-fir

Habit: A large tree 100' to 250' or more tall, and 3' to 6' in diameter; with a broad, pointed, pyramidal crown of dense foliage.

Leaves: About 1" long (1/2" to 1-1/2"), soft, slender, yellow-green, gray-green, or blue-green; linear and flattened; slightly grooved above, and with 2 white bands of stomatal bloom on the underside; apex blunt or pointed; base constricted into a petiole;

spirally arranged, but at times may be obscurely 2-ranked. Youngest branchlets often pendulous, especially on mature trees.

Cones: 3" to 4" long, ovoid-cylindrical; reddish-brown with semi-woody scales; trident bracts longer than the scales; pendent and borne throughout the crown.

Twigs: Young twigs at first minutely hairy but soon becoming smooth; yellowish-green, but becoming grayish-green with age.

Buds: About 1/4" long, spindle-shaped, pointed; lustrous, reddish-brown, nonresinous, imbricated scales.

Bark: On small trees gray or ashy-brown, thin, smooth, and with resin blisters; pole-size timber grayish-brown and somewhat mottled with lighter colored areas, and with broad, shallow fissures and broad, flat ridges; on mature trees 3" to 10" or more thick near the base, coarse, dark grayish-brown, deeply and irregularly ridged and fissured. Inner bark 2-toned; alternating layers of reddish-brown and cream-colored cork. On very old trees the bark is often yellowish-brown, and superficially scaly. The sloughing of the bark of very old trees may build up a mound around the bases of the trees.

" PITCHFORKS"

Douglas-fir

Habitat & Range: Will grow on a wide variety of soils, but in the Douglas-fir Region of western Oregon and Washington does best on deep, moist, sandy loams; poorest on gravelly soils. Ranges from central British Columbia and southwestern Alberta southward into the mountains of northern and central Mexico, and from the Pacific Coast to the Rocky Mountains. Elevational range: sea level to 5,000 feet along the coast; up to 7,200 feet in the Cascades and Sierras; and up to 11,000 feet in the southern Rocky Mountains. Douglas-fir is intermediate in tolerance, slightly tolerant in its youth, but becoming less tolerant with age.

Uses: Douglas-fir is the most important lumber tree in the nation. It is the principal wood for structural lumber and timbers; the leading veneer species for construction grades of plywood; and used extensively for ties, poles, piling, battery separators, flooring, general construction. It is finding increased use in the manufacture of pulp. There are species superior to Douglas-fir for certain uses, but it often takes over as an excellent substitue. Chemical derivatives of Douglas-fir **bark** include tannin, waxes, and dihydroquercetin (a food preservative). More than 20% of the sawtimber volume in the United States is Douglas-fir.

Remarks: Two forms of Douglas-fir are recognized, the Pacific Coast form, *P. menziesii* var. *menziesii,* and the Rocky Mountain form, *P. menziesii* var. *glauca.* Occurs in even-aged stands, or in mixture with western hemlock; grand, silver, noble and white firs; ponderosa pine, western larch and other species. It is the most common and most abundant tree in the Pacific Northwest.

Tsuga (Endl.) Carr.

hemlock

Habit: Tolerant, moist-site coniferous trees with pyramidal crowns, pendulous branchlets, and drooping leader.

Leaves: Persistent, linear, soft; spirally arranged, but frequently 2-ranked; flattened or thickened in cross section; apex round, and occasionally notched, or acute; base of the needle constricted to about the width of the midrib to form a petiole.

Flowers: Monoecious. Staminate cones axillary on previous season's growth; pistillate cones terminal.

Cones: Oblong to oblong-cylindrical, pendent; scales thin and semi-woody; mature in one season.

Twigs: Very slender, smooth or pubescent; roughened by slender, diagonally raised pegs to which the leaves are attached; buds small, and about 1/16" long, and covered with brown, imbricated scales.

Bark: Inner bark purplish-red to chocolate-red; rich in tannin.

Remarks: Hemlocks are found on moist sites in the temperate regions of the Northern Hemisphere. They are subject to attack by numerous insects and diseases. Because of their thin bark, hemlocks are easily damaged during logging. Very tolerant. There are four species of hemlock indigenous to the United States, two are native to the East and two are found in the West.

KEY TO HEMLOCKS

Leaves flat, varying in length; tend to be 2-ranked, yellow-green. Cones 3/4" to 1" long.   *T. heterophylla*

Leaves thickened, not 2-ranked; blue-green. Cones 1-1/4" to 3" long.   *T. mertensiana*

Tsuga heterophylla (Raf.) Sarg.

western hemlock

Habit: Large trees 125' to 200'tall, and 2' to 4' in diameter; with a pyramidal crown of somewhat pendulous branches and fine foliage.

Leaves: 1/4" to 3/4" long, linear, flat; dark glossy green and grooved above, with 2 white bands of stomatal bloom on the underside; apex round; short petiole; varying length of leaves conspicuous, the shorter ones arising from the top of the twig; tend to be 2-ranked.

Cones: 3/4" to 1" long, oblong, pend-
dent, sessile; purplish-red but
becoming reddish-brown at maturity; scales thin, semi-woody;
borne throughout the crown;
mature in one season.

Twigs: Slender, flexible, minutely pubescent; roughened
by raised, peglike leaf scars.

DROOPY TOP

Bark: Thin, superficially scaly,
brown to black on small
trees; on old trees about 1" thick, with flattened
ridges; inner bark dark red streaked with purple.

Habitat & Range: Does best on deep, moist, well-drained
soils. Ranges from southern Alaska southward
through western and southeastern British Columbia
through western Washington to northwestern California, eastward through northern Idaho and western
Montana. Elevational range: sea level to 2,700 feet
in Alaska; sea level to 5,000 feet in British Columbia;
sea level to 6,000 feet in Oregon and Washington.

Uses: Pulp, lumber for general construction, aircraft
veneer, plywood. Bark is a source of tannin.

Remarks: Very tolerant throughout its life. Found in
pure stands but most common in mixture with other
species. Common associates include Douglas-fir, Sitka
spruce, western redcedar, western white pine, grand
fir, silver fir, noble fir, mountain hemlock and Alaska
yellow-cedar. Thin bark makes it very susceptible to
logging and fire damage. Western hemlock is the principal pulpwood species in the Pacific Northwest.

Tsuga mertensiana (Bong.) Carr.

mountain hemlock

Habit: Coniferous tree 60' to 100' tall, and 2' to 3' in diameter; with a pyramidal crown of drooping branches and dense foliage.

Leaves: 1/2" to 3/4" long, linear, thickened (flatly tri-angular); dark green to blue-green with white stoma-tal bloom on all surfaces; apex blunt; petiole short; spirally arranged about the twig, but densest on the upper side; on the very short lateral branchlets the leaves appear to be grouped in starlike clusters.

Cones: 1-1/4" to 3" long, oblong-cylindrical, sessile; dark purplish-red but turning brown when mature; pendent, but occasionally may be erect; scales thin, semi-woody; borne in the upper portion of the crown. Resemble the cones of *Picea brewerana,* Brewer spruce, but are smaller and have conspicuous radial lines on the scales.

Twigs: Slender, or moderately stout when slow growing; light reddish-brown in color and covered with a minute pubescence; numerous short lateral twigs on the main branches.

Bark: Begins to break up early in life; on larger trees dull purplish-brown to dark reddish-brown, with nar-row round ridges; about 1" to 1-1/2" thick.

Habitat & Range: Usually a tree of high elevations or the cooler exposures of the middle slopes. It does best on moist, coarse, well-drained soils. Ranges from southern Alaska southward to central California, and east to northeastern Oregon, northern Idaho and western Montana. Elevational range: sea level to 3,200 feet in Alaska; 2,000 to 5,500 feet in British Columbia; 4,000 to 9,500 feet in the Cascade Moun-tains; and 6.000 to 11,000 feet in California.

Uses: Formerly not considered a commercial species. Mountain hemlock has recently come into its own and is being used for pulp and general construction.

Remarks: Very tolerant. Does best on northern exposures. Commonly found in mixture with lodgepole pine, subalpine and noble firs, Douglas-fir and Engelmann spruce. Bark rich in tannin.

Abies Mill.

fir

Habit: Tall, erect-coned, evergreen, moist-site trees with dense, conical crowns. The true firs usually have stiff, formal, layered appearance, because of the tendency of the branches to divide, re-divide, and subdivide, as many as seven times all in one plane.

Leaves: Linear, borne singly, spirally arranged, but usually clustered on the upper side of the twig; in some species 2-ranked; somewhat stiff, flattened or thickened in cross section; lines of white stomatal bloom on one or both surfaces; sessile (foliage slightly constricted at the base, but lacks a petiole). Leaves on cone-bearing (upper) branches are **not** typical.

Flowers: Monoecious. Staminate cones pendent, cylindrical, borne on the underside of the branches in the middle and upper crown; immature pistillate cones erect, borne near the top of the tree.

Cones: Borne erect in the top of the tree; bracts longer or shorter than the cone scales, if longer they are frequently reflexed; disintegrate when mature leaving an erect axis that may persist until the next spring; mature in one season.

Twigs: Smooth and a bit shiny, or pubescent; leaf scars large, round, flat; buds round to ovoid, more or less resinous (some exceptions), frequently in 3's at the tip of the twigs.

Bark: Resin blisters conspicuous on the bark of young trees.

Remarks: Six of the 11 true firs indigenous to the United States are native to the Pacific states.

KEY TO WESTERN FIRS

1. Leaves on underside of twig are hockey-stick-shaped (base parallels the twig); leaves 4-angled in cross section (flatly diamond-shaped on lower branches); tend to point upward; have bloom on both surfaces. Young twigs reddish. Cones 4" to 9" long and 2" to 3" in diameter. **RED FIRS 2**

1. Leaves straight, flat; base does not parallel the twig; may be 2-ranked or concentrated on upper side of twig; may have bloom on one or both leaf surfaces. Young twigs not reddish. Cones mostly 2" to 4" long (occasionally longer), and less than 2" in diameter (up to 2-1/2" diameter in *Abies amabilis;* mostly 3/4" to 1-3/4" in other species). **WHITE FIRS 3**

    2. Leaves grooved on upper surface (sometimes flat). Outside of cone almost completely covered with ends of long bracts. *A. procera*

    2. Leaves ridged on upper surface (occasionally flat). Bracts shorter than cone scales. *A. magnifica*

3. White bloom on all leaf surfaces. **4**

3. White bloom on lower leaf surfaces only; upper surface lustrous green. **5**

    4. Leaves erect, about 1" long. *A. lasiocarpa*

    4. Leaves tend to be 2-ranked; may curve out and upward in a boat-rib pattern; bloom on the upper surface at times may be seen in the groove only. *A. concolor*

5. Leaves 2-ranked (may be flat or V-shaped) and of
   unequal length. Cones cylindrical.   *A. grandis*

5. Leaves crowded on upper side of the twig (not 2-ranked);
   tend to point forward, sideward, and diagonally upward.
   Cones barrel-shaped. Buds heavily resinous.
                                                 A. amabilis

Abies amabilis (Dougl.) Forbes

Pacific silver fir   **silver fir**

Habit: Coniferous tree with a long conical crown of
dense foliage; thin, mottled ashy-gray to chalky-white
bark. Size 100' to 180' tall and 2' to 4' in diameter.

Leaves: 3/4" to 1-1/4" long, linear, flat, dark lustrous
green and grooved above, silvery-white below; apex
rounded and usually notched; spirally arranged, but
clustered on the upper side of the twig and tending to
point forward, sideward, and diagonally upward; foliage on cone-bearing branches thicker, pointed, stoma-
tiferous on all surfaces and tending to be erect.

Cones: 3-1/2" to 6" long, cylindrical to barrel-shaped;
purplish to purplish-brown in color; bracts shorter
than the scales, round shouldered, gradually narrow-
ing to a point.

Twigs: Moderately stout, fairly stiff; yellowish-brown,
covered with very short inconspicuous hairs when
new; buds spherical, purple under the pitch, usually
in 3's at the tip of the twig, very densely pitched
over.

Bark: Gray-green, smooth and with resin blisters on
young trees; older trunks have thin, mottled ashy-
gray to chalky-white bark that is superficially scaly;
on very old trees the bark may be furrowed near the
base.

Habitat & Range: Occurs on moist, well-drained, sand and gravelly soils from southeastern Alaska southward through western British Columbia, and western Washington and Oregon, also local area in northwestern California. Elevational range: sea level to 1,000 feet in Alaska; sea level to 5,000 feet in British Columbia; and 1,000 to 6,500 feet in Washington and Oregon.

Uses: Lumber for general construction.

Remarks: May occasionally be found in small, pure stands, but more commonly found in mixture with western hemlock, noble fir, grand fir, Douglas-fir and western redcedar; and in the upper elevations with mountain hemlock, Engelmann spruce, whitebark pine, Alaska yellow-cedar and lodgepole pine. Moderately tolerant. Seed germinates on duff or mineral soil.

Abies concolor (Gord. & Glend.) Lindl.

white fir

Habit: Coniferous tree up to 200' tall and 3' to 5' in diameter.

Leaves: 1-1/2" to 3" long; linear; rounded apex. Yellowish-green to green with white bloom on both surfaces (on upper surface bloom may be confined to central groove). Generally 2-ranked, but often upturned in a V or U shape.

Cones: 3" to 5" long, oblong to barrel-shaped; olive-brown in color; bracts shorter than the scales; very similar in appearance to *A. grandis,* grand fir.

Twigs: Moderately slender, yellowish-green to olive-brown and smooth; buds usually in 3's, the center bud is the most prominent, covered with a light gray pitch.

Habitat & Range: Occurs on moist, well-drained, coarse soils, or on dry soils, in the mountains. Primarily a tree of southwestern United States; most common in Rocky Mountains and Sierras. Ranges from northeastern and central Oregon southward into Lower California, eastward to western Wyoming and southern New Mexico. Elevational range: 3,000 to 8,000 feet in Oregon; and 3,800 to 10,000 feet in California.

Uses: General construction, boxes and crates, millwork, and pulpwood.

Bark: On young trees greenish-gray, thin and smooth, with resin blisters; on old trees ashy-gray and thick, with roughened, flattened ridges and irregular furrows; the inner bark is two-toned, with alternating layers of dark reddish-brown and light tan cork. The inner bark resembles that of Douglas-fir.

Remarks: The thick bark near the base of the tree makes it somewhat fire-resistant. White fir requires less moisture than any of the other western true firs. The seeds germinate satisfactorily on a variety of sites. It is very susceptible to diseases from pole size to maturity. It is very tolerant, especially in younger stages, hence it frequently replaces less tolerant pines in mixed stands. Seldom occurs in pure stands, but found associated with ponderosa and sugar pines, Douglas-fir, subalpine and California red firs, incensecedar and aspen.

Abies grandis (Dougl.) Lindl.

grand fir   **lowland white fir**

Habit: A large conifer 125' to 250' tall, and 2' to 6' in diameter; with a long, narrow open crown that is rounded or flat-topped.

Leaves: 3/4'' to 2'' long, linear; lustrous dark yellow-green and grooved on the upper side, and with two bands of white stomatal bloom on the underside; apex is rounded or notched; the leaves arise from all sides of the twigs, but due to a twist in the bases they appear to arise from the sides of the twigs; the leaf lengths vary; 2-ranked; the leaves in the middle and upper crown may tend to be erect, and on fertile branches they may be pointed.

Twigs: Brown to reddish-brown, initially with minute light brown hairs; buds resinous.

Bark: 2″ to 3″ thick on mature trees, furrowed, with flattened ridges; ashy-brown in color and mottled with lighter-colored areas, inner bark dark purplish-red.

Cones: Cylindrical, 2-1/2″ to 4″ long, green to greenish-purple.

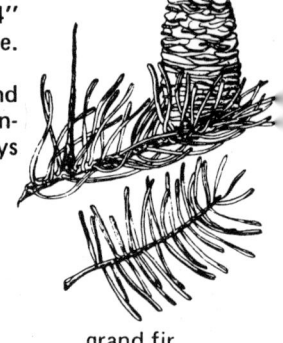

grand fir

Habitat & Range: Usually found on moist situations on mountain slopes and in the valleys and bottomlands. Ranges from southern British Columbia southward on the west side of the Cascade Mountains into northwestern California, eastward through northern Idaho and western Montana. Elevational range: sea level to 6,000 feet.

Uses: General construction, boxes and crates, millwork, and pulpwood.

Remarks: In Oregon, grand fir is widely distributed from the upper mountains down through the lowland valleys. It is the only true fir found at sea level in the state. Grand fir seldom occurs in pure stands, but is usually in mixture with other conifers, or in the lowlands with hardwoods. It is more tolerant than

Douglas-fir and the pines, but less tolerant than western hemlock, western redcedar, and silver fir. It is commonly attacked by the Indian paint fungus.

Abies lasiocarpa (Hook.) Nutt.

subalpine fir   **alpine fir**

Habit: A conifer of the higher elevations with a long, spirelike crown, and in open situations the branches are retained for nearly the full length of the tree. It is 40' to 100' tall, and 1' to 2' in diameter; at timberline may not attain a height of more than 5 or 6 feet.

Leaves: 1/2" to 1-1/2" long, linear; blue-green to silvery green, with bloom on all leaf surfaces; spirally arranged, but massed on the upper side of the twig and nearly erect; apex round or notched, pointed on fertile branches. Two resin ducts may be visible in the pulp of the leaf when viewed in cross section.

Cones: 2-1/2" to 4" long, cylindrical; purple, but becoming purplish-gray in color; frequently in clusters of 4 to 6 on the short, topmost branches; bracts shorter than the scales, rounded.

Twigs: Orange-brown, covered with minute hairs the first season or two, then becoming smooth; buds small, subglobose, resinous.

Bark: Ashy-gray to almost white; unbroken, except on the bases of older trees where it has shallow fissures and is reddish; if the bark is ridged or plated it may be superficially scaly. Resin pockets are scattered through the inner bark.

Habitat & Range: Found on subalpine slopes, ridges and valleys where there is adequate moisture. Ranges from southeastern Alaska and the Yukon southward through British Columbia and southeastern Alberta, in the Olympic Mountains, the Cascade Mountains of Washington and Oregon, eastward to the Rocky

Mountains from western Montana southward into New Mexico and southeastern Arizona, also local in Nevada. Elevational range: sea level to 3,000 feet in Alaska; 2,000 to 7,000 feet in Canada; 2,100 to 7,800 feet in the Cascades and Blue Mountains, 3,500 to 9,500 feet in the Rocky Mountains.

Uses: Used locally for fuel and corral poles; also for pulp.

Remarks: Occurrence seems to be governed by adequate moisture. Forms small pure stands, but commonly occurs in mixture with Engelmann spruce, lodgepole pine, mountain hemlock, western white pine, noble and silver firs, and whitebark pine. Requires less moisture than Engelmann spruce, but will grow on wetter sites. Very tolerant, only slightly less so than Engelmann spruce and mountain hemlock.

LIKE CHURCH SPIRE

subalpine fir

Abies magnifica **A. Murr.**

California red fir — red fir

Habit: A large conifer, 125' to 200' tall, and 2-1/2' to 5' in diameter; with thick, coarse, dark reddish-brown to purplish-black bark.

Leaves: 3/4" to 1-1/4" long, linear; spirally arranged, but massed on the upper side of the twig, pointing upward; silvery-green to blue-green, with white stomatal bloom on all surfaces; apex round or blunt, pointed on fertile (cone-bearing) branches; leaves on lower branches slightly thickened; higher up they are 4-angled in cross section; the leaf is shaped like a hockey stick, and its base tends to parallel the twig for a short distance; often have a slight ridge running longitudinally down the center of the top side.

Cones: 6" to 9" long, 2" to 3" in diameter, cylindrical; dark purple to purplish-brown or brown at maturity; bracts of the main species shorter than the cone scales.

Twigs: Moderately stout; yellow-green to olive-brown or light brown and lightly pubescent, later glabrous, reddish-brown and eventually ashy-gray in color; buds small, usually less than 1/4" long, brown, mostly non-resinous.

Bark: Ashy-white to chalky-white on pole and small saw-timber size trees; on old trees thick, coarse, deeply ridged and furrowed, dark-reddish brown to purplish-black; the ridges are broken into plates; inner bark dark reddish-brown.

Habitat & Range: Intermediate tolerance. Grows best on moist, well-drained soils in subalpine situations. The range of the main species is limited to California, extreme western Nevada and the Siskiyous of southern Oregon. The species is most abundant in the Sierra-Nevada Mountains as far south as Sequoia National Park at elevations of 7,000 to 9,000 feet. It has been found as low as 4,000 feet. It occurs in the northern part of the California Coast Range and in the northern and central Sierras.

Uses: General construction, boxes and crates, and mill-work.

Remarks: Forms large pure stands or occurs in mixture with white fir, mountain hemlock, western white pine, sugar pine, ponderosa pine and Douglas-fir. Red fir makes premium-priced Christmas trees. Crosses with noble fir where their ranges overlap. Some authors consider this cross a separate variety *(Abies magnifica* var. *shastensis).*

Abies procera Rehd.

noble fir

Habit: A tall, rather intolerant, straight tree with the trunk often clear of limbs for half to two-thirds its length. The crown is conical on open grown trees, but more rounded when crowded in mature stands. Size: 140' to 200' tall, and 3' to 5' in diameter.

Leaves: 3/4" to 1-1/4" long, linear, massed on the upper side of the twigs; blue-green with white stomatal bloom on all surfaces; thickened to 4-angled in cross section, slightly grooved on the upper surface, or sometimes flat; apex round or pointed; base not constricted; leaves arising from the underside of the twig shaped like a hockey stick, the base tending to parallel the twig.

Cones: 4" to 6" long, about 2" in diameter, cylindrical; green to olive-brown in color; bracts longer than the cone scales, margins serrated, spinose tip about as long as the exposed portion of the scale; the bracts are turned downward and almost completely ensheathe the cone scales.

Twigs: Moderately slender, reddish-brown in color, minutely pubescent the first few years; buds small, reddish-brown, often enclosed by clustered leaves, not pitched over, lateral buds not in the same plane, but attached somewhat below the main bud.

Bark: Smooth gray-green and blistered on young trees; on mature trees purplish-gray and eventually reddish-brown, the narrow ridges are broken into rectangular blocks which are superficially scaly.

Habitat & Range: Mountain slopes, benches and low ridges; moisture demanding, but not demanding in other soil requirements. Found in Washington and Oregon in the Coast Range and the Cascade Mountains, and as far south as the Siskiyou and Scott Mountains in northwestern California. Elevational range: 1,400 to 6,000 feet.

Uses: Lumber for general construction, boxes, crates, and millwork.

Remarks: The thin bark makes noble fir easily susceptible to fire damage. W.F. McCulloch reports "the dry heartwood and wet sapwood provides a curious phenomenon—trees with tops burned off in slash fires have been known to hold fire over winter, a great coal of fire working down the inside of the trunk as much as 40 feet to form a stove-pipe; this may break out as late as May or June following a fall slash fire."

Grows in pure stands, or in mixture with Douglas-fir; western and mountain hemlocks; silver, grand, subalpine, and California red firs; white and sugar pines. Intolerant, less tolerant than any of the other true firs. Crosses with California red fir where their ranges overlap.

Noble fir is commonly called "larch" by many loggers. Larch Mountain in northwestern Oregon supports a forest of noble fir, but no larch.

TAXODIACEAE — Baldcypress Family

Sequoia Endl.
Sequoiadendron Buchholz

Sequoia	redwood
Sequoiadendron	bigtree

Habit: Very large evergreen trees with thick fibrous bark and soft, porous, durable, reddish wood.

Leaves: Persistent, of 2 types: (a) flatly linear and 2-ranked, and (b) awl-like to lanceolate, somewhat appressed to the twig and tending to point forward. Dead leaves fall in sprays, not singly, leaving an oblong twig scar.

Flowers: Monoecious.

Cones: Pendent, barrel-shaped; scales spirally arranged, peltate and wrinkled; cones attain full size the first season, but in one species require an additional year to mature.

Remarks: In early geological periods trees of this family were common throughout much of North America and Europe. Today two genera remain which are restricted in range almost wholly within the state of California. Both attain an immense size and are generally recognized as being the largest living plants. These genera derive their names from a half-breed Cherokee Indian, Sequoiah, who developed the first alphabet used by that tribe.

Sequoia sempervirens (D. Don) Endl.

redwood   coast redwood

Habit: A large tree 180' to 370' tall, and 8' to 23' in diameter, with dark reddish-brown fibrous bark. In young trees the crown is conical in shape and the lateral branches tend to curve downward; in old trees the crown is often short, round or flat-topped, with a few large lateral branches. The boles of old trees are often buttressed at the base.

Leaves: Linear, flat, 1/2" to 1" long, spirally arranged, 2-ranked; dark yellow-green above and with two bands of white stomatal bloom on the underside; apex acute; petiole absent, but the base of the leaf is firmly attached to the twig below the point of union. On the topmost branches the leaves are closely appressed to the twig, and at first glance appear to resemble the foliage of the giant sequoia or bigtree. Dead leaves fall in sprays.

Cones: Oblong or barrel-shaped, 3/4" to 1" long, about 1/2" or 5/8" in diameter; reddish-brown to dark brown; scales spirally arranged, peltate, and wrinkled; mature in one growing season.

Twigs: Moderately slender, round, green at first but later turning brown.

Bark: Bark reddish brown or brick-colored; outer layer sometimes weathered to grayish-brown; fibrous, 3" to 12" thick.

Habitat & Range: Found on moist, well-drained, sandy and clayey-loam soils, in the fog belt area along the Pacific Coast, from southern Curry County in extreme southwestern Oregon southward to Monterey County in mid-California. Range varies in width from 10 to 40 miles, and the continuity of the north-south range is broken in several places along the coast. Elevational range: sea level to 3,000 feet.

Uses: Lumber and dimensional stock for homes, industrial building, bridges, trestles and heavy construction; siding, sashes, doors, sills, paneling, tanks, silos, caskets, cigar boxes, storm gutters, outdoor furniture, grape stakes, posts and numerous other uses. The wood is very durable and requires no preservative treatment when in contact with the soil. The bark is used in insulating board and as an ingredient in linoleum.

Remarks: Redwood occurs in pure stands, but is more commonly found in mixture with Douglas-fir, Sitka spruce, Port-Orford-cedar, grand fir, western hemlock, western redcedar, California laurel, tanoak, torreya, red alder and bigleaf maple. Heavy fogs and rain appear to restrict the species to its present range. Moderately tolerant. It is the only western conifer which will stump sprout, and that is an important method of natural regeneration. Small detached burls will sprout when placed in water.

Redwood attains the greatest height of any living plant. The Founder's Tree in northwestern California is 364' tall and 12.6' in diameter.

Dawn redwood, *Metasequoia glyptostroboides,* resembles coast redwood but has deciduous foliage, opposite leaf arrangement, and opposite cone scales.

Sequoiadendron giganteum (Lindl.) Buchholz

giant sequoia   **bigtree**

Habit: Mammoth trees 200' to 300' tall, and 10' to 20' in diameter. Young trees have long conical crowns extending nearly to the ground; in large old trees the crown is irregular in shape and often broken, the base is often buttressed and fire-scarred.

Leaves: Spirally arranged, awl-like to lanceolate, 1/4'' to 1/2'' long; blue-green to green, stomatal bloom on all surfaces; somewhat appressed to the twig or spreading; rigid and sharp-pointed; turn brown at the end of the 3rd or 4th year, but may persist for some time. Dead leaves fall in sprays.

Cones: Barrel-shaped, 2'' to 3'' long; yellowish-brown to reddish-brown; scales peltate, spirally arranged, and wrinkled; seeds covered with a red pigment. Cones attain full size the first year but require an additional year to mature.

Bark: 12 inches or more thick at the base of old trees, but thinner higher up the bole; orange-brown to cinnamon-red in color, fibrous and spongy.

FAMOUS
CALIFORNIA
VISITOR

bigtree

Habitat & Range: Deep, moist, well-drained sandy and gravelly soils on middle and upper slopes of the Sierra Nevada Mountains in central California from Placer County to Tulare County. Range spotty. Elevational range: 5,000 to 8,500 feet.

Uses: Giant sequoia is seldom cut for commercial purposes. Most groves are being preserved in state and national parks for their esthetic value.

Remarks: Giant sequoia may occur in small pure groves, but it more commonly is found growing in mixture with white fir, red fir, Douglas-fir, ponderosa pine, sugar pine, and incense-cedar. Intermediate tolerance. Reproduction is best on mineral soil. Fire scars are common on all the older trees.

The wood is very brittle, but durable in contact with the soil. Bigtree does not attain the height of the coast redwoods, but it will grow to a larger diameter and older age. The General Sherman Tree in Sequoia National Park has the largest volume of all trees. It is 273' tall and 36-1/4" in diameter. The tree is estimated to be between 3,000 and 4,000 years old and to have a volume of 600,000 board feet. Also may be called Sierra redwood.

COMPARISON OF IDENTIFYING CHARACTERS OF FOUR "CEDARS"
Of Family CUPRESSACEAE

	Patterns on under side of leaves	Branch sprays	Cones	Bark
Port-Orford-cedar *Chamaecyparis lawsoniana*	White lines of stomata form X's or X's with elongated centers	Flat, soft, with uniform branchlets blue-green; about 1/16" wide	About 1/4" to 1/3" diam., round; 6 to 8 wedge-shaped, peltate, wrinkled, decussate scales. Cones mature in one year.	Up to 10" thick on old trees, ridged, brown with gray outer layer.
Alaska yellow-cedar *Chamaecyparis nootkatensis*	None	Pendent, to give waterfall effect; rough; often very dark green	About 1/3" diam., round; 4 to 6 wedge-shaped, decussate, convex, peltate scales, each with a short knob or point. Cones mature in 2 years.	Less than 3/4" thick even on old trees, somewhat scaly, ashy-brown outside, intense brown inside.

western redcedar *Thuja plicata*	White lines of stomata form bow ties or butterflies	Flat, large and more rigid than in P-O-C, rough, yellow-green. About 1/8" wide	Like Dutchman's pipe; about 1/2" long; 8 to 12 decussate cone scales (of which 6 are fertile) in valvate pairs. Cones mature in one year.	Less than 1" thick in long strips, bright cinnamon red beneath, gray outside.
incense-cedar *Calocedrus decurrens*	Leaf pattern forms wine-glass; stem end toward main trunk of tree	Twisted, fanlike, at right angles to branch, or diagonal; rough, thick stems; dark yellow-green or green	Like duck bill when closed, flying goose when open; oblong about 1-1/4" long; 3 large cone scales evident (2 are fertile). Cone matures in one year.	Reddish-purple and scaly on young trees; up to 8" thick, bright reddish-brown, ridged on old trees.

CUPRESSACEAE Cypress Family

Thuja L.

thuja arborvitae

Habit: Tolerant, moist-site, evergreen trees or shrubs with scalelike foliage arranged in flattened sprays; wood aromatic.

Leaves: Persistent, scalelike, decussate, and closely appressed to the twig; facial scales flattened, lateral scales folded or keeled; with or without glands; frequently, but not always, with a white stomatal bloom on the lower scales. Dead leaves fall in sprays.

Flowers: Monoecious. Staminate cones small and inconspicuous; pistillate cones terminal.

Cones: Ovoid-cylindrical, erect, brownish; scales decussate, thin, semi-woody or leathery, with a weak spine offset from the apex; scales in valvate pairs; cones mature in one season.

Twigs: Young twigs and branchlets flattened in cross section; older branches round and frequently roughened with dead leaves, slender, tough and flexible.

Remarks: There are five species of arborvitae; two are native to North America, and the others are found in China, Japan, and Korea. The wood is light in weight, aromatic, and durable.

Thuja plicata Donn.

western redcedar

Habit: Large trees 150' to 200' high, and 3'to 10' in diameter; with an open pyramidal crown of pendulous, frond-like lateral branchlets; on large trees the base is fluted and swell-butted.

Leaves: 1/16'' to 1/8'' long (up to 1/4'' long on older twigs), scalelike, in opposite pairs, closely appressed to the twig; facial scales flattened and with an indistinct gland near the apex, lateral scales folded or keeled; foliage sprays flattened, about 1/8" wide; white stomatal pattern on the lower surface resembles a butterfly or bow tie.

Cones: About 1/2" long, erect, ovoid-cylindrical; decussate scales semi-woody, thin, and with a small reflexed spine near the apex, scales 10 to 12 in number but only 6 are fertile; all are in valvate pairs.

Twigs: Younger twigs and branchlets flattened, older twigs are round, slender and flexible, slightly zigzag; reddish-brown in color.

Bark: 1/2" to 3/4" thick, fibrous; brown, but weathered to a grayish-brown on the outside, finely ridged and furrowed; outer bark breaks up into long narrow strips or shreds.

BUTTERFLIES UNDERNEATH

western redcedar

Habitat & Range: Found on moist sites along river bottoms, flats and benches, and mountain slopes. Ranges from southeastern Alaska southward to northwestern California, also northeastern Washington, northern Idaho, and western Montana. Elevational range: sea level to 4,000 feet in the Pacific Northwest; 1,500 to 7,000 feet in the Inland Empire.

Uses: Lumber for siding, interior finish, greenhouse construction and flumes; boat building, caskets, poles, posts, boxes and crates, sash and doors. 80% of the shingles and shakes manufactured in Oregon and Washington are made from western redcedar. Wood extremely durable.

Remarks: Very tolerant. Occurs in small pure patches, but more commonly in mixture with Sitka spruce, western hemlock, grand fir, Douglas-fir and western white pine. It attains the largest size of any of the species in the genus. The wood is aromatic and durable.

The Indians made more use of this species than any other. Various parts of the tree were used for canoes, baskets, thongs, shelter, and clothing.

Calocedrus **Kurz***

incense-cedar

There are three species of *Calocedrus*, only one is native to western United States, one is found in South China and the other is found along the Burmese border and in Formosa. Because there is but one native species the generic description is omitted.

Calocedrus decurrens **(Torr.) Florin***

incense-cedar

Habit: Evergreen trees 70' to 110' tall, and 3' to 5' in diameter, with a conical crown of frond-like branches.

Leaves: Persistent, appear whorled (actually decussate) scale-like. 1/4'' to 1/2'' long (up to 7/8'' on some older twigs); yellow-green; closely appressed to the twig, with only the tip sticking out; the facial scales are flattened, with inconspicuous translucent glands; the lateral scales are folded or keeled; the overlapping of the lateral scales on the facial scales results in a wineglass outline on the latter; aromatic when crushed. Foliage arranged in flattened, elongated, fingerlike sprays. Dead leaves fall in sprays.

---

*Formerly *Libocedrus* — 1979 Checklist still has listed as *Libocedrus* but most botanists and current publications have changed to *Calocedrus*.

Flowers: Monoecious. Staminate cones oblong-rectangular and yellowish; pistillate cones small, yellowish-green with 6 scales.

Cones: Pendent, 3/4″ to 1-1/4″ long, ovoid, somewhat flattened; leathery or semi-woody in texture; yellowish-brown; appear to be composed of 3 scales, but actually have 6; the two basal ones are aborted, the central pair is fused together, and the two large remaining scales are the only ones which are fertile; mature in one season. The closed cone resembles a duck's bill, and the open cone resembles a flying goose.

Twigs: Moderately stout, at first flattened but eventually becoming round; reddish-brown to grayish-brown in color.

Bark: Purplish-red, 3″ to 4″ thick near the base; much thinner higher up; inner bark is rich reddish-brown, weathering to grayish-brown on the outside; furrowed, with long interlacing ridges.

Habitat & Range: Does best on moist porous soils, but is able to adapt itself to various soil types. Although available moisture determines its locale in the southern part of its range, it apparently is less moisture demanding than the other "cedars." Found on both slopes of the Cascades in Oregon, the northern Coast Range and the length of the Sierra Nevada Mountains in California; also Lower California. Elevational range: 1,000 to 6,600 feet in Oregon; 1,000 to 8,000 feet in California; and above 7,500 feet in Lower California.

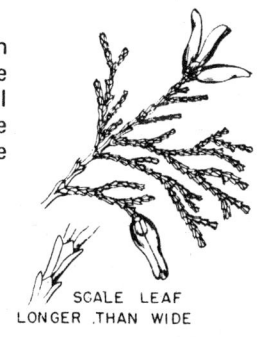

SCALE LEAF LONGER THAN WIDE

incense-cedar

Uses: Extensive use of incense-cedar for lumber is impaired by a fungus which attacks the heartwood, producing the condition known as "pecky cedar" or "peck." This condition does not impair the great durability of the wood, and it makes excellent fence posts. Has limited use for lumber, ties, mothproof chests, venetian blinds, grape stakes, and shakes. Primary species used in making pencils.

Remarks: "The thick bark at the base of old trees makes the species less susceptible to fires that may often kill its thinner barked associates. When mixed stands are selectively logged for the better species and when the slash is left unburned, the advance reproduction of incense-cedar takes over the site in many cases. Essentially a drought-resisting tree, incense-cedar occurs in the pine-oak mixed forest of the dry foot-hill county in California and southern Oregon; found in the pine-white fir mixed forest of the Sierra and Cascades; also encroaches into the drier sites in the Douglas-fir-western hemlock types. It is a vigorous seed producer, seedlings grow well on a wide variety of sites, and incense-cedar would probably take over more forests were it not slow growing." (W.F. McCulloch)

Chamaecyparis Spach.

white-cedar

Habit: Tolerant, moist-site evergreen trees with decussate, scalelike foliage arranged in flattened sprays; the cone is small and spherical.

Leaves: Persistent, scalelike, in opposite pairs, imbricated, and closely appressed to the twig; facial scales flattened, lateral scales folded or keeled, about 1/8" long; glandular near the tip but not always distinctly so. Sprays about 1/16" wide. Dead leaves fall in sprays, not singly.

Flowers: Monoecious; inconspicuous; staminate cones terminal, ovate to oblong, yellow to reddish; pistillate cones round, green to blue-green.

Cones: Small, round, with peltate, decussate scales. Mature in one or two growing seasons.

Twigs: Smaller twigs and branchlets distinctly flattened, round on older branches. Leader droops.

Remarks: There are 6 species of white-cedar; three are native to the United States, two to Japan, and one to Formosa. The durable wood is heavier than that of the redcedars, often with a distinct odor, especially when freshly cut or dampened.

KEY TO WHITE-CEDARS

Leaf sprays flat, with white "X" pattern on underside. Cones have 6 or 8 wrinkled scales without prominent bosses (points).   *C. lawsoniana*

Leaf sprays have no white stomatal pattern; youngest sprays flat; older sprays thickened, often 4-angled in cross section. Cones have 4 or 6 convex scales, each with a prominent boss (point).
                                    C. nootkatensis

Chamaecyparis lawsoniana (A. Murr.) Parl.

Port-Orford-cedar   **Port-Orford-white-cedar**

Habit: Trees 125' to 200' tall, and 3' to 6' in diameter; with a pyramidal crown of pendulous, frond-like branches.

Leaves: 1/16" to 1/8" long, scalelike, arranged in opposite paris, imbricated and closely appressed to the twig; mostly blue-green; glands on facial scales translucent when held up to the light; white X's on the underside of the foliage sprays. Foliage sprays flat, finer, denser and more lacy than those of western red-cedar or incense-cedar.

Cones: Round, average about 1/4" in diameter, reddish-brown and glaucous; 6 or 8 peltate, decussate scales which are wrinkled on the surface; mature in one season.

Twigs: New twigs and branchlets distinctly flattened, older branches round, with thin brown bark.

Bark: Brown, but weathered to a grayish-brown on the outside; fibrous, ridged and furrowed; the outer bark often splits into long narrow strips; 4" to 8" thick near the base, but thinner higher up the bole. It has the thickest bark of the so-called "cedars."

Habitat & Range: Tolerant. Most commonly found on moist, well-drained soils in the coastal fog belt region of southwestern Oregon and northwestern California. It occurs chiefly in Coos and Curry Counties in Oregon, and in Del Norte and Humboldt counties in California. It is found in the coast ranges and Siskiyou mountains; it occurs in small areas in western Lane and Douglas Counties, Oregon, and in the Trinity Mountains and on Mt. Shasta in California. The range forms a narrow strip 10 to 40 miles wide. Elevational range: sea level to 5,000 feet.

WHITE X'S
UNDERNEATH

Port-Orford-cedar

Uses: At one time the durable, easily-worked wood was commonly used for battery separators and venetian blinds; however, Douglas-fir has replaced it for the former use and metal for the latter. Most now exported to Japan as a substitute for Japan's own *C. obtusa* now in short supply.

Remarks: Port-Orford-cedar will form small pure stands, but is more commonly found in mixture with western redcedar, Sitka spruce, western hemlock, Douglas-fir, grand fir, and occasionally with coast redwood and California-laurel. Susceptible to *Phytophthora* root rot, especially on poorly drained soils. On suitable soils it is a fine species for ornamental planting. It is the largest species in the genus.

Chamaecyparis nootkatensis (D. Don) Spach.

Alaska-cedar   **Alaska yellow-cedar**

Habit: Medium-sized tree 70' to 100' tall, and 2' to 4' in diameter, with a shaggy conical crown of pendulous, frond-like branches.

Leaves: Scalelike, closely appressed to the twig imbricated and in opposite pairs, about 1/16" to 1/8" long long; yellow-green to gray-green or blue-green; tips of the lateral scales may not be closely appressed to the twig, thus resulting in a serrated edge on the foliage sprays; glands indistinct; **no** stomatal markings.

Cones: Round, 1/4" to 1/3" in diameter; glaucous green, but becoming purplish-brown to reddish-brown at maturity; 4 to 6 convex peltate scales, smooth except for a central boss; mature in two growing seasons.

Twigs: Younger twigs and branchlets flattened, older branches round and frequently roughened with dead, persisting leaves. Leader droops.

Bark: Thin; inner bark reddish to cinnamon-brown, but weathered to a gray-brown on the outside; shallowly ridged and furrowed, except for the younger trees which may be scaly.

Habitat & Range: Does best on moist, rocky and gravelly soils in the mountains. Ranges from southeastern Alaska southward through western British Columbia, to the Cascade Mountains in Washington and Oregon and the Siskiyou Mountains in southwestern Oregon and northern California, also the Olympic Mountains in Washington and the Blue Mountains in northeastern Oregon. Elevational range: sea level to 3,000 feet in Alaska; sea level to 5,000 feet in British Columbia; near sea level to 3,500 feet in the Olympics; and 2,000 to 7,500 feet in the Cascades.

Uses: Interior finish, furniture, boat hulls, cabinet work, novelties, pattern stock and canoe paddles.

Remarks: Sometimes occurs in small pure stands, but more frequently in mixture with mountain hemlock; lodgepole and western white pine; subalpine, noble and silver firs; Engelmann spruce and Douglas-fir. Further north it is associated with Sitka spruce, western hemlock and western redcedar. Moderately tolerant, but tolerance varies with age and site conditions. The wood is durable, has a yellowish cast, and an obnoxious odor when freshly cut or moist.

Juniperus L.

juniper

Habit: Intolerant, evergreen, dry-site trees and shrubs, with aromatic, scalelike and/or awl-like foliage, and berrylike cones.

Leaves: Persistent; decussate or ternate; scalelike and closely appressed to the twig, often glandular-pitted on the bark; and/or awl-shaped, or linear-lanceolate and somewhat spreading; aromatic.

Flowers: Mostly dioecious; inconspicuous.

Cones: Small, berrylike, fleshy, subglobose with fused decussate, peltate scales (cones rarely open);

blue-black, blue, or reddish-brown and covered with a white bloom; contains one to many seeds; mature in one to three growing seasons.

Bark: Thin and breaking up into long fibrous or shreddy strips; usually reddish-brown.

Remarks: Indigenous to the Northern Hemisphere. The wood is quite colorful—red—and is very durable. Junipers occur mainly on sites too dry for ponderosa pine.

KEY TO FOUR JUNIPERS

1. Leaves uniformly awl-shaped to linear-lanceolate, in whorls of 3, radially spreading, not glandular; chalky-white on upper surface. Sprawling shrub or small tree. *J. communis*

1. Leaves scalelike and appressed to twig; or leaves awl-like, often spreading (divergent); or both scalelike and awl-like on same tree. 2

    2. Leaves conspicuously resin-dotted, usually scalelike, commonly in whorls of 3. *J. occidentalis*

    2. Leaves not resin-dotted. 3

3. Branchlets 4-angled in cross section, with leaves in 4 ranks; awl-shaped and divergent or scalelike and appressed; glands absent or inconspicuous. *J. scopulorum*

3. Branchlets round or 6-angled in cross section; leaves usually scalelike, glandular-pitted, in whorls of 3. *J. californica*

Juniperus communis L.

common juniper

Habit: Mat-forming shrubs, sometimes erect, or small trees up to 30' tall and 6" to 12" in diameter.

Leaves: 1/3" to 1/2" long, linear-lanceolate, sessile; white on the upper surface, dark shiny green below; apex acute, callus tipped; arranged in whorls of three, and nearly perpendicular to the twig.

Cones: About 1/4" in diameter, subglobose; bluish-black, covered with a white bloom; requires 3 growing seasons to mature.

Twigs: Slender, smooth and often shiny; triangular in cross section between the nodes.

Bark: Less than 1/4" thick, gray-reddish brown and shreddy.

Habitat & Range: Found on sandy or rocky flats, slopes and ridges. Indigenous to Europe, Asia and North America. In North America: Alaska, Canada, Washington southward to central California, eastward into Ohio and Virginia, and then south through the mountains to Georgia; also portions of Arizona and New Mexico.

Uses: Extracts from the fruit used to flavor gin. May be planted as an ornamental. Foliage has diuretic properties for many domestic animals, therefore not good browse. Hitchcock and Cronquist (1973) recognize 4 varieties.

Juniperus californica Carr.

California juniper

Habit: Shrub, or small tree up to 30' tall, and 10" to 20" in diameter; with a conical crown and a fluted trunk.

Leaves: Scalelike, about 1/8"
long, usually in 3's; yellow-
green; closely appressed to
the twig; keeled and
glandular-pitted on the
back; apex round; awl-
shaped on vigorous
branches, up to 1/3" long,
rigid, sharply pointed,
white on the upper
surface.

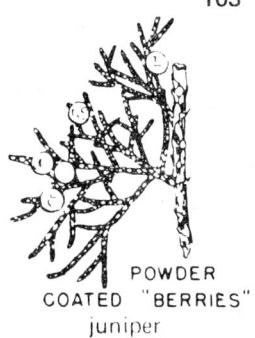

POWDER
COATED "BERRIES"
juniper

Twigs: Almost round, stout; after the leaves fall the
bark is thin, scaly, and ashy-gray.

Cones: Round, 1/4" to 5/8" in diameter; reddish-brown
and covered with a white bloom; surface smooth
except for a slight projection from the center of each
scale; contains one or two grooved and ridged seeds;
requires two seasons to mature.

Bark: Gray to gray-reddish brown; thin and breaking
into long shreddy scales or strips; inner bark reddish-
brown.

Habitat & Range: Dry, sandy, rocky or gravelly soils;
from Shasta county, California south to Baja California, mostly in the Coast Range. Not found in Oregon. Elevational range: 2,000 to 5,000 feet.

Remarks: Occurs in pure stands or in mixture with
mountain-mahogany, ponderosa pine, digger pine,
piñon pine, manzanita, mesquite, and yucca. Probably very intolerant. Used locally for fuel and fence
posts.

Juniperus occidentalis **Hook.**

western juniper   **Sierra juniper**

Habit: Strong-scented small dry-site trees 20' to 60' tall, and 1' to 3' in diameter; bole short and thick.

Leaves: Scalelike, in whorls of 3 and tightly appressed to the twig, and/or awl-shaped with the tips standing free from the twig; grayish-green to blue-green; back side of scales rounded, glandular and resin-dotted.

Cones: Round 1/4" or slightly larger in diameter; bluish-black and covered with a white bloom; skin tough; contains two or three ridged and grooved seeds; mature in two growing seasons.

Twigs: Round, smooth and reddish-brown, later becoming scaly.

Bark: Cinnamon-brown to reddish-brown, but often weathered to a gray-brown on the outside; 1/2" to 1" thick, with broad shallow furrows and flattened ridges.

Habitat & Range: Dry, sandy to rocky soils; from eastern Washington southward into southern California and western Nevada, eastward into western Montana. Elevational range: 500 to 5,000 feet in Oregon and Washington; 2,500 to 10,500 feet in California.

Uses: Fuel and fence posts.

Remarks: Intolerant. Occurs in pure open stands or in mixture with ponderosa and Jeffrey pines on marginal sites for the pines.

Fruit is eaten by birds, and deer browse the foliage. The wood is durable. The most extensive juniper stands in the world are formed by this species in eastern Oregon.

Juniperus scopulorum **Sarg.**

Rocky Mountain juniper

Habitat: Bushy shrubs up to 20' tall and 6'' to 10'' in diameter, or small trees 25'to 30' tall and 1' to 1-1/2' in diameter.

Leaves: Scalelike, in alternating pairs, closely appressed to the twig, indistinctly glandular on the backside; and/or awl-shaped and divergent; yellow-green to green.

Cones: Round, about 1/4'' in diameter; bluish-black and covered with a white bloom; seeds 2, triangular and grooved; mature in two growing seasons.

Twigs: 4-angled or square in cross section.

Bark: Thin, shallowly ridged and furrowed and breaking into long shreds; outer bark grayish to graying brown, inner bark reddish-brown.

Habitat & Range: Found on dry, sandy or gravelly soils, but does best in moist canyons in the semi-arid areas of southern British Columbia and southwestern Alberta, eastern Washinton southward to southern Nevada, and eastward to western Dakotas, northwestern Texas, and eastern New Mexico. In Oregon found near Wallowa Mountains. Elevational range: 350 to 6,500 feet.

Uses: Locally for fuel and fence posts. Wood is very durable.

Remarks: Probably very intolerant. Associated species include mountain-mahogany, narrowleaf cottonwood, sagebrush, pinyon pine and several junipers.

Cupressus L.

cypress

Habit: Evergreen trees, or occasionally shrubs, with overlapping, scale-like, decussate, leaves closely appressed to the twigs; branches are erect or spreading.

Leaves: Persistent, scalelike, appressed to and arranged in opposite pairs on the twig, lateral scales folded or keeled; margins finely toothed; awl-shaped or linear-lanceolate foliage on the vigorous growth. Glandular and commonly resin-dotted.

Flowers: Monoecious; staminate cones cylindrical and terminal; pistillate cones round.

Cones: Round to subglobose, woody or leathery in texture, mostly 1/2" to 1-1/4" in diameter; 3 to 6 pairs of peltate scales, the surface of each scale is somewhat wrinkled and has a central boss (projection); mature at the end of the second growing season but often persists on the tree for an indefinite period.

Twigs: Young twigs that are clothed with living foliage are **4-angled** in cross-section, with one exception (Chinese weeping cypress). Older branches are round and are covered with a thin scaly bark.

Remarks: There are 12 species of cypress found in North America, Europe, and Asia. There are six species native to the United States, and all are found in the West, from southwestern Oregon southward into Mexico and Lower California. Each species has a very limited natural range. With the exception of Monterey cypress, none of the native species seems to have any potential as a timber tree, but they are frequently planted as ornamentals, or may be used in erosion control. The wood is durable and is used locally for fence posts. Monterey cypress, *C. macrocarpa* Hartw., is not native to Oregon, but is sometimes planted along the southern coast.

Cupressus bakeri Jeps.

Baker cypress   **Siskiyou cypress**

Habit: A small tree, usually under 50' tall. Open, spreading branches with aromatic twigs.

Characteristics: Its leaves are flat and closely appressed; obtuse and with a noticeable dorsal resin gland; gray-green in color; short and pointed. Its cones are round, gray-brown to silver, 1/2" to 3/4" in diameter at maturity; commonly with 6 scales, each with a prominent umbo above the middle. The uppermost pair of cone scales are longest, and often curve inward.

Habitat & Range: Open woods and poor, dry slopes of Jackson and Josephine Counties in Oregon, and in

page 107

TAXACEAE   **Yew Family**

Taxus L.

yew

Habit: Evergreen trees and shrubs with dark green foliage; the fruit is one-seeded, fleshy.

Leaves: Persistent, linear; spirally arranged, in some species 2-ranked; apex acute, often with a spinose callus tip; smooth and dark green above, pale green below; petiolate.

Flowers: Dioecious; staminate flowers globose, borne in the leaf axils on the underside of the twig; pistillate flowers solitary.

Fruit: 1/4" to 1/3" long, subglobose to oblong, orange-red aril (fleshy, gelatinous fruit open at the upper end and containing one large seed); matures in one season.

Twigs: Round, slender and green.

Bark: Thin, brown to purplish-brown.

Remarks: Yews are indigenous to the Northern Hemisphere. Three species are native to the United States, two in the East and one in the West. Very tolerant.

Taxus brevifolia Nutt.

Pacific yew

Habit: Small trees 30' to 50' (sometimes up to 80') tall, and 1' to 2' in diameter, with a dark green crown of pendulous branches. The bole is frequently asymmetrical and fluted. Usually a moist-site, understory tree.

Leaves: 1/2" to 1" long, linear, rigid; dark green or yellow-green above, paler beneath; apex pointed; midrib stout; petiolate; commonly 2-ranked.

Fruit: Fleshy, orange-red aril, 2/8" to 5/8" long, oblong-oval.

Bark: About 1/4" thick, dark purplish or reddish-brown, scaly; inner bark reddish-purple.

Habitat & Range: Pacific yew is a common understory tree in the Pacific Coast forests. Very tolerant. Grows in moist, well-drained sites in the sun or shade. Ranges from extreme southeastern Alaska southward to northern California, and in the Sierra Nevada Mountains to central California; northeastern Oregon, northern Idaho and western Montana. Range similar to that of western hemlock, except for the Sierra Nevada region of California.

Uses: The wood is very durable and very hard; it requires no preservative treatment even when in contact with the soil. Used for special fence posts; gate posts and corner posts. It makes good archery bows.

Pacific yew

KEY TO BROADLEAF TREES AND SHRUBS

1. Trees or shrubs with leaves.   2

1. Shrubs with leaves reduced to spines.
   Ulex europaeus p. 197

    2. Leaves opposite.   3

    2. Leaves alternate.   16

3. Leaves compound.   4

3. Leaves simple.   5

    4. Twigs flattened at nodes, strong; fruit a single, straight-winged samara. *Fraxinus latifolia* p. 241

    4. Twigs round at nodes, weak; pith large and spongy; fruit small berries. *Sambucus* p. 244

5. Leaves palmately lobed and veined; double-samara fruit. *Acer* p. 202

5. Leaves not lobed; arcuately or pinnately veined, or with netted veins.   6

    6. Leaves persistent; thick and leathery or stiff.   7

    6. Leaves deciduous (*Shepherdia* leaves somewhat leathery).   10

7. Leaf margins entire and 1-1/2" to 2-1/2" long, elliptical, oval, or broadly ovate. Margin irregularly revolute in one species. *Garrya* p. 224

7. Leaf margins serrate or spinose-toothed or entire and clustered.   8

    8. Leaf margins finely serrate; leaves 1/2" to 1-1/2" long, round or ovate to elliptical.   9

8. Leaf margins smooth or with sparse spinose teeth; leaves 1/4″ to 1″ long, obovate, cuneate or spatulate. *Ceanothus* p. 207

9. Erect shrub, up to 4 feet high; leaves elongated, ovate to elliptical *Pachistima myrsinites* p. 217

9. Very low, trailing vinelike shrub; leaves round, lustrous, (1/2″ to 1″). *Linnaea borealis* p. 251

10. Fruit a white, persistent, waxy berry; twigs very slender; pith brown, mostly hollow. *Symphoricarpos* p. 247

10. Fruit not white; twigs slender to stout; pith white (in most genera) and solid. 11

11. Leaf margins toothed or lobed. 12

11. Leaf margins smooth or wavy. 13

12. Leaf margins with a few, small, widely spaced, glandular teeth; 3 (rarely 5) main veins from near base of blade; buds minute, naked. *Philadelphus* p. 156

12. Leaf margins coarsely serrate or dentate; buds about 1/4″ long, mostly stalked. *Viburnum* p. 249

13. New twigs and branchlets scurfy (flaky). *Shepherdia* p. 218

13. New twigs and branchlets not scurfy. 14

14. Branchlets 4-ribbed or 4-ridged, appearing square; leaves obovate or oval. *Lonicera* p. 243

14. Twigs and branchlets round. 15

15. Leaves have arcuate veins; leaves 2″ to 6″ long. *Cornus* p. 221

15. Leaves have 3 (rarely 5) main veins from base; may have a few widely spaced teeth.
Philadelphus p. 156

   16. Leaves simple.   17

   16. Leaves compound.   68

17. Leaves palmately lobed and veined, i.e., maple-like.   18

17. Leaves not palmately lobed and veined.   22

   18. Branches and stems armed with prickles or spines.   19

   18. Branches and stems unarmed.   20

19. Stems abundantly armed with irritating, long prickles; leaves large; veins and petiole armed.
Oplopanax horridum p. 220

19. Stems bear spines at nodes, and often prickles on internodes; leaves small (1″ to 2″).
Ribes p. 158

   20. Leaves large, mostly 4″ to 8″ in diameter; stems weak.   *Rubus parviflorus* p. 187

   20. Leaves small, mostly 1-1/2″ to 3″ in diameter.   21

21. Bark tan-colored, shreddy, exfoliating in long strips; flowers (and follicles) borne in hemi-spherical clusters.   *Physocarpus* p. 173

21. Bark smooth or shreddy, but not peeling in long strips. Tubular or funnel-shaped flowers in small racemes; Fruit is a berry. Petiole often as long as leaf blade.
Ribes p. 158

22. Branches and twigs armed with thorns; buds red; fruit a pome. *Crataegus* p. 165

22. Branches and twigs unarmed. 23

23. Leaves with 2 to 4 distinct glands on the petiole and/or lowest serration. *Prunus* p. 176

23. Leaves without distinct glands on the petiole or lowest serration. 24

24. Leaves wedge-shaped; apex 3-lobed; tend to persist. 25

24. Leaves not wedge-shaped; apex not 3-lobed; deciduous or persistent. 26

25. Leaves aromatic (sage odor), gray-green; margins not revolute. *Artemisia tridentata* p. 252

25. Leaves not aromatic, green above, whitish below; margins revolute. *Purshia tridentata* p. 172

26. Leaves distinctly 3-veined from base of blade (see underside of leaf). *Ceanothus* p. 207

26. Leaves not 3-veined from base. 27

27. Leaves grass-like, not more than 1/16" wide, linear; tend to persist. *Chrysothamnus* p. 254

27. Leaves not grass-like. 28

28. Leaves persistent, thick and leathery, or stiff. 29

28. Leaves deciduous, not leathery. 47

29. Leaf margins smooth. 30

29. Leaf margins serrated and/or lobed. 39

30. Leaves distinctly aromatic when rubbed or crushed. *Umbellularia* p. 155

30. Leaves not aromatic. 31

31. Leaves with golden scurfiness on underside. *Castanopsis* p. 141

31. Leaves lack golden scurfiness on underside. 32

32. Buds naked, dark brown. *Rhamnus californica* p. 214

32. Buds covered with imbricate scales 33

33. Leaves less than 3" long. 34

33. Leaves 3" long or longer. 37

34. Leaf margins revolute. 35

34. Leaf margins not revolute. 36

35. Leaves borne on spur shoots; leaves 1/2" to 1-1/4" long, light brown on underside. *Cercocarpus ledifolius* p. 164

35. Leaves not on spur shoots; leaves 3/4" to 2-1/4" long, white on underside. *Ledum glandulosum* p. 234

36. Buds clustered at tip of twig; leaves often have spinose-toothed margins. *Quercus* p. 145

36. Buds not clustered. Bark dark red. Leaves entire. Fruit looks like tiny apple. *Arctostaphylos* p. 228

37. Bud scales fuzzy; leaves oblong, stiff, prominently penniveined, often toothed. *Lithocarpus densiflorus* p. 144

37. Bud scales not fuzzy; leaf margins entire.   38

    38. Brown scaly bark exfoliates, exposing smooth reddish-brown or orange-brown layer. Flowers small, urn-shaped. A tree.
Arbutus menziesii p. 226

    38. Bark does not exfoliate; green to brown. Flowers large, trumpet-shaped. A shrub.
Rhododendron p. 235

39. Buds naked, dark brown. Leaves finely serrate.
Rhamnus californica p. 214

39. Buds have imbricate or valvate scales.   40

    40. Buds clustered at tip of twig; leaf margins spinose-toothed.   *Quercus chrysolepis* p. 147

    40. Buds not clustered.   41

41. Leaves ovate or oval; margins very finely serrate.   42

41. Leaves oblong, oblanceolate, or obovate.   43

    42. Leaves 1-1/2" to 4" long, broadly ovate or oval; twigs round in cross section, tend to zigzag.   *Gaultheria shallon* p. 232

    42. Leaves 1/2" to 1-1/2" long, ovate; dark green and waxy above; appear to have been folded along midrib; youngest slightly ridged.   *Vaccinium ovatum* p. 239

43. Leaves less than 2" long.   44

43. Leaves 2" long or longer.   45

    44. Leaf margins revolute; leaves oblanceolate to obovate.   *Baccharis pilularis* p. 253

44. Leaf margins not revolute; leaves obovate, conspicuously penniveined.
Cercocarpus betuloides p. 163

45. Leaves narrow, willowlike, oblanceolate to oblong-lanceolate, dark green; base wedge-shaped; petiole about 1/2'' long.
Myrica californica p. 128

45. Leaves broad; oblong, oblong-elliptical, or oblong-ovate.   46

46. New leaves and twigs fuzzy; leaves conspicuously penniveined with one coarse tooth per vein; leaf margins occasionally entire.
Lithocarpus densiflorus p. 144

46. New leaves and twigs smooth; leaf veins not conspicuous; leaf margins entire or with very fine serrations.   *Arbutus menziesii* p. 226

47. Young twigs distinctly ribbed or ridged, green.   48

47. Young twigs round in cross section.   49

48. Both simple and trifoliate leaves present.
Cytisus scoparius p. 195

48. All leaves are simple, elliptical to oblong; buds red.   *Vaccinium parvifolium* p. 240

49. Leaf petiole distinctly flattened laterally; blade round or triangular or rhomboid.
Populus p. 122

49. Leaf petiole (if present) round, not flattened.   50

50. Leaf margins smooth, unlobed.   51

50. Leaf margins toothed or lobed (entire in some species of *Salix*).   54

51. Buds naked, dark brown; leaves conspicuously penniveined. Bark smooth, gray.
Rhamnus purshiana p. 215

51. Buds with imbricate scales. 52

   52. Leaves ovate to lanceolate, 2″ to 6″ long, with underside silvery-white and/or with rusty areas. *Populus* p. 122

   52. Leaves elliptical to obovate or oblanceolate. 53

53. Pith chambered. Leaves light green, soft, tapered at both ends; taste like cucumbers.
Oemleria cerasiformis p. 169

53. Pith solid. Leaves bright green above, paler below, elliptical to obovate.
Rhododendron occidentale p. 237

   54. Leaves 2-ranked (phyllotaxy 1/2). 55

   54. Leaves in 3 or more ranks (phyllotaxy 1/3 or 2/5, or indeterminate). 57

55. Leaves singly serrate, with netted veins; upper leaf-surface sandpapery. Pith very finely chambered at nodes. *Celtis reticulata* p. 151

55. Leaves doubly serrate, prominently penniveined; pith solid. 56

   56. New twigs pubescent (soft-hairy); zigzag; no spur shoots; leaves broadly and irregularly rounded, sparsely hairy on upper surface, soft-hairy below. *Corylus* p. 140

   56. New twigs smooth or resin-dotted; buds on spur shoots after first season; leaves not hairy. *Betula* p. 136

57. Buds stalked, 3-ranked; pith triangular; leaves conspicuously penniveined. Nutlets borne in small semi-woody cones with spirally arranged scales. *Alnus* p. 130

57. Buds sessile; phyllotaxy 2/5 or indeterminate. 58

    58. Leaves pinnately 5- to 9-lobed. Fruit an acorn. Buds clustered. *Quercus* p. 145

    58. Leaves not lobed, or if lobed, lobes not more than 3. 59

59. Buds naked or with single, caplike bud scale. 60

59. Buds with imbricate or valvate scales. 61

    60. Buds naked, brown; leaves oblong, with very fine teeth (or entire). *Rhamnus purshiana* p. 215

    60. Buds with single, caplike scale; leaves lanceolate, elliptical, or spatulate; leaf margins serrate (or entire). *Salix* p. 121

61. Buds borne on spur shoots; leaves ovate to oval, serrate; may have one to three small lobes. Fruit a pome (apple). *Pyrus fusca* p. 171

61. Buds not on spur shoots. 62

    62. Petiole more than 1/4" long. 63

    62. Petiole 1/8" to 1/4" long. 65

63. Leaves round or oval or slightly oblong, 1-1/4" to 2" long, with teeth on outer (apical) portion of blade, but not on basal portion. Fruit a small pome (apple). *Amelanchier* p. 161

63. Leaves ovate or lanceolate. 64

64. Leaves prominently penniveined; margins coarsely toothed or with a few small toothed lobes; leaf base obtuse or wedge-shaped. Dense terminal clusters of flowers or follicles. *Holodiscus discolor* p. 168

64. Leaves netted-veined; margins crenate-serrate to smooth; leaf base round; underside silvery-white and/or with rusty areas. *Populus* p. 122

65. Leaves ovate to elliptical or oblong. 66

65. Leaves obovate or oblanceolate. 67

66. Leaf margins finely, sharply serrate; teeth ending in gland-tipped hairs; leaves elliptical, thin. Twigs have green pith. *Vaccinium membranaceum* p. 238

66. Leaf margins have few, large teeth; leaves ovate to oblong. Twigs have white pith. *Spiraea* p. 193

67. Teeth on only the outer 1/2 or 1/3 of leaf blade; leaves obovate to oblanceolate. *Myrica gale* p. 129

67. Teeth on all of leaf margin; nipple-like tip of midrib protrudes beyond blade. Leaf obovate to elliptical. *Menziesia ferruginea* p. 235

68. Twigs and stems armed. 69

68. Twigs and stems unarmed. 71

69. Twigs armed only at nodes, with paired stipular spines; youngest twigs angular; buds submerged. 7 to 19 leaflets. *Robinia pseudoacacia* p. 196

69. Entire twig or stem armed, with prickles. 3 to 9 leaflets. 70

70. Leaflets small, round or oval, 1/2" to 3/4" long. Usually 5 to 9 leaflets. Rachis usually unarmed. Fruit an orange-red hip (containing achenes). *Rosa* p. 180

70. Leaflets large, mostly 1-1/2" to 3-1/2" long. Usually 3 to 5 leaflets. Rachis usually armed with prickles. Fruit an aggregate of drupelets. *Rubus* p. 184

71. Leaves persistent; leaflets stiff, with spinose margins. *Berberis* p. 152

71. Leaves deciduous. 72

72. Leaves 1/2" to 1" long; branches green and distinctly ribbed. *Cytisus scoparius* p. 195

72. Leaves 2" long or longer. 73

73. Leaflets usually 3. 74

73. Leaflets 7 to 21. 75

74. Lateral leaflets only 1/4 to 1/3 the size of ther terminal leaflet; terminal leaflet broadly obovate to round-rhombic, with wedge-shaped base, but no (sub-) petiole. Flower buds in spikes; foliage buds submerged. Fruit red. *Rhus trilobata* p. 199

74. Lateral leaflets at least 1/2 the size of the terminal leaflet; leaflets ovate to obovate; terminal leaflet irregularly toothed to lobed, with distinct (sub-) petiole. Buds naked. Fruit whitish, with meridian lines.
Rhus diversiloba p. 200

75. Leaf margins entire or wavy. Young twigs angular; buds submerged.
Robinia pseudoacacia p. 196

75. Leaf margins serrate. 76

    76. Leaflets oblong or oblong-elliptical; flowers and fruit in broad, flat-topped, terminal clusters. *Sorbus* p. 191

    76. Leaflets lanceolate to oblong-lanceolate; flowers and fruit in elongated terminal clusters. *Rhus glabra* p. 199

SALICACEAE   Willow Family

Salix L.

willow

Habit: Rapidly growing, thicket-forming trees and shrubs.

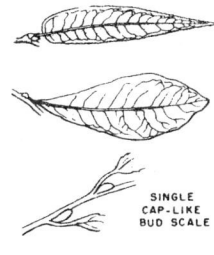

Leaves: Deciduous, alternate, 5-ranked, simple, stipulate; lanceolate, elliptical, or spatulate in shape; margins entire, wavy, or serrate; apex round, acute or accuminate; sessile or with short petiole. In many species, stipules are persistent.

SINGLE CAP-LIKE BUD SCALE

Flowers: Dioecious; in upcurving aments (catkins); sometimes fragrant.

DIFFERENT SPECIES

willow

Fruit: Two-valved, 1-celled capsule, ovate with an accuminate tip; 1/4″ or less in length; contains several minute, hairy seeds. Fruit matures and disseminates its seed in the late spring or early summer. Seed very short-lived; needs moist mineral soil to germinate.

Buds: 1/8″ to 5/8″ long, usually closely appressed to the twig; the bud has but a single, cap-like scale; scale smooth or pubescent. Terminal bud absent.

Twigs: Slender to moderately stout, flexible; smooth or occasionally pubescent; green, red, brown, yellow, orange or purple in color; lenticels usually prominent; twig scar evident in late summer or early fall on the side of the twig opposite the last lateral bud; pith round and solid. Phyllotaxy 2/5.

Habitat & Range: Along streams and standing water in the full sun. On all continents except Australia and Antarctica, but most abundant in the Northern Hemisphere, where it will be found growing as far north as the Arctic Circle.

Remarks: Very intolerant. Occurs on many types of soil. Comparatively short-lived, but prolific sprouters. Easily propagated by cuttings. Useful for erosion control.

Willows are very good to excellent browse plants for game animals and domestic stock. Grouse and quail feed on the buds. Twigs are used for basketry.

There are many species, varieties, and hybrids, often very difficult to distinguish. In some instances both male and female specimens are essential if the species is to be identified.

Populus **L.**

cottonwood   **poplar**

Habit: Rapidly growing trees. Commonly found growing in moist, well-drained situations.

Leaves: Deciduous, alternate, simple, 5-ranked; ovate, ovate-lanceolate, deltoid, or rhomboid in shape; upper surface smooth and glossy; margins entire, dentate, serrate, or occasionally lobed; petiole usually long, terete or laterally flattened.

Flowers: Dioecious; borne in drooping aments (catkins); appear before the leaves.

Fruit: 2- to 4-valved, 1-celled capsule; ovate, sub-globose, or conical in shape; usually less than 1/4" long, smooth or finely pubescent; contains several minute, hairy seeds. Fruits mature in late spring; seeds very short-lived unless they reach moist mineral soil promptly.

Twigs: Stout to slender; yellowish-brown, olive-drab, or reddish-brown in color; smooth or pubescent, pith stellate. Phyllotaxy 2/5. Spur shoots on some older branches.

Buds: Lateral buds appressed or divergent; terminal buds present, slightly larger than the lateral buds; aromatic in some species; scales imbricate; resinous or nonresinous.

Uses: Wood used for pulp, boxes and crates, excelsior, veneer, matches, and factory lumber.

Remarks: Indigenous to the temperate and cooler regions on the Northern Hemispere; 15 species are native to the United States. Very intolerant, fast growing. Moisture-demanding, but found on a variety of soils. Short-lived, but vigorous sprouters. Many species propagate readily from cuttings.

The litter caused by fallen flowers, the obnoxious quantity of the cottony seed, and the tendency of the roots to break through sewer joints and clog the lines, militates against the use of *Populus* for ornamental planting.

KEY TO THE COTTONWOODS

1. Petiole laterally flattened. Leaves broadly ovate to round; bark smooth, greenish-white.

P. tremuloides

1. Petiole round.   2

2. Leaves ovate, whitish or rusty on the underside.   *P. trichocarpa*

2. Leaves narrow; ovate-lanceolate; petiole short.
                                      P. angustifolia

Populus tremuloides Michx.

quaking aspen   **aspen**   **trembling aspen**

Habit: Small to medium-sized tree 30' to 80' tall and 1'
to 2' in diameter; with smooth white to greenish-
white bark, tends to grow in small pure stands or in
thickets.

Leaves: 1-1/2" to 3" in diameter, broadly ovate or
almost round; margins crenate-serrate; apex acute;
base rounded or cordate; shiny light green to yellow-
green and smooth above, paler below; turns bright
yellow in autumn; petiole slender, 1-1/2" to 3" long,
laterally flattened.

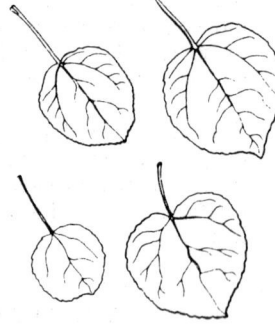

Fruit: A conical capsule
about 1/4" long; stalk
minutely pubescent.

Twigs: Moderately slender,
shiny, reddish-brown;
later becoming grayish;
buds appressed, slightly
resinous, reddish-brown,
about 1/4" to 3/8" long.

Bark: Smooth silvery-white
to greenish- or yellowish-
white, with scattered
roughened areas; the
bases of large trees are
dark, ridged, and fur-
rowed.

FLAT LEAF
STEMS CAUSE
TREMBLING

aspen

Habitat & Range: Found along streams and on moist benches and mountain slopes, on a variety of soils, but doing best on sandy loams.Widespread in Alaska, Canada, the mountains of western United States, and the northern half of eastern United States, also in northern Mexico. It is the most widely distributed tree in North America.

Forage Value: Rates as fair to good browse for sheep and cattle. Highly palatable to many western wildlife species, including deer, elk, moose, beaver, pika, mountain-beaver, snowshoe hare, and porcupine. It is perhaps the most important single woody browse species on western ranges.

Uses: Paper pulp, lumber, excelsior, matches, boxes, baskets, and crates. Used locally for fuel.

Remarks: In the Lakes State Region it commonly becomes established following logging of the pines, or after a fire. It plays a part silviculturally in that region similar to that of red alder in the coastal area of the Douglas-fir Region in the Pacific Northwest. Aspen is very intolerant, grows rapidly, sprouts vigorously when cut; and is host to many destructive insects and diseases.

Populus trichocarpa Torr. & Gray

black cottonwood

Habit: A large tree 100' to 200' high, and 3' to 6' in diameter, with a broad, open crown.

Leaves: 3" to 6" long, ovate to ovate-lanceolate; margins wavy to crenate-serrate; apex acute; base round to subcordate; dark lustrous green and smooth above, silvery-white and commonly with rusty areas on the underside; petiole round, 1-1/2" to 3" long.

Fruit: Subglobose, 3-valved, 1-celled, pubescent capsule, 1/3" to 1/2" long.

Twigs: Moderately stout, greenish-brown to olive-drab in color, slightly ribbed or terete; lenticels distinct, spur shoots are common on the older branches; buds resinous, aromatic, with dark reddish-brown imbricated scales; terminal bud about 3/4" long, ovoid-conical; lateral buds smaller and often divergent, leaf scars semi-circular.

STICKY FRAGRANT BUDS

black cottonwood

Bark: Smooth, yellowish-tan to gray on young trees; on old trees gray to grayish-brown, and broken into deep furrows and narrow flattened ridges, 1-1/2" to 2-1/2" thick.

Habitat & Range: Occurs on moist sites along streams, bottomlands, river islands and benches. Ranges from southern and southeastern Alaska and the southern Yukon, southward to northern Lower California and western Nevada, eastward to central Montana, local in Wyoming and southwestern North Dakota. Elevational range: near sea level to 4,500 feet in Washington and Oregon; 500 to 6,000 feet in California.

Uses: Paper pulp, plywood cores, excelsior, dairy and poultry boxes, crates and coops, laundry appliances and toys.

Remarks: Very intolerant. Grows rapidly and will sprout from the stump. Occurs in small pure stands or associated with red alder, bigleaf maple, Oregon ash, Douglas-fir, and grand fir.

Black cottonwood is the largest of the American poplars, and is the largest hardwood indigenous to the West. The first forest plantations in Oregon were of black cottonwood. The plantations were established along the Willamette River and on some of the river islands.

In the spring as the buds begin to swell and burst, the air in the vicinity of the trees is filled with a honey-like fragrance.

Populus angustifolia Janes

narrowleaf cottonwood

Characteristics: Very similar to black cottonwood, except that the leaves are narrower, 2'' to 5'' long, lanceolate to narrow-ovate. Leaf base rounded to wedge-shaped; petiole short, 1/2'' to 1'' long.

Fruit: Broadly ovate, 2-valved capsule.

Uses: May be used locally for fuel.

Habitat & Range: Moist, well-drained sites in the sun. Found in southern Alberta and Saskatchewan southward through Montana to eastern New Mexico westward into eastern Washington, extreme southeastern Oregon, Nevada and Arizona, and in the Black Hills and western Nebraska, also in northern Mexico. Elevational range: 2,500 to 5,000 feet. In Oregon it is found only on Steens Mountain in the extreme southeastern part of the state.

MYRICACEAE   Wax-Myrtle Family

Myrica L.

bayberry

Habit: Aromatic, small trees or shrubs with deciduous or persistent foliage.

Leaves: Deciduous or persistent, alternate, 5-ranked, simple; margins entire or serrate; petiole short.

Flowers: Dioecious or monoecious; borne in aments (catkins).

Fruit: Small, round or ovoid drupes that may be either waxy or fleshy.

KEY TO THE BAYBERRIES

Leaves deciduous, 1" to 2-1/4" long, with scattered yellowish glands on underside. Shrub less than 6' tall. *M. gale*

Leaves persistent, 2" to 4" long, with pale green, smooth underside, often with minute black specks. Small tree up to 30' tall, or large shrub. *M. californica*

Myrica californica **Cham.**

Pacific bayberry   **Pacific waxmyrtle**

Habit: Large, evergreen shrub or small tree up to 30' or 40' tall, and 8" to 12" in diameter; with a dense, dark green, round crown of slender willowlike foliage.

Leaves: Persistent, alternate, simple; oblanceolate to oblong-lanceolate or oblanceolate-cuneate, 2" to 4" long, 1/2" to 3/4" wide; dark green, smooth and lustrous above, paler beneath and with very minute black specks (often not visible to the naked eye); margins remotely serrate except for the base which is entire; apex acute; base wedge-shaped; petiole short, about 1/2" long, minutely pubescent.

Flowers: Monoecious. Aments (catkins) borne in the leaf axils; staminate aments 1/2" to 1" long; pistillate aments borne above the staminate aments, 1/2" to 1-1/2" long.

Fruit: Round, dark purple to grayish-white, waxy drupe about 1/6" in diameter, usually borne in clusters.

Twigs: Moderately stout, dark green, pubescent the first year, slightly ridged; older twigs round, brownish-green, eventually becoming ashy-gray.

Bark: Very thin, dark gray or grayish-brown and often mottled with white areas.

Habitat & Range: Found on moist, well-drained, sandy or gravelly soils in the sun or shade near the Pacific Coast from Washington southward to southern California. Elevational range: sea level to 300'.

Remarks: Very tolerant. Associated with evergreen huckleberry, rhododendron, salal, hairy manzanita, lodgepole (shore) pine, Sitka spruce and western hemlock.

Planted as an ornamental. Early settlers gathered the fruits and rendered the wax to make candles.

Myrica gale L.

sweetgale

Habit: Shrubs up to 6' tall.

Leaves: Deciduous, alternate, simple; obovate to oblanceolate, 1" to 2-1/4" long, dark green and smooth above; paler beneath, with conspicuous scattered yellowish glands, and usually slightly pubescent; margins serrate along the upper 1/3 to 1/2, entire below; apex acute to round; base wedge-shaped; petiole very short, about 1/8" long.

Flowers: Dioecious. Stamens and pistils in separate aments in axils of bracts.

Fruits: Very small waxy drupe.

Twigs: Dark grayish-brown and slender; buds about 1/16" long.

Bark: Grayish to grayish-brown.

Habitat & Range: Found on moist sites in the sun, often on acid soils. From Alaska southward to west central Oregon, the East Coast and Europe.

BETULACEAE   Birch Family

Alnus B. Ehrh.

alder

Habit: Moist-site trees and shrubs with nitrogen-fixing bacteria on the roots. Intermediate tolerance.

Leaves: Deciduous, alternate, simple, 3-ranked; ovate, obovate or oval in shape; margins serrate, doubly serrate or dentate, rarely entire. The leaves fall in the autumn without changing color.

Flowers: Monoecious. Flowers borne in aments (catkins), 2 to 5 in a cluster; staminate aments are **preformed**, i.e., the male flowers emerge from the bud during the current growing season, but hang from the twigs unopened until the next growing season.

Fruits: Winged nutlets; borne on the scales of a semi-woody strobile or cone. The strobiles persist on the tree long after the seeds have been released.

Twigs: New twigs are round or triangular in cross section; olive drab, reddish or reddish-brown in color, lenticels more or less conspicuous; pith is triangular in cross section.

Buds: Stalked or sessile; scales valvate or imbricated, brown to reddish-brown, slightly resinous or waxy.

Remarks: Inhabit moist areas from sea level to high mountain slopes in the temperate and cooler regions of the Northern Hemisphere, also found in Central and South America. Geologically an ancient genus.

KEY TO THE ALDERS

1. Leaf margins revolute.   *A. rubra*

1. Leaf margins not revolute.   2

  2. Leaf apex round or obtuse; margins finely, usually singly, serrate, with glandular teeth.
          A. rhombifolia

  2. Leaf apex acute; margins doubly serrate.   3

3. Larger serrations resemble small lobes. Underside of leaf not sticky.   *A. incana*

3. Larger serrations usually not lobelike; leaves thin and almost papery. Underside of leaf often sticky.   *A. sinuata*

Alnus rhombifolia Nutt.

white alder

Habit: A tree 40′ to 80′ tall and 1′ to 2′ in diameter; with a broad, dome-shaped, open crown, and grayish-brown scaly bark.

Leaves: 2″ to 3-1/2″ long, ovate to ovate-rhombic or oval, margins finely serrate to doubly serrate and indistinctly glandular; apex round to bluntly pointed; base obtuse to broadly wedge-shaped; green to yellow-green and initially slightly sticky above, paler and smooth to somewhat pubescent along the veins on the underside; petiole short, 1/2″ to 1″ long, grooved above.

Fruits: Winged nutlets; borne in a semi-woody strobile or cone; 1/2″ to 3/4″ long; brown in color.

Twigs: New twigs slender, light green and somewhat pubescent, but soon becoming smooth, olive-drab to yellowish-brown in color; slightly triangular in cross section; lenticels evident, buds stalked, about 1/2'' long, slender, red to reddish-brown, slightly pubescent; scales valvate.

Bark: On old trunks about 1'' thick, whitish to grayish-brown, with flat, plated ridges which are superficially scaly.

Habitat & Range: Found on moist sites along stream bottoms and on lower mountain slopes, from southern interior British Columbia southward to northern Lower California, and in northern Idaho.

Uses: Not commercially important.

Remarks: Intermediate tolerance. Forms pure stands, or is associated with bigleaf maple, western dogwood, Oregon ash, and California sycamore.

Alnus rubra Bong.

red alder

Habit: A tree 30' to 120' tall and 1' to 3' in diameter; with a fairly straight bole and a moderatley open, broadly pyramidal or dome-shaped crown.

Leaves: 3'' to 6'' long and about half as wide, ovate to ovate-elliptical, shiny green to yellow-green and smooth above; paler and pubescent along the veins on the underside; margins doubly serrate to slightly lobed and serrate, revolute (i.e., the margins are rolled down and under); petiole about 1'' long, grooved on the upperside. Apex acute.

red alder

Fruit: Tiny nutlets with thin lateral wings or one encircling wing; borne on the scales of a semi-woody cone, 1/2" to 1" long, cylindrical, brown to gray.

Twigs: New twigs are distinctly triangular in cross section; olive drab to reddish-brown in color, lenticels prominent; buds stalked, about 1/2" long; scales valvate, red and somewhat waxy. Lammas shoots (twigs with leaves in the axil of a leaf) frequently may be found on vigorous shoots.

Bark: Ashy gray to grayish-brown; comparatively smooth along the upper bole, and near the base with flattened, irregularly plated ridges which are superficially scaly; inner bark tan, becoming reddish-brown upon exposure to the air.

Habitat & Range: Occurs along streams and in moist bottoms, and on moist mountain slopes. Ranges from southeastern Alaska southward through western British Columbia, and on the west side of Cascade Mountains as far south as southern California. Elevational range: sea level to 3,500 feet in the Pacific Coast states.

Uses: Furniture (often disguised as maple or some other species), core stock and cross bands in plywood, woodenware, millwork, plugs for paper rolls, and to a limited extent for pulp.

Remarks: Intermediate tolerance. Forms pure stands, or occurs in mixture with cottonwood, bigleaf maple, vine maple, Oregon ash, willows, Douglas-fir and grand fir.

Red alder is the largest and most important of the Pacific Coast alders. The total volume of this species is greater than any other western hardwood.

Alnus sinuata (Reg.) Rydb.

Sitka alder

Habit: A thicket-forming erect shrub, or a small tree 20' to 40' tall and 5" to 10" in diameter; with grayish or grayish-green bark.

Leaves: 1-1/2" to 5" long, ovate to ovate-oval, thin and papery; margins sharply, double serrate to slightly lobed and serrate; apex acute; base obtuse; shiny green to yellow-green above, paler and smooth beneath, or slightly pubescent in the vein axils.

Fruit: Winged nutlets; borne in a broadly ellipsoidal or barrel-shaped, semi-woody cone or strobile, about 1/2" to 3/4" long.

Twigs: New twigs round to slightly ribbed; shiny light brown to yellow-brown; at first slightly pubescent and glandular-dotted, later becoming smooth; lenticels conspicuous; buds acute, spindle-shaped with reddish-brown valvate scales, slightly stalked or sessile.

Bark: Gray to grayish-green in color, with warty lenticels.

Habitat & Range: Found in moist sites in the mountains. Ranges from the Yukon, and western and southern Alaska southward to northern California, eastward to southwestern Alberta and western Montana, also northeastern Oregon. Elevational Range: in the United States usually above 3,000 feet.

Alnus incana (L.) **Moench***

thinleaf alder   **mountain alder**

Habit: A shrub or small tree up to 25' tall, with slender branches and grayish-brown bark; tends to form thickets.

Leaves: 2'' to 4'' long, ovate to ovate-oval or oblong-ovate; dark green and smooth above, paler and smooth or slightly pubescent beneath; margins sharply and doubly serrate, or coarsely toothed and serrate; apex acute to round; base broadly obtuse to somewhat rounded, or abruptly narrowed and wedge-shaped; petiole 1/2'' to 1'' long, grooved above, at first green but becoming dark reddish-brown on the upper side; midrib light yellow-green.

Fruit: Narrow-winged nutlets; borne in a barrel-shaped, semi-woody cone or strobile, about 1/2'' long.

Twigs: Slender, round to slightly ridged; at first slightly hairy but becoming grayish-brown; lenticels orange colored; buds stalked or sessile, conical, about 3/8'' long; bud scales dark reddish-brown.

LITTLE TEETH ON BIG TEETH

LOOK FOR THESE

mountain alder

Bark: Greenish-gray to gray-reddish brown, thin and smooth on small trees, becoming scaly near the base when older.

Habitat & Range: In the mountains near streams, springs, and seeps. Ranges from central Alaska southward through eastern Oregon to central California and western Nevada, eastward to western Montana and northern New Mexico. Elevational range: in the States from 3,000 to 7,000 feet.

Remarks: Less tolerant than other alders. Forms pure thickets, and commonly associates with lodgepole pine, vine maple, willows, aspen and black cottonwood. The most widely distributed western alder and the most common alder in eastern Oregon, the Rocky and Sierra-Nevada Mountains.

*Sometimes called *Alnus Tenuifolia* Nutt.

Betula L

birch

Habit: Intolerant, moist-site trees and shrubs with thin, papery bark and prominent horizontal lenticels.

Leaves: Deciduous, alternate, simple, 2-ranked; ovate to triangular in shape; margins serrate, doubly serrate, lobed and serrate or dentate; petiolate.

Flowers: Monoecious, both sexes borne in aments (catkins); staminate aments preformed, usually 2 to 3 in a cluster; pistillate aments usually solitary.

Fruit: Winged nutlets; borne on the papery scales of a cylindrical strobile or cone; strobile is usually pendent and distintegrates when mature.

Twigs: Slender; 1/2 phyllotaxy; green to reddish-brown in color; in some species aromatic (winter-green odor) when bruised; spur shoots abundant on older branchlets; pith round or slightly triangular. Twigs may appear to be crooked, i.e., they tend to zigzag.

Buds: Terminal buds absent; lateral buds ovate to ovate-conical, with brown or reddish-brown imbricated scales.

Bark: Papery. May or may not peel horizontally; prominent horizontal lenticels.

Remarks: Ancient in origin. Widely distributed through the temperate and cooler regions of the Northern Hemisphere. In the United States there are 19 species attaining tree size, and several others are shrubs. In the West the shrubby species are browsed, their palatability ranging from fair to very good.

KEY TO THE BIRCHES

1. New twigs resin-dotted. Leaves 1/2" to 2" long. 2

1. New twigs smooth. Leaves 2" to 3-1/2" long, with doubly-serrate margins. *B. papyrifera*

   2. Leaf margins serrate to dentate; leaves ovate to diamond-shaped. *B. occidentalis*

   2. Leaf margins crenate; leaves obovate to round. *B. glandulosa*

Betula glandulosa Michx.

bog birch   **scrub birch**

Habit: An erect (occasionally almost prostrate), much-branched shrub up to 12' in height; with glandular branchlets and grayish to dark grayish-brown bark.

Leaves: Broadly obovate to almost round, 1/2" to 1-1/2" long and nearly as wide; margins crenate; apex round; base round or broadly wedge-shaped; dark green and smooth above, paler and somewhat glandular below; petiole up to 1/4" long, reddish.

Fruit: Winged nutlets; borne in a cylindrical cone or strobile, about 3/4" long.

Twigs: Slender and usually crooked; dark grayish-brown to reddish-brown; very sticky when new, resin later solidifies into tiny globules.

Bark: Smooth and thin, dark grayish-brown or gray; doesn't peel horizontally.

Habitat & Range: Occurs in mountain meadows and bogs, and around springs and seeps. Ranges from Alaska southward through British Columbia, east of the Cascade and Sierra Nevada Mountains in

Washington and Oregon, and northern California; also the Rocky Mountains, the Great Lakes area, and the New England states.

Remarks: One of the most common and widely distributed western birches. Buds eaten by grouse, quail and ptarmigan. Browse qualities rated as poor to good. Hitchcock and Cronquist (1973) recognize 2 varieties.

Betula occidentalis **Hook.**

red birch   **water birch**

Habit: Loosely branched shrub, or small tree up to 30' tall, with slender branches which are resin-dotted on the new growth; bark dark reddish-brown.

Leaves: Broadly ovate to diamond-shaped, 3/4" to 2" long, and 1/2" to 1-1/4" wide; green to yellow-green above, initially sticky but becoming smooth, paler below and somewhat glandular; margins coarsely serrate, but entire near the base; apex acute to rounded; base broadly obtuse to rounded; petiole about 1/2" long, yellowish and glandular-dotted, flattened above.

Fruit: Winged nutlets; borne in a cylindrical cone or strobile, 1" to 1-1/2" long.

Twigs: New twig green and sticky, becoming reddish-brown, and resin-dotted, eventually grayish-brown and smooth.

Bark: Reddish-brown to copper-colored, smooth and with conspicuous lenticels. On older plants the bark may loosen and curl slightly, but it does not peel horizontally.

YOUNG TWIGS WARTY

water birch

Habitat & Range: Found along streams from central British Columbia southward on the east side of Cascade Mountains in Washington and Oregon, and the Sierra Nevada Mountains to central California, eastward to southwestern Manitoba, the Rocky Mountains and the mountains of the southwest.

Remarks: Palatability fair to good. Bark more durable than the wood. Hitchcock and Cronquist (1973) recognize 2 varieties.

Betula papyrifera Marsh.

paper birch   **white birch**

Habit: Tree 30′ to 70′ tall, and up to 2′ in diameter; with white or grayish-white bark marked with prominent horizontal lenticels.

Leaves: 2″ to 3-1/2″ long, ovate to ovate-elliptical; yellow-green and smooth above, paler and slightly hairy beneath, especially in the vein axils; margins doubly serrate; apex acute; base rounded to subcordate; petiole 3/4″ to 2-1/2″ long.

Fruit: Winged nutlets, wings minutely pubescent; borne in a pendent, cylindrical, disintegrating cone or strobile, 1″ to 1-1/4″ long.

Twigs: Brown and smooth, lenticels ivory-colored.

Bark: On young trees may be bronze-colored to light reddish-brown; older trees white or creamy-white, and peeling in horizontal strips; lenticels prominent, horizontal, flattened-ellipsoidal.

Habitat & Range: Occurs on cool, moist, well-drained sites in the sun. Primarily a Canadian tree, but common in northern United States, especially the Northeast. In the west it occurs from British Columbia and Alberta southward through eastern Washington and into the Wallowa Mountains of northeastern Oregon, and eastward to western Montana.

Remarks: The least common of the birches in Oregon and perhaps the rarest broadleaf tree species in the state. In the Northeast, an important timber tree, used for furniture and flooring, and articles of turnery. Because of a former special use by Indians, this species is sometimes known as canoe birch. Hitchock and Cronquist (1973) recognize 2 varieties.

Corylus L.

hazel

Habit: Shrubs or small trees.

Leaves: Deciduous, alternate, 2-ranked, simple; ovate to oval; margins doubly serrate; surfaces more or less pubescent; petiole short and pubescent.

Flowers: Monoecious, borne in aments (catkins); staminate aments preformed; pistillate flowers in a tiny cluster, stigmas red.

Fruit: A nut partially or wholly surrounded by an involucre or husk, commonly paired.

Twigs: Moderately slender, tend to be crooked, new twigs pubescent; terminal buds absent, lateral buds with imbricated scales.

Remarks: Some species are raised commercially for their nut crop. Nuts commonly known as filberts or hazel nuts.

Corylus cornuta var. *californica* (A. DC.) Sharp

California hazel

Habit: Open and spreading shrubs up to 15' tall, or small trees up to 30' tall and 6" to 12" in diameter.

Leaves: Broadly ovate or obovate to almost round, 2" to 4" long and 1-1/2" to 3" broad; pubescent; dark green above; paler below; margins sharply and doubly serrate; apex broadly acute to almost round; base sub-cordate; petiole up to 3/4" long, pubescent.

Fruit: Subglobose nuts about 3/8" to 5/8" long, wholly surrounded by tan-colored, somewhat hairy, beaked or elongated papery husk; often paired on the twig.

Twigs: Current year's twigs slender, brownish and pubescent; branchlets tend to zig zag. Phyllotaxy 1/2'.

ZIG-ZAG TWIGS
HAIRY FRUIT
California hazel

Habitat & Range: Occurs in the understory of coniferous forests, on burned-over and logged-over lands, and along streams. Ranges from southern British Columbia southward to central California on the west side of the Cascade and Sierra Nevada Mountains.

Remarks: Tolerant to very tolerant. At times it may inhibit reproduction of desirable tree species. Preformed staminate aments commence elongating very early in the spring before the leaves appear. Nuts edible. Browse value poor to fair.

FAGACEAE   Beech Family

Castanopsis (D. Don) Spach

chinkapin   **chinquapin**

Habit: Tolerant trees or shrubs with persistent leaves, and seeds that are borne in a spiny bur.

Leaves: Persistent, alternate, 5-ranked, simple, leathery; margins entire (native species).

Flowers: Monoecious; borne in erect aments (catkins). The pistillate flowers occur on the basal portion of an otherwise-staminate stalk, forming a bisexual ament. All staminate aments also occur.

Fruit: 1 to 4 edible nuts, resembling small chestnuts, borne in a bur with sharp, branched spines; requires two growing seasons to mature.

Twigs: Round; pith stellate; bud scales imbricated; phyllotaxy 2/5.

Remarks: There are about 30 species, of which only two are indigenous to the United States; the remainder are found in southeastern Asia. The genus is closely related to the chestnuts (*Castanea* spp.).

Castanopsis chrysophylla (Dougl.) A.DC.

golden chinkapin   **western chinquapin**

Habit: Evergreen trees 90′ to 150′ in height, and 3′ to 6′ in diameter, with a round or conical crown; or at the northern and southern limits of its range commonly shrubby.

Leaves: 2-1/2″ to 4-1/2″ long, lanceolate or oblong-elliptical, leathery; pale green or yellow-green, glabrous and usually lustrous above, with a golden scurfiness (occasionally pale green or silvery) below; margins entire and at times slightly revolute; apex acute; base acute to rounded; petiole up to 1/2″ long, scurfy.

Flowers: Borne in erect aments; staminate flowers grayish-yellow, scurfy and tomentose; pistillate aments short and attached to the basal portion of an otherwise staminate ament, or merely constituting that basal portion.

Fruit: 1 or 2, somewhat triangular nuts; borne in a 4-parted bur with sharp, branched spines, light brown when mature.

Twigs: Slender, initially coated with a golden scurfiness, reddish-brown, older branchlets darker and smooth; pith yellow, stellate in shape; buds occasionally clustered at the tip of the twig; bud scales imbricated, light brown and papery, hairy along the margins.

Bark: On young trees grayish-brown and mottled with large white areas; later, shallowly fissured with broad, flat, dark ridges; on older trees 1″ to 2″ thick, deeply furrowed and ridged.

Habitat & Range: Found on dry, sandy and gravelly soils, in western portions of the Pacific states. In Washington, golden chinkapin occurs on the eastern slopes of the Olympic Mountains. In Oregon, it occurs in the Coast Range and on both sides of the Cascade Mountains, especially on the west side. In California it occurs in the Coast Range and on the western slopes of the Sierra Nevada Mountains. Elevational range: 2,000 to 5,000 feet in Oregon; 3,000 to 10,000 feet in California.

Uses: Although the lumber does not find wide use it has been utilized for building construction, boxes and crates, furniture and cabinet work.

Remarks: Tolerant to intermediate in tolerance. Occurs in dense thickets or associated with Douglas-fir, noble fir, redwood, ponderosa and Jeffrey pines, and canyon live oak. Vigorous sprouter. Through experiments it has been found susceptible to chestnut blight, the disease which has practically eliminated the American chestnut in the East.

golden chinkapin

Lithocarpus **Blume**

tanoak

Habit: Tolerant, evergreen, moist-site trees, or occasionally shrubs, having acorn fruit.

Leaves: Persistent, alternate, 5-ranked, simple, stiff, entire or with coarse teeth; pinnately veined; stipulate.

Flowers: Monoecious; borne in erect aments (catkins). Pistillate flowers are on the basal portion of an otherwise staminate ament, called a bisexual ament.

Fruit: Nut (acorn) borne in a bristly cup; matures in two growing seasons.

Twigs: Round and stout; pith stellate.

Remarks: Intermediate in characteristics between the chestnuts (*Castanea* spp.) and the oaks (*Quercus* spp.), but more closely related to the latter. There are numerous species, most of which are found in southeastern Asia. Only one species is indigenous to the United States.

Lithocarpus densiflorus **(Hook. & Arn.) Rehd.**

tanoak

Habit: Evergreen trees 60' to 100' tall and 1' to 3' in diameter, with a dense, broad, round crown, or when growing in a forest stand with a narrow, spikelike crown of ascending branches; or a shrub up to 10' in height.

Leaves: Oblong to oblong-ovate, 3" to 5" long, thick, stiff, and leathery; dark green and with a tawny tomentum when first unfolded, later pale green, lustrous and smooth, or with a slight tomentum on the upper surface, lower surface initially tomentose, later becoming smooth and bluish white; margins entire or coarsely toothed and frequently revolute; apex acute; base obtuse to round; petiole stout, 1/2" to 1" long, tomentose.

Fruit: Nuts (acorns) oval to ovate, borne singly or paired, 3/4" to 1-1/4" long, with a scurfy tomentum; cup shallow, bristly-scaled on the outside, tomentose on the inside.

Twigs: Stout and round, tomentose, becoming smooth the second or third year, reddish-brown and occasionally glaucous; pith stellate; buds ovate, about 1/2" long, protected by loosely imbricated, tomentose scales. Phyllotaxy 2/5.

Bark: 3/4" to 1-1/2" thick, with narrow furrows and broad, rounded or flattened ridges checkered with square plates which are superficially scaly, reddish-brown to grayish-brown in color.

Habitat & Range: Found on moist, well-drained, sandy and gravelly soils, from southwestern Oregon southward to southern California, also in the Sierra-Nevada Mountains (where it is commonly shrubby). Elevational range: from near sea level to 4,700 feet.

Uses: Locally for fuel, furniture and mine timbers. Bark is a commercial source of tannin. The wood has a potential value for flooring and other uses similar to that of oak.

Remarks: Tolerant. Found in small pure stands, but more commonly associated with redwood, Douglas-fir and canyon live oak. Vigorous stump sprouter. Birds and rodents feed on the acorns.

Quercus **L.**

oak

Habit: Sturdy upland trees or shrubs; mostly intermediate in tolerance.

Leaves: Deciduous or persistent, alternate, simple; margins entire, pinnately lobed or serrate.

Flowers: Monoecious; staminate flowers borne in unisexual aments (catkins). Pistillate flowers solitary or in 2- or 3-flowered spikes.

Fruit: Nuts (acorns) partially enclosed by a scaly cup or involucre; bitter to the taste because of the tannin content; matures in one or two seasons.

Twigs: Slender to stout, ridged; pith stellate in shape. Buds are commonly clustered at the tips of the twigs. Phyllotaxy 2/5.

Remarks: The oaks are the most important and the most abundant group of hardwoods in the United States. They are of early geological origin, and today there are between 200 and 300 species, varieties, and hybrids to be found throughout the world. In addition to the very strong wood, the various species are important as a source of tannin and dyes, cork, pharmaceutical extractives and other types of products.

There are seven oaks native to Oregon, however, only the three most common ones are included in this manual.

KEY TO THE OAKS

1. Leaves lobed, deciduous.   2

1. Leaves not lobed; margins spinose or entire; persistent.   *Q. chrysolepis*

   2. Lobes rounded or blunt-pointed, not bristle-tipped; bark light colored.   *Q. garryana*

   2. Lobes pointed, bristle-tipped; bark dark, with pink fissures.   *Q. kelloggii*

Quercus chrysolepis Liebm.

canyon live oak

Habit: Evergreen trees 30' to 80' tall and 1' to 2' in diameter, with a short trunk and spreading crown; or a shrub up to 15' tall.

Leaves: Persistent, 1" to 3-1/2" long, and 1/2" wide, oblong-ovate or elliptical, thick and leathery; fuzzy when they first appear, becoming yellow-green, lustrous, and smooth above; initially fuzzy below, becoming bluish-white and smooth; margins entire or with a few to many spinose teeth (hollylike), apex acute; base obtuse to rounded; petiole yellowish, seldom more than 1/2" long. The species has two types of leaves, and it is quite common for both types to be on the same plant, even on the same twig.

Fruit: Nut (acorn) ovoid to oblong, 1/2" to 2" long, and about half as wide, initially somewhat fuzzy; cup cylindrical or saucer-shaped; requires two seasons to mature.

Twigs: Slender, rigid or flexible, fuzzy when new; older twigs mostly smooth, reddish-brown, eventually becoming grayish-brown.

Bark: Grayish-brown tinged with red, mostly smooth, with small closely appressed scales, 3/4" to 1-1/2" thick.

Habitat & Range: Occurs on dry, well-drained sites in the sun, in open woods, in canyon bottoms, and on mountain slopes. From southwestern Oregon southward to northern Lower California, local in western Nevada. Elevational range: 2,000 to 8,000 feet.

Remarks: Tolerant. Occurs in pure patches, but more commonly associated with ponderosa pine, Douglas-fir, incense-cedar, black oak and various live oaks.

Vigorous sprouter. The species is considered to be the most ancient of the existing American oaks.

The wood has had only limited use; it is heavy, hard and strong.

Quercus garryana Dougl.

Oregon white oak

Habit: Trees 40' to 80' tall and 2' to 3' in diameter, with a broad compact crown.

Leaves: Deciduous, 3" to 6" long, 2" to 4-1/2" broad, obovate or oblong, thick and leathery; dark green and pubescent when new, becoming glabrous and somewhat lustrous above, paler and smooth or slightly pubescent below; margins 7- to 9-lobed, lobes round or bluntly pointed; sinuses frequently narrow, rounded at the bottom; apex round; base wedge-shaped; petiole 1/2" to 1" long, pubescent. The lobes often touch or overlap.

Fruit: Nut (acorn) oval or barrel-shaped, 3/4 to 1-1/2" long half to 2/3 as wide; cup shallow; matures in one season.

Twigs: Stout, ridged, initially pubescent, becoming smooth; greenish-brown or olive-drab, becoming reddish-brown and eventually gray; pith stellate; several buds are usually clustered at the end of the twigs; bud scales yellowish-brown and tomentose. Phyllotaxy 2/5.

Oregon white oak

Bark: White to light brown or grayish-brown; shaggy

or with short, broad ridges and shallow furrows, less than 1'' thick.

Habitat & Range: On dry to moist, well-drained gravelly soils in the valleys and lower foothills from southwestern British Columbia and Vancouver Island southward principally on the Westside (west of the summit of the Cascades and Sierras) to north-central California. Elevational range: from near sea level in the north to 4,000 feet in the south.

Uses: Has had only limited use other than for fuel. Potentially valuable for flooring, furniture, cooperage, cabinet work, interior trim and ship building.

Remarks: Oregon white oak is the most abundant and widely distributed oak in Oregon. It is the only native oak found in eastern Oregon (Sherman County) where it is associated with ponderosa pine and western juniper. It is the only oak native to Washington and British Columbia.

Intolerant in Oregon; intermediate in tolerance in California. Forms pure stands, or is associated with madrone, Oregon ash, bigleaf maple, Douglas-fir, ponderosa pine and black oak. Heavy seeder and vigorous sprouter. The foliage is rich in protein.

Quercus kelloggii Newb.

California black oak

Habit: Trees 40' to 80' tall and 1' to 2-1/2' in diameter, with an open, rounded crown; at high elevations it may be a shrub up to 15' high.

Leaves: Deciduous, 3'' to 6'' long, 2'' to 4'' wide, oblong to obovate; greenish-red and pubescent when they first unfold, becoming yellow-green, smooth and somewhat lustrous above, paler below, margins mostly 7-lobed, lobes 3-toothed and bristle-tipped;

sinuses shallow to deep, rounded at the bottoms; base obtuse or wedge-shaped; petiole 1" to 2" long. Lobes often touch or overlap.

Fruit: Nut (acorn) oblong to oblong-ovoid, 1" to 2-1/2" long, chestnut-brown; cup encloses about half the nut; requires two growing seasons to mature.

Twigs: Reddish-brown, ridged, smooth or minutely pubescent; buds about 1/4" long, chestnut-brown; the scales minutely hairy along the edges; the buds are commonly clustered at the ends of the twigs.

Bark: Dark gray or black and smooth on young trees; on old trees dark brown, and often with a reddish tinge or almost black, with broad, irregularly plated ridges, about 1" thick.

Habitat & Range: On dry, sandy, gravelly, or rocky soils in the valleys, foothills and lower mountain slopes on the west side of the Cascade and Sierra Nevada Mountains from south central Oregon southward to southern California. Does not occur on the west slope of the Coast Range in California. Elevational range: from 1,000 feet in Oregon to 9,000 feet in southern California.

Remarks: Intermediate tolerance. Occurs as a scattered tree or in open, pure stands, but more commonly associated with ponderosa pine, Douglas-fir, incense-cedar, Oregon white oak, and canyon live oak.

Not yet commercially important. However it is

California black oak

sometimes used for furniture and flooring and occasionally for posts and tool handles. Deer feed on the leaves and the acorns.

ULMACEAE   Elm Family

Celtis L.

hackberry

Habit: Mostly deciduous trees occurring in the temperate and tropical regions of both hemispheres.

Leaves: Deciduous, alternate, simple; margins mostly serrate, occasionally entire. Netted veins.

Flowers: Both perfect and unisexual flowers on the same tree.

Twigs: Slender, crooked; phyllotaxy 1/2; pith very finely chambered at the nodes; terminal buds absent.

Celtis reticulata Torr.

netleaf hackberry

Habit: Shrubs or small trees up to 30' tall.

Leaves: Deciduous, alternate, simple, 1" to 3-1/2" long, ovate to ovate-lanceolate; dark green and "sand papery" above, paler and pubescent along the veins on the underside; margins serrate; apex acute to accuminate and often falcate (sickle-shaped); base rounded or subcordate, asymmetrical; 3-veined from the base of the leaf; petiole 1/3" to 3/4" long.

Fruit: Dark brown or orange-red drupe, globose, about 1/4" in diameter.

Twigs: Round, crooked or zigzag; pith chambered at the nodes; terminal buds absent; bud scales imbricated.

Bark: Grayish-brown, ridged and furrowed.

Habitat & Range: Found on dry, gravelly soils, near streams, from Washington southward on the east of the Cascade Mountains in Oregon to eastern and southern California; eastward to Wyoming, Colorado, Oklahoma, and Texas.

BERBERIDACEAE   Barberry Family

Berberis

Oregon-grape   **holly-grape**

Habit: Evergreen shrubs with pinnately compound leaves, leaflets hollylike.

Leaves: Persistent, alternate, pinnately compound with 3 to 21 leaflets which are stiff and leathery; margins spinose; leaflets sessile or petiolate.

Flowers: Perfect; yellow.

Fruit: Dark blue berry, about 1/4" in diameter.

Remarks: Inner bark and wood is yellow. Some species susceptible to black-stem wheat rust. Genus formerly called *Mahonia.*

KEY TO THE OREGON-GRAPES

1. Prostrate shrub, leaflets 3 to 7, mostly 5.   *B. repens*

1. Erect shrubs.   2

    2. Leaflets 11 to 21; midrib not prominent; clustered at the end of the stems.   *B. nervosa*

    2. Leaflets 5 to 9; midrib prominent; leaves alternate.   *B. aquifolium*

Berberis aquifolium **Pursh.**

tall Oregon-grape

Habit: Erect, evergreen shrubs 3' to 10' tall, with dark green glossy leaves.

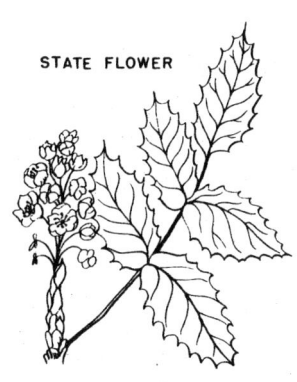

STATE FLOWER

tall Oregon-grape

Leaves: 6" to 12" long, alternate, pinnately compound with 5 to 9 leaflets, leaflets broadly lanceolate to ovate; dark glossy green above, paler beneath; leaflet margins spinose; terminal leaflet petiolate, lateral leaflets mostly sessile; midrib distinct.

Fruit: Dark blue berries about 3/16" in diameter.

Habitat & Range: Found on dry to moist, well-drained sites in the sun or shade; from British Columbia southward on the Westside to northern California; also northeastern Oregon.

Remarks: Tolerant. The state flower of Oregon. Fruit is eaten by many birds and mammals. Makes good jelly. Nurserymen and florists use the foliage for greenery.

Berberis nervosa **Pursh**

dwarf Oregon-grape

Habit: Low, evergreen shrub with pinnately compound leaves; seldom over 30" high.

Leaves: 10" to 16" long, pinnately compound with 11 to 21 leaflets, leaflets ovate to ovate-lanceolate,

154

sessile, except for the terminal leaflet which is petiolate; dark glossy green above, paler beneath and without a distinct midrib; the leaves are clustered at the ends of the stems.

Fruit: Dark blue berries about 3/16" in diameter.

Twigs: Stout; numerous, light brown, lanceolate bud scales persist at the ends of the stems.

Habitat & Range: Moist, well-drained sites in the sun or shade; on the west side of the Cascade and Sierra Nevada Mountains from British Columbia southward into northern California, also northeastern Oregon, and Idaho.

Remarks: Very tolerant. Common in the understory in the Pacific Coast forests. Florists use the foliage for greenery. Birds and small mammals eat the fruit.

dwarf Oregon-grape

Berberis repens **(Lindl.) G. Don.**

creeping Oregon-grape

Habit: An evergreen, prostrate, creeping shrub seldom over 10" high.

Leaves: 4" to 8" long, pinnately compound with 3 to 7 leaflets, mostly 5; ovate, ovate-oblong or oblong; dull green above, smooth and paler beneath; margins spinose; lateral leaflets sessile, terminal leaflet petiolate; midrib prominent.

Fruit: Dark blue berries about 3/16" in diameter.

Twigs: Slender, often taking root at the nodes.

Habitat & Range: Found on dry, well-drained sites in the sun or shade in the mountains, from southern British Columbia southward on the east of the Cascade and Sierra Nevada Mountains to northern California, also the Rocky Mountains and the Black Hills.

Remarks: Probably the most common and widely distributed *Berberis* in the West. Browsed some by deer.

LAURACEAE   Laurel Family

Umbellularia (Nees) Nutt.

California-laurel

NOTE: Umbellularia is a monotypic genus and the features are described under the species.

Umbellularia californica (Hook. & Arn.) Nutt.

California-laurel   **bay**   **Oregon-myrtle**

Habit: Large, evergreen trees 60' to 100' tall and 2' to 5' in diameter, with aromatic foliage; often multiple-stemmed when growing in the open, and with a dome-shaped crown; or a prostrate to erect shrub up to 15' high.

Leaves: Persistent, alternate, simple, aromatic, 2-1/2" to 5-1/2" long and up to 1" wide, elliptical to oblong-lanceolate; dark green glabrous and shiny above, paler and smooth below; margins entire; apex acute, base broadly acute to round; petiole round, yellow-green, 1/2" to 3/4" long. Very strong-scented when crushed.

Flowers: Perfect, inconspicuous, yellowish.

Fruit: Bluish-black, olivelike drupe, about 3/4" in diameter, with a conical, golf-tee stalk; seed large.

Twigs: Round, slender, light green and smooth, eventually grayish-brown.

Bark: On young trees smooth and dull grayish-brown; on old trees thin, dark reddish-brown and scaly.

Habitat & Range: Found on moist, well-drained sites in the sun or shade, on bottomlands, hillsides, and mountain slopes; from southwestern Oregon southward in the Sierra and Coast Ranges to southern California.

Uses: Turnery items, novelties, veneer, furniture, cabinet work, keel blocks and friction blocks.

Remarks: Tolerant to very tolerant. Vigorous sprouter. Occurs in pure stands or associated with bigleaf maple, red alder, tanoak, madrone, California sycamore and Douglas-fir, also with the chaparral species in the Sierra-Nevada Mountains.

The aromatic leaves and volatile oils will irritate the tender membranes of the eyes and nose.

The burls and wood of this species exhibit the greatest range in color and figure of any of the American woods.

Contrary to what is claimed by some individuals, this is **not** the same species (or even the same genus) that grows in the Holy Land.

HYDRANGEACEAE   Hydrangea Family

Philadelphus **L.**

mockorange

Habit: Opposite-branched, moist-site shrubs with showy flowers.

Leaves: Deciduous, opposite, simple; margin entire to remotely serrate.

Flowers: Perfect, white, solitary or clustered.

Fruit: 4-celled capsule.

Remarks: Considerable variation occurs in many of the species and it is quite likely that several of the species will cross.

mockorange

Philadelphus lewisii Pursh

mockorange

Habit: Loosely branched shrub up to 12' tall.

Leaves: 1" to 3" long, ovate to elliptical-ovate; light green and smooth above, paler and smooth beneath; margins nearly entire or with a few glandular serrations; apex acute; base rounded; 3- to 5-veined from the base or near the base; petiole about 1/2" long.

Flowers: White, 3/4" to 1" broad.

Fruit: Light brown capsule about 1/4" long.

Twigs: Slender, opposite, tan or light brown; branching often widely-dichotomous.

Bark: Light brown and smooth.

Habitat & Range: Occurs on moist, well-drained sites in the sun; in the Cascade and Sierra Nevada Mountains from British Columbia southward to Central California, eastward to Montana. Usually found at the lower elevations.

Remarks: Browsed by deer. Planted as an ornamental.

GROSSULARIACEAE   **Currant Family**

Ribes L.

currants; gooseberries

Habit: Shrubs.

Leaves: Deciduous, alternate, simple, small, palmately lobed and veined; leaves of some species have velvety underside.

Flowers: Perfect; in racemes; petals united to form a tube or funnel.

Fruit: Smooth or glandular berry; edible.

Twigs: Smooth or armed with simple or forked spines at the nodes, and often with prickles or bristles between the nodes. Lenticels horizontal; bark tends to exfoliate in some species.

Remarks: Shrubs. Most species with spines and prickles are called gooseberries. Unarmed species are called currants. Nearly all species are the alternate host of white pine blister rust.

KEY TO CURRANTS AND GOOSEBERRIES

1. Stems armed with spines at nodes, and often with prickles or bristles between nodes.   2

1. Stems unarmed.   3

   2. Spines 3 to several parted, weak; berries fall free from their stalks when ripe; calyx saucer-shaped.   *R. lacustre*

   2. Spines mostly single, stiff; berries fall with stalks attached; calyx not saucer-shaped, often with spreading lobes.   GOOSEBERRIES (*R.* spp.)

3. Leaves 1-1/2'' to 3'' (or larger), 3- to 5-lobed;
   velvety underside.   Flowers red; berries blue-
   black.   *R. sanguineum*

3. Leaves less than 1" in diameter, round; lobes sometimes
   indistinct; doubly serrate margins; upper surface whitish,
   waxy. Flowers greenish-white to pink; berries red or
   orange.   *R. cereum*

Ribes sanguineum Pursh

red-flowering currant

Habit: Loosely branched shrub
up to 10' tall.

Leaves: 1-1/2'' to 3'' (occasionally up to 4-1/2'') in diameter; dark green and somewhat
pubescent above; paler and
with a velvety pubescence
beneath; palmately 3- to 5-
lobed and veined, lobe margins serrated; base cordate,
petiole 1'' to 1-1/2'' long,
glandular, pubescent.

Flowers: Red, borne in long,
showy racemes.

red-flowering currant

Fruit: Dark blue berry with stalked glands, covered
with a white, waxy coating.

Twigs: Round, green and pubescent, becoming smooth
and reddish-brown.

Bark: Reddish- to grayish-brown; splits longitudinally
revealing vertical rows of horizontal lenticels.

Habitat & Range: Occurs on dry to moist, well-drained
sites in the sun or shade, on the west side of the Cascade and Sierra Nevada Mountains from Washington
southward to central California.

Ribes lacustre (Pers.) Poir.

prickly currant   **swamp currant**

Habit: Tolerant, moist-site spiny shrub, up to 4' tall, sometimes trailing.

Leaves: 3/4" to 2-1/2" broad; palmately 3- to 5-lobed, deeply incised and serrate. Underside rather velvety.

Stems: Armed at nodes with 3- to several-parted spines; prickles sometimes present between nodes.

Flowers: Greenish, in racemes; saucer-shaped calyx.

Fruit: Purplish-black berry; falls free from its stalk when ripe.

Habitat & Range: Moist woods. Widely distributed from California to Alaska and to Atlantic states. Eastern and western Oregon.

Ribes cereum Dougl.

wax currant   **squaw currant**

Habit: Much-branched shrubs, up to 6' tall.

Leaves: Very small, round, usually less than 1" in diameter; white waxy upper surface; margin doubly serrate; not distinctly lobed.

Stems: Unarmed; bark smooth, light gray.

Flowers: Tubular, greenish-white to pinkish.

Fruit: Red to orange berries.

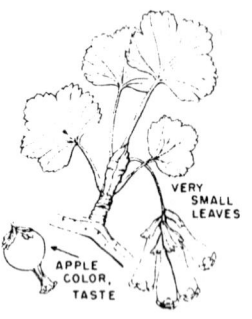

VERY SMALL LEAVES

APPLE COLOR, TASTE

wax currant

Habitat & Range: Dry woods or rocky slopes. Eastern Oregon and Washington, the Siskiyous; also California, British Columbia, and eastward to South Dakota. Hitchcock and Cronquist (1973) recognize 3 varieties.

ROSACEAE   Rose Family

Amelanchier Med.

serviceberry

Habit: Shrubs or small trees.

Leaves: Deciduous, alternate, simple, prominently penniveined; 1" to 2" long, oval to oblong-oval; upper 1/4 to 3/4 of margin serrate; lower part of margin entire; apex rounded; base round or subcordate; petiole about 1/2" long.

Flowers: Perfect. White, with long, straplike petals; in short racemes.

Fruit: Small, red to dark purple to black pome (apple), up to 1/2" in diameter.

Remarks: Serviceberries are found in North America, Europe, and Asia. Several species are attractive ornamentals. Many species are so similar that it is difficult to distinguish among them. All are hosts of the cedar apple fungus.

Amelanchier alnifolia Nutt.

Pacific serviceberry   **western serviceberry**

Habit: Large shrubs or small trees up to 40' tall and 6" in diameter.

Leaves: As described for the genus. Veins tend to run out to the teeth.

Flowers: As described for the genus.

Fruit: Smooth, dark blue pome (apple) 1/4" to 1/2" in diameter.

Twigs: Slender, smooth; reddish-brown when young, becoming grayish-brown; buds about 1/2" long with dark reddish-brown imbricated scales that are hairy along the margins.

Bark: Thin, light brown and tinged with red; smooth or shallowly fissured.

Habitat & Range: Occurs on moist, well-drained sites in the sun or partial shade, from southern Alaska to northwestern California, and eastward throughout the Rocky Mountains.

Remarks: Hitchcock and Cronquist (1973) recognize 5 varieties of this species. All varieties generally form pure thickets, or commonly associated with aspen, chokecherry, bitter cherry, western crab apple, and manzanita. The foliage and young twigs are relished by deer and elk; many birds and mammals feed on the fruits.

UPPER $\frac{1}{2}$ - $\frac{1}{3}$ MARGIN TOOTHED

Pacific serviceberry

Cercocarpus **H.B.K.**

mountain-mahogany   **cercocarpus**

Habit: Deciduous or evergreen shrubs or small trees with short spurlike lateral branchlets, and a 1-seeded fruit that has a long, plumed tail.

Leaves: Deciduous, semi-persistent or persistent, alternate, simple; petiole very short.

Flowers: Perfect; borne singly or in clusters; petals absent; the sepals are united into a tube which expands or flares out at the top into a funnel.

Fruit: A slender elliptical or narrow-oblong achene, with a long curled or twisted plume.

Twigs: Somewhat stiff, spur shoots common on older branches.

Remarks: This genus is restricted to western United States and Mexico, and consists of about 20 species. The scientific name is derived from the plumed or tailed fruit; the common name has reference to the mountainous habitat, and to the hard and heavy character of the wood.

KEY TO THE MOUNTAIN-MAHOGANIES

Leaves elliptical; margins smooth and revolute.
C. ledifolius

Leaves obovate; margins serrated above, smooth and wedge-shaped below. *C. betuloides*

Cercocarpus betuloides **Nutt.**

birchleaf mountain-mahogany   birchleaf cercocarpus

Habit: An erect evergreen shrub up to 15' tall, or occasionally attaining tree size and up to 40' in height.

Leaves: Persistent, alternate, but commonly clustered at the ends of spur shoots, 1/2'' to 1-1/2'' long, and about 2/3 as wide, obovate; conspicuously penn-veined; dark green or yellow-green and smooth above, paler and occasionally slightly pubescent on the underside; margins serrated above the middle, entire below; apex round; base wedge-shaped; petiole less than 1/4'' long.

Flowers: Small, inconspicuous, reddish-tinged.

Fruit: Slender achene, 1/3" to 1/2" long, tipped with a plumose tail up to 3" long.

Twigs: Very slender, reddish-brown and glaucous, becoming gray-reddish-brown and eventually grayish-brown; numerous spur shoots on older twigs.

Habitat & Range: Occurs on the drier foothills and lower mountain slopes in the sun, from southern Oregon southward into lower California, eastward to central Arizona.

Remarks: Used locally for fuel and turnery items. Good deer browse.

Cercocarpus ledifolius **Nutt.**

curlleaf mountain-mahogany   **curlleaf cercocarpus**

Habit: An erect evergreen shrub up to 15' tall, or occasionally a small tree up to 40' tall and 1' to 2' in diameter.

Leaves: Persistent; alternate, or clustered on the ends of spur shoots, 1/2" to 1" long, narrowly elliptical; pubescent when they first unfold, becoming smooth and dark green above, paler and more or less pubescent on the underside; thick and leathery; margins entire and revolute; both ends acute; petiole very short.

Flowers: Small, inconspicuous, trumpet-shaped, pubescent.

Fruit: Cylindrical to elliptical hairy achene, 1/3" to 1/2" long; plumed tail 1-1/2" to 2" long, twisted.

Twigs: New twigs reddish-brown and somewhat pubescent, but later becoming smooth and sometimes glaucous; older twigs silvery-gray to grayish-brown, stout. Spur shoots and short stiff lateral branches common.

Bark: On larger specimens reddish- to grayish-brown, with deep wide furrows, and ridges that break up into thin plate-like scales.

Habitat & Range: Found on warm, dry, rocky, ridges; from eastern Oregon southward to southeastern California, eastward to western Montana, Colorado and northern Arizona, also northern Lower California. Elevational range: 2,000 to 9,000 feet.

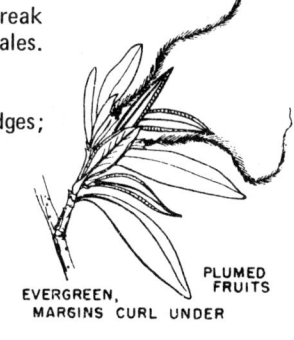

PLUMED FRUITS

EVERGREEN, MARGINS CURL UNDER

curlleaf mountain-mahogany

Remarks: Curlleaf mountain-mahogany attains the largest size of any of the species in the genus, and is the one most likely to attain tree size. Used locally for fuel and for smoking meats.

In some localities it is an important browse for deer and elk. Patches of curlleaf mountain-mahogany are reputed to be likely places to jump buck deer during the hunting season. Hitchcock and Cronquist (1973) recognize 2 varieties.

Crataegus L.

hawthorn

Habit: Trees or shrubs with scaly bark and armed twigs.

Leaves: Deciduous, alternate, simple, membraneous or thickened; petiolate; stipulate.

Flowers: Perfect; borne in clusters, white to red in color.

Fruit: Round to ovoid pome (apple), 1/4'' to 1'' in diameter.

Twigs: Armed with thorns; lack terminal buds; bud scales red or reddish-brown and lustrous.

Remarks: This genus has an abundance of species, varieties and hybrids taxonomically very difficult to identify with any great degree of certainty.

KEY TO THE HAWTHORNS

Thorns an inch long or longer; fruit red.   *C. columbiana*

Thorns usually less than 1'' long; fruit black.

C. douglasii

Crataegus columbiana Howell

Columbia hawthorn

Habit: Thicket-forming shrubs.

Leaves: 1-1/4'' to 2-1/2'' long, obovate to nearly oval; alternate or clustered at ends of spur shoots; dark green, lustrous and smooth above, paler and smooth beneath; apex rounded; base wedge-shaped; upper margin doubly serrate, lower margin finely serrate or entire; petiole up to 1/2'' long.

Fruit: Dark red pome, about 1/4'' in diameter.

Twigs: Similar to *C. douglasii*.

Bark: Similar to *C. douglasii*.

Habitat & Range: Dry to moist sites in the sun; from southeastern British Columbia southward on the east side of the Cascade Mountains to northeastern California; eastward from the Cascades, along the Columbia River, and its tributaries to Idaho. Hitchcock and Cronquist (1973) recognize 2 varieties.

Crataegus douglasii **Lindl.**

black hawthorn

Habit: A thicket-forming, erect shrub up to 10' tall, or occasionally a small tree 20' to 30' tall and 3" to 6" in diameter with stiff branches armed with thorns.

Leaves: 1-1/2" to 4" long, obovate, obovate-elliptical or ovate; alternate, or clustered on spur shoots, dark green or yellow-green, smooth and commonly lustrous, paler beneath; margins doubly serrate or lobed and serrate; apex acute; base wedge-shaped; petiole 1/2" to 1" long, grooved above, green but turning red when exposed to the sun.

Flowers: White and clustered.

Fruit: Black, round pome, about 1/4" in diameter.

Twigs: New twigs brown to reddish-brown and smooth, grayish-brown on older growth; terminal buds absent, lateral buds subglobose with red imbricated scales; spur shoots commonly found on older branches; armed with sharp, reddish-brown thorns.

black hawthorn

Bark: Thin, dark reddish-brown, shallowly fissured and scaly near the base of the plant.

Habitat & Range: Found on moist, well-drained, sandy or gravelly soils; from extreme southeastern Alaska southward, on both sides of the Cascades, to central California and western Nevada, eastward to northern Michigan and Wyoming.

Remarks: Grows in dense thickets, or associated with chokecherry, willow, red alder, bigleaf maple, Oregon white oak, Oregon ash, bitter cherry, Douglas-fir and grand fir.

Thickets provide excellent cover for birds and small mammals; the pomes are eaten by birds and small mammals. Browse value variable. Hitchcock and Cronquist (1973) recognize 2 varieties.

Holodiscus Maxim.

ocean spray

Habit: Deciduous shrubs.

Leaves: Deciduous, alternate, simple; margins entire, serrated or shallowly lobed and serrated; petiole short.

Flowers: Perfect; small; borne in conspicuous, dense, terminal clusters.

Fruit: 1-seeded follicle.

Remarks: A small genus of 5 species and varieties; confined to western North America.

Holodiscus discolor (Pursh) Maxim.

ocean spray

Habit: Erect, loosely branched shrub up to 15' tall.

Leaves: 3/4" to 2-1/2" long, ovate; green and minutely pubescent above, paler and more or less pubescent beneath; margins coarsely toothed or very shallowly lobed and serrate, entire near the base; apex acute; base broadly obtuse or wedge-shaped; prominently pinnately veined (venation pattern resembles a set of chevrons); petiole up to 3/4" long.

Flowers: Very small, white- or creamy-white, borne in dense terminal clusters.

Fruit: Light brown, tiny, 1-seeded follicle; fruit clusters persist into the winter, or until the next growing season.

Twigs: Slender, initially minutely pubescent, becoming smooth; slightly ribbed when young; pith large, white and spongy. Phyllotaxy 2/5.

Habitat & Range: Tolerant. Found on well-drained to dry sites in the sun and shade; from south central California northward to British Columbia, eastward to Idaho.

LOOK FOR
THESE IN WINTER

ocean spray

Remarks: Browsed by Olympic elk and deer. The Indians used the straighter stems for arrow shafts, hence one of the common names for the species is "arrowwood."

Oemleria Reichb.

Indian-plum

NOTE: This is a monotypic genus (see the species description).

Oemleria cerasiformis (H. & A.) Landon

Indian-plum   **osoberry**

Habit: Erect shrub with light green foliage, up to 15' tall.

Leaves: Deciduous, alternate, simple, oblong-elliptical, oblong-lanceolate or oblong-ovate, 1-1/2" to 5" long, up to 1-1/4" wide; light green and smooth above, paler beneath; margins entire to slightly wavy; apex and base both acute; petiole up to 3/4" long. Fresh foliage has the taste of cucumbers. Leafs out very early in the spring, usually in advance of other species.

Flowers: Dioecious; whitish-green.

Fruit: Ovoid, bluish-black, plumlike drupe, up to 1/2" long.

Twigs: Slender, green, becoming reddish-brown; pith chambered; buds about 1/4" long, ovoid-conical; bud scales green, eventually becoming reddish-tinged. Conspicuous orange lenticels.

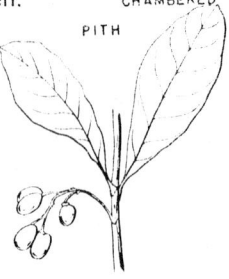

CHAMBERED PITH

Indian-plum

Bark: Smooth, reddish-brown to dark gray.

Habitat & Range: Grows on moist, well-drained sites in the sun or shade; from British Columbia southward into California, on the west side of the Cascade Mountains.

Remarks: Poor forage. Birds often eat the fruit before it matures.

Pyrus L. (*Malus* Mill.*)

apple and pear

Habit: Trees or shrubs, many species of which produce edible fruits.

Leaves: Deciduous to semi-persistent, simple, alternate or clustered on the ends of spur shoots; margins entire, serrate or lobed and serrated; petiolate; stipulate.

Flowers: Perfect, borne singly or in clusters, white to pink in color.

Fruit: Small to large pome (apple).

Twigs: Slender to stout; spur shoots or spinose lateral branchlets are to be found on the older branches.

Remarks: Widely distributed throughout the northern hemisphere. Many species, varieties, and hybrids make positive identification of individual specimens difficult.
*Note: Some authors classify pears as *Pyrus* and apples as *Malus;* others group them under *Pyrus.*

Pyrus fusca Raf.

western crabapple

Habit: Large shrubs often growing in thickets, or small trees up to 40' tall and 10" to 18" in diameter.

Leaves: Deciduous, 1" to 4" long, ovate, ovate-lanceolate, oblong-ovate, oval or elliptical; pubescent on both surfaces where new, becoming dark green to yellow-green and glabrous above, paler and slightly pubescent below; margins serrate or 1- to 3-lobed and serrate; apex acute; base broadly wedge-shaped to rounded; petiole stout, 1" to 1-1/2" long, smooth or minutely pubescent.

Flowers: About 1/2" across, white, clustered.

Fruit: Globose to oblong-ovate pome, 5/16" to 3/4" in diameter, yellow-green to red.

Twigs: Moderately slender, pubescent the first season, becoming reddish-brown and smooth, later grayish-brown; spur shoots abundant on older branches.

Habitat & Range: On moist sites near streams and other wet places, in the sun or partial shade; from southern Alaska southward to northwestern California (on the west side of the Cascade Mountains in the Pacific Northwest.

Remarks: Fruits eaten by birds.

Purshia **D.C.**

Habit: Shrubs.

Leaves: Persistent (deciduous under special circumstances); simple, alternate, or clustered on spur shoots; cuneate (wedge-shaped); apex 3-lobed; margins revolute (curled under).

Flowers: Yellow, tube-shaped.

Fruit: Tear-shaped, bitter tasting achene.

Remarks: There are two species in this genus, and both are indigenous to western United States.

Purshia tridentata **(Pursh) D.C.**

bitterbrush   **antelope brush**

Habit: An erect, much-branched, evergreen shrub, 2' to 10' high, with small, 3-lobed, wedge-shaped leaves.

Leaves: Wedge-shaped, 1/4" to 3/4" long; persistent; alternate but commonly clustered on short spur shoots; green to grayish-green above and finely pubescent above, white to grayish-white and pubescent below; margins smooth and revolute (rolled under); apex 3-lobed; base wedge-shaped;

LEAF MARGINS ROLLED UNDER

bitterbrush

petiole very short. The foliage is similar in shape to that of big sagebrush, but is smaller, darker and non-aromatic.

Flowers: Small, tubular, yellow, borne singly.

Fruit: Single or paired, elliptical or tear-shaped achene with a tapered tip or beak, bitter tasting.

Twigs: Spur shoots abundant; main twigs slender, reddish-brown and smooth, becoming gray-reddish brown, bitter.

Bark: Thin, gray to grayish-brown or brown.

Habitat & Range: Found on sandy to gravelly and rocky soils in the dry plains, foothills and mountain slopes; found in the intermountain region between the Cascade and Sierra Nevada Mountains and the Rocky Mountains. Elevational range: 200 to 9,000 feet.

Remarks: An important winter browse for elk, deer, and antelope.

Although bitterbrush is normally evergreen, in some localities, and in some years, it is deciduous.

Physocarpus Maxim.

ninebark

Habit: Loosely branched shrubs with thin, exfoliating bark.

Leaves: Deciduous, alternate, simple, palmately lobed and veined; petiolate.

Flowers: Perfect. White or occasionally pink, borne in terminal clusters.

Fruit: Follicle.

Remarks: Essentially a North American (1 Asiatic species) group.

KEY TO THE NINEBARKS

Leaf lobes acute; leaves smooth or slightly pubescent.   *P. capitatus*

Leaf lobes round; leaves usually pubescent on both surfaces.   *P. malvaceus*

Physocarpus capitatus (Pursh) Ktze.

ninebark

Habit: Large erect, spreading shrubs up to 12' high; with maplelike leaves and thin, shreddy bark.

Leaves: 1-1/2" to 3-1/2" long, nearly as wide, oval to round-ovate in outline; dark green, glabrous and somewhat shiny above, paler and somewhat pubescent beneath; margins 3- to 5-lobed; lobes pointed and their margins are serrated; petioles 3/4" to 1-1/2" long.

Flowers: Small, white, borne in a dense hemispherical cluster.

Fruit: Follicle reddish-brown to brown, 1/4" to 1/3" long.

Bark: Thin, orange-brown or gray-yellowish brown, breaks up into long strips or shreds and eventually exfoliates.

Habitat & Range: Occurs on moist, well-drained sites in

SHREDDED BARK
ninebark

the sun or shade; from British Columbia south to central California, east into western Montana.

Remarks: An inferior browse plant.

Physocarpus malvaceus (Greene) Ktze.

mallow ninebark

Habit: Erect, loosely branched shrub up to 8' tall, with maplelike leaves and shreddy bark.

Leaves: Orbicular, 1'' to 2-1/2'' in diameter; dark green and pubescent above, paler and pubescent beneath; palmately 3-lobed (occasionally 2 smaller basal lobes) lobe margins doubly serrate, lobe apices round or broadly acute; base subcordate; petiole 1/2'' to 3/4'' long.

Flowers: Small, white, borne in a hemispherical cluster; stems pubescent.

Fruit: Follicle, 1/4'' to 1/3'' long, brown.

Twigs: Reddish-brown to gray-ish-brown, splits longitudinally into long strips, eventually exfoliates.

Habitat & Range: Found on dry rocky slopes in the sun or under open timber; British Columbia south to Nevada, eastward to Montana and Wyoming.

SHREDDY LOOSE BARK

mallow ninebark

Remarks: Poor to fair browse: low palatability for cattle; but good nutritive qualities. Rootstocks yellow inside. Probably the most common and widely distributed ninebark in the West.

Prunus L.

cherry and plum

Habit: Trees or shrubs.

Leaves: Deciduous (or persistent), alternate, simple; with prominent glands at the base of the leaf blade and/or on the petiole.

Flowers: Perfect. Solitary or clustered, white to pink.

Fruit: Fleshy drupe.

Twigs: Slender to stout; spur shoots common on older branches; bitter to the taste.

Bark: Scaly or curling; lenticels frequently conspicuous.

Remarks: Cyanic compounds in the foliage at certain seasons may be toxic to stock. Genus includes peaches, apricots, and almonds, not native to Oregon.

KEY TO SOME CHERRIES AND PLUMS

1. Flower and fruit stalk long raceme; leaves ovate; glands on leaf petiole only.   *P. virginiana*

1. Flowers and fruits not borne on an elongated stalk.   2

    2. Leaves broadly ovate to oval.   *P. subcordata*

    2. Leaves elliptical or oblong-elliptical, usually thin.   *P. emarginata*

Prunus emarginata Dougl.

bitter cherry

Habit: Trees 20' to 50' tall and 5" to 18" in diameter, crown oblong to somewhat conical; bark bronze colored.

Leaves: 1″ to 3″ long, elliptical, obovate-elliptical or oblong-obovate; dark green and glabrous above, paler and initially minutely pubescent below but soon becoming smooth; margins finely serrate; minute glands on the basal serrations (occasionally on the petiole).

Flowers: White, borne in a loose, round cluster.

Fruit: Bright red, juicy, bitter drupe, about 1/4″ in diameter.

Twigs: Round and slender, initially minutely pubescent, but soon becoming smooth and dark reddish-brown; spur shoots are common on the older twigs and branches.

Bark: Thin, dark reddish-brown or grayish-bronze, smooth, but tending to break and curl crosswise; horizontal slitlike lenticels prominent.

Habitat & Range: Found on dry to moist and well-drained, sandy and gravelly soils in the sun or partial shade; from British Columbia southward to southern California, eastward to western Montana and southwestern New Mexico. Elevational range: from about 150 feet in the northern part of its range to 9,000 feet in southern California.

bitter cherry

Uses: Wood suitable for fine furniture.

Remarks: Tends to form thickets, or is associated with Douglas-fir, dogwood, grand fir, bigleaf maple, and cascara buckthorn. Intolerant to intermediate in tolerance. Deer and elk browse the leaves and twigs, and numerous birds and mammals feed on the fruits. Hitchcock and Cronquist (1973) recognize 2 varieties.

Prunus subcordata Benth.

Klamath plum

Habit: Thicket-forming shrubs or small trees up to 25' tall.

Leaves: 1" to 3" long, broadly ovate or oval, somewhat thickened; minutely pubescent when they first unfold, but soon dark green, smooth and lustrous above, paler below; margins serrate to doubly serrate; apex and base both rounded. Glands on the petiole; frequently on the lowest serration as well.

Flowers: White, borne in a loose, round cluster.

Fruit: Oblong, 1/2" to 1-1/4" long, yellow, dark red or purple in color; seed about 1/2" to 3/4" long, ridged on one side.

Twigs: Slender, eventually smooth and reddish-brown with conspicuous lenticels, older branches grayish-brown and with numerous spur shoots.

Bark: Grayish-brown, fissured and broken into plates which may be scaly, about 1/4" thick.

Habitat & Range: Found on dry to moist and well-drained, sandy and gravelly soils; from southern Oregon south to central California. In Oregon most abundant in Klamath and Lake counties.

Remarks: Intolerant. Tends to form pure thickets or is associated with black hawthorn, Oregon crab apple, chokecherry and ponderosa pine.

Attempts are being made to improve and domesticate the species. The fruits make an excellent jelly or preserves.

Good browse.

Prunus virginiana L.
common chokecherry

Habit: Large shrub, or a small tree up to 30′ tall.

Leaves: 2″ to 4″ long, 1″ to 2″ wide, oblong-ovate, obovate or obovate-elliptical; dark green or yellow-green, smooth and somewhat lustrous above, paler below and occasionally minutely pubescent; margins serrate; apex acute; base round; petiole about 1″ long, grooved above, and with 2 or 3 prominent glands just below the leaf blade.

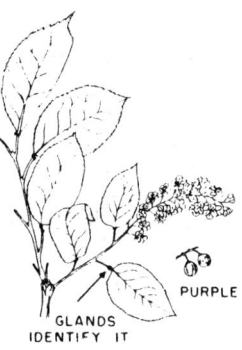

PURPLE

GLANDS
IDENTIFY IT

common chokecherry

Flowers: White, borne in an elongated raceme, 3″ to 6″ long.

Fruit: Round drupe, 1/4″ to 3/8″ in diameter, dark purple, juicy.

Twigs: When new, green-brown, smooth or pubescent, later reddish-brown and smooth; spur shoots common on older branches.

Bark: Thin, broken and scaly; lenticels not evident.

Habitat & Range: Found on dry or moist, well-drained, sandy, gravelly or rocky soils. Ranges across Canada and Northern United States, in the West south to southern California, Arizona and New Mexico. Elevational range: near sea level to 4,000 feet in Oregon and Washington; up to 7,000 feet in California.

Remarks: Good browse for deer and elk. Many birds eat the fruit. Fruit is used for jellies and wines. Hitchcock and Cronquist (1973) recognize 2 varieties.

Rosa L.

rose

Habit: Erect or climbing shrubs with pinnately compound leaves; stems usually armed.

Leaves: Deciduous (rarely persistent), alternate, pinnately compound with serrated leaflets; stipulate.

Flowers: Perfect; usually large and showy, borne singly or in clusters.

Fruit: Bony, hairy achenes borne in a pulpy body termed a "hip"; calyx deciduous or persistent.

Stems: Usually armed with fine or coarse prickles.

Remarks: This is a large genus containing numerous species, varieties, and hybrids which at times may be difficult to identify with any great degree of certainty. The hips are rich in vitamin C and are important winter feed for birds.

KEY TO THE ROSES

1. Stems armed with coarse, oval-based prickles. Calyx persists on hip.   2

1. Stems armed with fine, needlelike prickles. Calyx deciduous.   *R. gymnocarpa*

2. Stems tend to be crooked; bruised foliage does not have a sweet ciderlike odor. *R. multiflora*

2. Stems straight or slightly crooked; bruised foliage has a sweet ciderlike odor. *R. eglanteria*

Rosa gymnocarpa **Nutt.**

little wood rose

Habit: Finely branched, tolerant, moist-site shrub up to 6' tall; stems armed with fine prickles.

Leaves: 2" to 3-1/2" long, with 5 to 7 oval or elliptical-ovate leaflets which are 1/2" to 3/4" long; dark green and smooth above, paler and smooth beneath, or rarely minutely pubescent; margins doubly serrate; leaflets petiolate; rachis and petioles minutely glandular-pubescent; paired stipules at the base of the rachis glandular-pubescent.

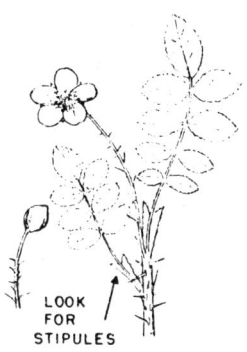

little wood rose

Flowers: Pink, borne singly or up to 4 in a cluster.

Fruit: Hip (containing achenes) is orange-red, glabrous, elliptical or flask-shaped; calyx deciduous.

Stems: Armed with numerous straight, slender prickles, or rarely with few prickles.

Habitat & Range: Occurs on moist sites in the wood or in the open. Widely distributed throughout the West from the Rocky Mountains to the Pacific Coast, and from British Columbia to southern California.

Remarks: The hips are eaten by most birds; deer and elk browse the foliage. The most important of the native roses on western ranges.

Rosa multiflora **Thumb.**

Habit: An erect shrub with arching or drooping stems.

Leaves: 2″ to 4″ long, with 5 to 9 obovate to obovate-oblong leaflets; dark green above, pale and pubescent beneath; margins serrate; apex round; base acute; rachis and petioles pubescent; paired stipules at the base of the rachis sharply serrate.

Flowers: White, borne singly or clustered.

Fruit: Orange-red, round hip containing several hairy achenes; calyx persistent.

Stems: Round and crooked, yellowish-green, turning red on the surfaces exposed to the sun; armed with coarse, oval-based, recurved prickles; arching.

Habitat & Range: Introduced from Japan and Korea.

Remarks: Extensively planted as an ornamental. Planted on farms and range land to provide cover and food for game birds.

Rosa eglanteria **L.**

sweetbriar rose

Habit: Erect shrub up to 8′ tall; stems armed with coarse, recurved prickles.

Leaves: 2-1/2″ to 4″ long, with 5 to 7 oval or obovate-oval leaflets; dark green and smooth above, pale and pubescent below; emit a sweet ciderlike odor when bruised; margins doubly serrate; both apex and base round; rachis and petioles glandular-pubescent; paired stipules sharply pointed, about 1/2″ long, margins finely serrate, lower surfaces glandular pubescent.

Flowers: Mostly pink, but occasionally white, borne singly or in clusters of 2 to 4; stalks glandular-hairy.

Fruit: Hairy achenes borne in a red or scarlet, smooth, ovoid to ellipsoidal hip which is 1/2″ to 3/4″ long; calyx persistent.

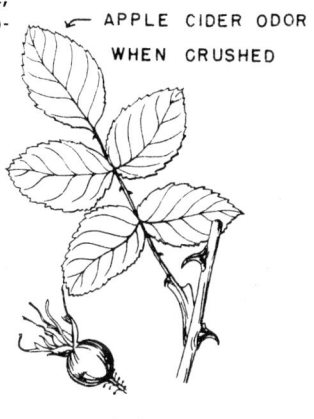

APPLE CIDER ODOR WHEN CRUSHED

sweetbriar rose

Stems: Round, light green or reddish-green on the surfaces exposed to the sun; straight or slightly crooked; armed with large, oval-based, recurved prickles; buds divergent, about 1/8″ long, ovoid, pointed; bud scales light green but turning red near the tips, imbricated.

Habitat & Range: Introduced from Europe and widely planted in many places in the United States and Canada. In this region it is found on the west of the Cascade Mountains from British Columbia to northern California. It has escaped from cultivation and is quite common along roadsides and in pastures.

Remarks: Considered a good plant for erosion control. Provides cover and food for game birds. Generally considered good browse.

Rubus L.

blackberry and close relatives

Habit: Shrubs or trailing vines, mostly with prickly stems.

Leaves: Deciduous or persistent, alternate; simple, or pinnately or palmately compound; stipulate.

Flowers: Perfect, complete; white to red, borne singly or in clusters.

Fruit: An edible aggregate of druplets which adheres to or pulls free from the torus (the swollen receptacle).

Remarks: This is another genus with a great abundance of species, varieties, and hybrids. Many are useful for erosion control, and to provide cover and food for game. The fruits of many are used for making jams, jellies, and wines.

KEY TO THE RUBUS SPECIES

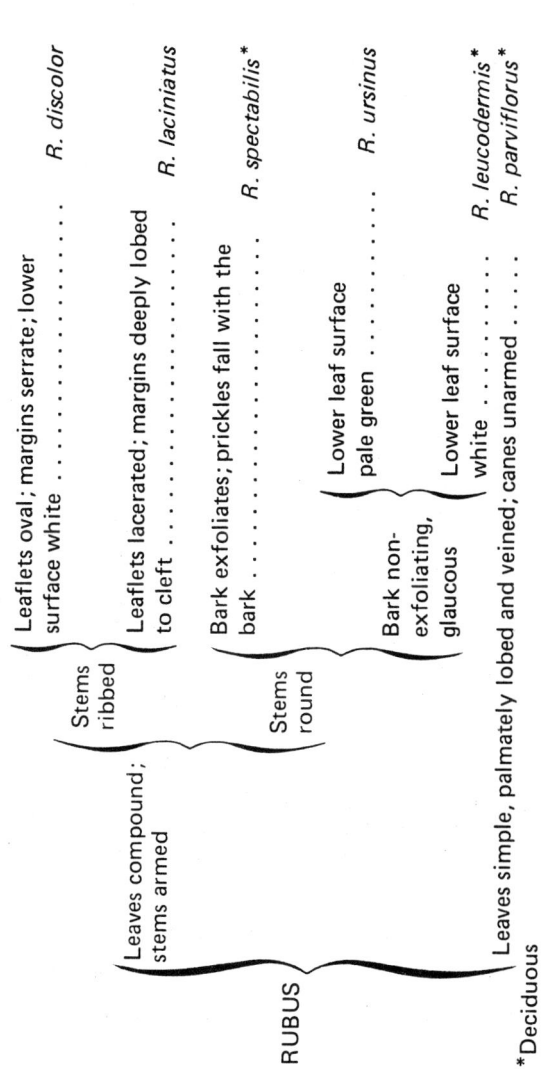

RUBUS

Leaves compound; stems armed

Stems ribbed
- Leaflets oval; margins serrate; lower surface white . . . . *R. discolor*
- Leaflets lacerated; margins deeply lobed to cleft . . . . *R. laciniatus*

Stems round
- Bark exfoliates; prickles fall with the bark . . . . *R. spectabilis* *
- Bark non-exfoliating, glaucous
  - Lower leaf surface pale green . . . . *R. ursinus*
  - Lower leaf surface white . . . . *R. leucodermis* *

Leaves simple, palmately lobed and veined; canes unarmed . . . . *R. parviflorus* *

*Deciduous

Rubus laciniatus **Willd.**

evergreen blackberry

Habit: Shrubs with heavy, angular, trailing or climbing stems up to 10′ in length. The stems are armed with large, flattened, recurved prickles.

Leaves: Persistent, palmately compound with 3 to 5 lacerated leaflets; green to reddish-green above and paler beneath; rachis and petiole armed.

Flowers: White to pink in color.

Fruit: Black aggregate of small drupelets; adheres to the torus.

Stems: Red to purple in color, stout, ridged, armed with large, recurved oval-based prickles.

Habitat & Range: Commonly found on barren and infertile soils on burns, old fields, logged-over areas and along roadsides; on the westside from Washington southward into California. It was introduced from Europe and has escaped from cultivation.

evergreen blackberry

Remarks: The fruit is made into jams and jellies. It has little forage value. The dense thickets provide food and excellent cover for birds and small mammals.

Rubus leucodermis **Dougl.**

blackcap   western raspberry

Habit: A semi-erect shrub with round, armed trailing stems.

Leaves: Deciduous, palmately compound leaves, with 3 (sometimes 5) ovate leaflets that are doubly serrate or lobed (1 to 3 lobes) and serrate; dark green and occasionally somewhat pubescent above and with a heavy white **tomentum** below.

Flowers: White, borne in small clusters.

Fruit: Red, dark purple, or black aggregate of drupelets, about 1/2″ in diameter; pulls free from the torus.

Stems: The first year's growth usually erect, thereafter trailing, round; green to reddish bark covered with a blue-white bloom; armed with stout prickles which occasionally may be recurved.

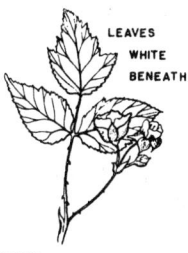

LEAVES WHITE BENEATH

STEMS HAVE WHITE POWDER

blackcap

Habitat & Range: Southern Alaska southward through British Columbia and western United States.

Remarks: The fruit is eaten by humans, birds, and mammals. It is a fair browse plant.

Rubus parviflorus **Nutt.**

thimbleberry

Habit: An erect shrub 3′ to 6′ high, with weak, canelike, unarmed stems, and simple palmately lobed leaves.

Leaves: Deciduous, simple, broad, 3″ to 8″ in diameter; palmately 3- to 5-lobed and serrate; dark green, minutely hairy on both surfaces, petiole with bristly hairs and more or less glandular.

Flowers: White or occasionally whitish-pink, borne singly or in terminal clusters.

Fruit: Red, flattened hemispherical, aggregate of drupelets which pull free from the torus.

Stems: Light brown or grayish-brown, canelike, weak, and unarmed; bark thin and papery; new stems green and glandular.

thimbleberry

Habitat & Range: Widely distributed on moist sites from the Great Lakes westward to the Pacific Coast, from Alaska southward into Mexico. Elevations ranging from sea level to 9,000 feet.

Remarks: A fair to outstanding browse plant. The fruit is eaten by birds, mammals, and humans.

Rubus spectabilis Pursh

salmonberry

Habit: An erect, tolerant, moist-site shrub 3' to 10' high, with light-brown, exfoliating bark.

Leaves: Deciduous, pinnately compound with 3 ovate leaflets, 1" to 3" long; shiny dark green and smooth to wrinkled above, paler and pubescent along the veins beneath; margins double serrate, or 1- or 2-lobed and doubly serrate. The rachises, petioles, and midveins often armed.

Flowers: Pink to dark red, borne singly.

Fruit: An aggregate of drupelets; salmon colored to red or reddish-purple.

Stems: New stems green with a reddish tinge, and armed; on older stems the bark is orange-brown and armed; bark (with prickles) exfoliates.

Habitat & Range: Occurs on moist sites; from Alaska southward to the Santa Cruz Mountains in California, eastward to Idaho and Montana. Very abundant near coast of Oregon.

salmonberry

Remarks: Provides food and cover for birds and small mammals. The watery, poorly flavored fruit is eaten, but seldom gathered, by humans.

Rubus discolor Weihe & Nees

Himalaya berry

Habit: An erect, spreading or trailing shrub; with stout, heavily ridged and armed stems.

Leaves: Persistent to semi-persistent, palmately compound with 3 to 5 oval leaflets about 1-1/2" to 2-1/2" long, dark green to reddish-green and smooth (or occasionally coarsely hairy) above, and with a heavy white bloom and tomentum below; margins serrate. Rachis and petioles armed.

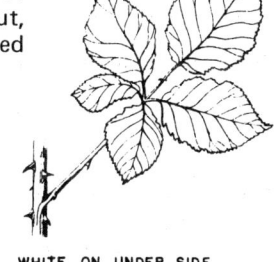

WHITE ON UNDER SIDE
STEMS REDDISH-BROWN

Himalaya berry

Flowers: Large, white, borne in clusters.

Fruit: A black aggregate of drupelets, about 1" long; adheres to the torus.

Stems: Heavily or coarsely ridged, purplish-red; armed with heavy, red, broad-based, recurved prickles.

Habitat & Range: A native of the Old World and of uncertain origin. It has been widely planted in the U.S. and has escaped from cultivation.

Remarks: The fruit is widely utilized for making jams and jellies. Birds and mammals feed on the fruit, and seek protection in the tangled thickets.

Rubus ursinus Cham & Schlecht.

wild blackberry

Habit: Evergreen, climbing or trailing shrub, with long slender branches often 10' to 20' long.

Leaves: Persistent, pinnately compound with 3 to 5 leaflets, **doubly** serrate or lobed and serrate; dark green and smooth or sparsely hairy above, paler on the under side.

Flowers: White, borne in clusters.

Fruit: Large, black, tasty aggregate of drupelets which adheres to the torus.

Stems: Round, slender, green to reddish; armed with slender, small based, straight or recurved prickles; glaucous—the bloom is easily rubbed off.

Habitat & Range: Occurs in open woods, on old burns and cut-over areas; from Idaho westward to the Coast, and from British Columbia to southern California.

Remarks: The fruit is highly prized for jams and jellies. A large number of birds and mammals feed upon the fruit, and many seek cover in the dense thickets. It grows well on poor, eroded soils, the stems taking root at intervals, making it a worthwhile shrub for erosion control.

Sorbus L.

mountain-ash

Habit: Trees or shrubs.

Leaves: Deciduous, alternate, pinnately compound; margins serrate; stipulate.

Flowers: Perfect; mostly white; borne in terminal flat-topped clusters.

Fruit: Small pome.

KEY TO THE MOUNTAIN-ASHES

Leaflet margins serrate almost full length; tips acute.
S. scopulina

Leaflet margins rarely serrate more than 3/4 length; tips rounded or truncate.　　　*S. sitchensis*

Sorbus scopulina **Greene**

Greene mountain-ash　　　　　**western mountain-ash**

Habit: Erect shrub or small tree to 15' tall.

Leaves: Pinnately compound with 9-13 leaflets. Leaflet tips acute, margins finely serrated for almost entire length. Leaflets generally less than 1/3 as broad as they are long. Lateral leaflets mostly sessile; terminal leaflet petiolate.

Buds: Winter buds more or less glutinous and only sparsely pubescent.

Flowers: Flowers borne in nearly flat-topped corymbs usually containing 70-200 flowers.

Fruit: Round, orange to scarlet, glossy pomes about 1/2" in diameter.

Habitat & Range: Widespread throughout the mountains of the western U.S. and Canada.

Remarks: Hitchcock and Cronquist (1973) recognize 2 varieties of this species.

Sorbus sitchensis Roem.

Sitka mountain-ash

Habit: An erect, much branched shrub up to 10' tall, or occasionally a small tree up to 25' tall.

Leaves: 5" to 10" long, with 7 to 11 oblong to oblong-elliptical leaflets, leaflets 1" to 3" long; green and smooth above, paler below; margins serrate, except for near the base where they are entire; terminal leaflet petiolate, lateral leaflets mostly sessile; both the apex and the base are acute to round.

Flowers: White, borne in large, dense, flat-topped clusters.

Fruit: Round, orange-red to red pome, 1/2" to 1/3" in diameter.

Stems: Stout, olive drab, glaucous and with light-colored vertical lenticels, becoming gray-greenish-brown; terminal bud 1/2" to 3/4" long, oblong-ovate, with lustrous, reddish-brown imbricated scales which are pubescent along the margin, lateral buds smaller.

Bark: Thin, smooth, grayish-green to brownish-green.

Habitat & Range: Found on dry to moist, well-drained sites in the sun; from the Yukon and southern Alaska, south to central California (in the Sierra-Nevada Mountains) and western Nevada, east to northern

Idaho and northwestern Montana. Elevational range: in the United States, 2,500 to 10,000 feet.

Remarks: Planted as an ornamental. Forage value fair. The fruit provides food for many birds. Hitchcock and Cronquist (1973) recognize 2 varieties of this species.

Spiraea L.

spiraea

Habit: Erect or prostrate shrubs.

Leaves: Deciduous, alternate, simple; petiole short.

Flowers: Mostly perfect; small but commonly borne in loose or dense clusters.

Fruit: Follicle.

KEY TO THE SPECIES

Leaves serrate along the upper 1/4 to 1/2 of the margin only; flowers pink or reddish, borne in dense elongated clusters. *S. douglasii*

Leaf margins serrate to doubly serrate; flowers white, borne in flat-topped cluster. *S. betulifolia*

Spiraea douglasii **Hook.**

Douglas spiraea

Habit: An erect shrub 2′ to 4′ tall.

Leaves: 1-1/4″ to 3″ long, 1/2″ to 1″ wide, oblong-elliptical, oblong-ovate or elliptical; green above, paler and with a silvery pubescence below; margins serrated along the upper 1/4 to 1/2, entire below; apex round; base broadly acute to narrowly rounded; petiole not over 1/4″ long, often shorter.

Flowers: Very small, pink or reddish, borne in dense elongated terminal clusters (panicles).

Fruit: Smooth follicle, about 1/8" long. Persists through most of the winter.

Twigs: Slender, light yellow-brown, becoming reddish-brown, lightly ribbed.

Habitat & Range: Occurs on moist sites in ditches, along streams, in swales and around seeps on mountain slopes; from British Columbia southward into northern California, eastward into Idaho. Hitchcock and Cronquist (1973) recognize 3 varieties.

Spiraea betulifolia Pall.

shiny-leaf spiraea

Habit: Erect, sparsely branched shrub up to 3' high.

Leaves: 1" to 3-1/2" long, broadly ovate, ovate-elliptical or oblong; light green and smooth above, paler below; margins serrate to doubly serrate; apex round to acute; base round to broadly wedge-shaped; petiole about 1/4" long.

Flowers: Very small, white, borne in a dense flat-topped cluster.

Fruit: Small follicle, about 1/8" long, usually 5 in a cluster.

Stems: Slender, light yellow-brown and smooth when young, becoming reddish-brown, and eventually gray-reddish brown.

Habitat & Range: Found on dry to moist, well-drained sites in the sun; from British Columbia to southern Oregon, eastward to the Rocky Mountains.

LEGUMINOSAE   **Legume Family**

NOTE: The three species of legumes described here
were **introduced** from Europe or eastern United
States. Each of these species is the **only** one of its
genus introduced into the Pacific Northwest, so the
generic descriptions are omitted.

Cytisus scoparius L.

Scotch broom

Habit: Erect, loosely, branched shrub with slender green
branches, 3' to 10' tall.

Leaves: Deciduous. Very small, simple leaves 1/4'' to
1/2'' long and trifoliate leaves up to 1'' long; smooth
and light green above paler and minutely pubescent
or smooth below; elliptical to oblong-lanceolate;
margins entire.

Flowers: Perfect. About 3/4'' long, bright yellow, pealike.

Fruit: Dark brown to black, hairy legume or pod, about
1'' long.

Twigs: Very slender, green to dark green, distinctly
ribbed.

Habitat & Range: Introduced as an ornamental from
Scotland and has now become well established in
the moister parts of the Northwest and California,
also the east coast from Nova Scotia to Virginia.

Remarks: Regarded as toxic to livestock—affects the
nervous system. It is regarded as a good renovator of
denuded and barren lands. Planted as an ornamental
and to stabilize road banks. The leaves are rich in
potash. Nitrogen-fixing bacteria on the roots.

Robinia pseudoacacia L.

black locust

Habit: Eastern tree 40' to 80' tall and 2' to 3' in diameter, with dark brownish-black, coarsely ridged and furrowed bark.

Leaves: 8" to 14" long, pinnately compound with 7 to 19 elliptical to ovate-oblong leaflets; green to yellow-green and smooth above, paler beneath; margins entire; leaflet apex and base rounded; leaflets petiolate; rachis swollen at the base.

WELL-KNOWN VISITOR

black locust

Flowers: White, pealike, borne in racemes. Look and smell like white sweet peas.

Fruit: Brown legume, 2" to 4" long, about 1/2" wide.

Twigs: Angled or ridged when new, eventually becoming round; initially green, becoming brown; paired stipular spines present on young twigs, but may be absent on large trees. Buds naked and submerged in the leaf scars.

Bark: On mature trees brown, deeply furrowed, with round, coarse, interlacing, stringy ridges, 1" to 2" thick. Orange or yellow color in fissures.

Habitat & Range: Grows on dry to moist, well-drained sites in the sun. Ranges in the Appalachian Mountains from Pennsylvania to northern Georgia and Alabama, west to Missouri, Arkansas and eastern Oklahoma. Extensively planted in the West, where it has escaped from cultivation in many localities.

Uses: Fence posts, insulator pins, tree nails (for wooden ship and barge construction), tool handles, posts, mine timbers and fuel.

Remarks: Very tolerant. Prolific sprouter. Makes good growth on a number of different types of soils, and is somewhat tolerant of alkali soils. There are nitrogen fixing nodules of bacteria on the roots. The twigs and inner bark are toxic. The wood is very durable, heavy and hard.

The trees have a deep, wide spreading root system that makes them used for erosion control. Extensively planted in shelterbelts.

Ulex europaeus **L.**

gorse   **furze**

Habit: A much-branched, spiny shrub up to 10' tall.

Leaves: Most of the leaves have been reduced to spines, 1/2'' to2'' long, dark green, ribbed.

Flowers: Yellow and pealike. In the spring the shrub may be one large mass of blooms.

Fruit: Legume or pod; seeds very hardy.

Twigs: Green to gray-green, ribbed.

Habitat & Range: The shrub was introduced from Europe and planted along the coast in Oregon. It is now reported from Astoria, Oregon, south to Mendocino County in California.

Remarks: This shrub forms impenetrable thickets and constitutes a serious pest wherever it is found. It contributed to the burning of Bandon, Oregon in 1936. Volatile oils in the stems and spines account for its high flammability. Strict control measures are necessary to prevent the shrub from extending its range. Nitrogen-fixing bacteria nodules are present on the roots.

ANACARDIACEAE   Cashew Family

Rhus **L.**

sumac

Habit: Shrubs or small trees having a milky, acrid or resinous sap.

Leaves: Deciduous, alternate, simple or pinnately compound with 3 to 23 leaflets.

Flowers: Dioecious or polygamous; small but usually borne in dense terminal clusters.

Fruit: Small, dry to fleshy, smooth or tomentose drupe.

Buds: Naked.

Remarks: The genus is native to both hemispheres. The sumacs are a source of tannin, waxes, dyes, varnishes, and medicinal compounds. Some species cause a serious skin inflammation.

KEY TO THE SUMACS

1. Leaflets commonly 3 in number.   2

1. Leaflets 9 to 21.   *R. glabra*

2. Lateral leaflets only 1/4 to 1/3 the size of the terminal leaflet; terminal leaflet broadly obovate to round-rhombic, with wedge-shaped base, but no (sub-) petiole. Flower buds in spikes; foliage buds submerged. Fruit red.
R. trilobata

2. Lateral leaflets at least 1/2 the size of the terminal leaflet; leaflets ovate to obovate; terminal leaflet irregularly toothed to lobed, with distinct (sub-) petiole. Buds naked. Fruit whitish, with meridian lines. *R. diversiloba*

Rhus glabra L.

smooth sumac

Habit: Shrubs up to 15' tall.

Leaves: Deciduous, 8" to 14" long, pinnately compound with 9 to 21 lanceolate to oblong-lanceolate leaflets; leaflets 1-1/2" to 3" long, dark green above, pale green or whitish-green below; margins serrate; apex acute; base round; terminal leaflet petiolate, lateral leaflets sessile; rachis pubescent, later becoming smooth.

Flowers: Small, white, borne in dense, elongated, terminal clusters.

Fruit: Bright red, glandular drupe about 3/16" in diameter. Persist the year round.

Twigs: Stout, pubescent and light reddish-brown, later becoming smooth and grayish-brown.

Habitat & Range: Found on dry to moist, well-drained sites in the sun. Ranges from British Columbia south on the east of the Cascade Mountains to central Oregon, east to Illinois.

BRIGHT CRIMSON FALL COLOR
BIG RED FRUIT CLUSTER

smooth sumac

Remarks: Browsed by deer. Many game birds eat the fruits. The foliage turns a bright red in the fall.

Rhus trilobata Nutt.

skunkbush

Habit: A loosely branched shrub up to 7' tall.

Leaves: Deciduous, 1-1/2" to 3" long, trifoliate; terminal leaflet broadly obovate to round-rhombic, upper margin irregular serrated or 3-lobed, lower margin entire, apex round, base wedge-shaped, petiole indistinct or lacking; lateral leaflets oval, about 1/4 the size of the terminal leaflet, margins wavy to lobed, sessile; leaflets green above, pale beneath, initially pubescent, later becoming smooth; emit an obnoxious odor when crushed.

Flowers: Small, pale yellow, borne in terminal clusters up to 1/2" long, appear before the leaves.

Fruit: Orange to red, glandular-hairy drupe, about 1/4" in diameter. Persist.

Stems: Slender, light yellow-brown, becoming light grayish-brown.

Habitat & Range: Found on dry, well-drained sites in the sun or shade. Ranges from southern Oregon (on the east side of the Cascade Mountains) south to lower California, east to the Rocky Mountains.

Remarks: Birds eat the fruit. Poor browse.

Rhus diversiloba T. & G.

poisonoak

Habit: Erect shrubs 3' to 10' in height, or tree-climbing vines, with shiny, dark green leaves which turn varying shades of red and yellow in the fall.

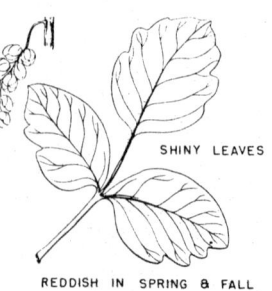

SHINY LEAVES

REDDISH IN SPRING & FALL

poisonoak

Leaves: Deciduous, alternate, pinnately compound, with 3 (rarely 5) ovate to ovate--rhombic or obovate leaflets, the terminal leaflet is larger than the lateral leaflets and has a distinct petiole, the lateral leaflets are subsessile; margins wavy to shallowly lobed or rarely smooth; surfaces smooth and shiny, initially reddish-green in the early spring, but soon turning green; red or yellow in the fall.

Flowers: Small, long-stemmed, inconspicuous, yellowish-green; borne in loose, pendulous clusters (panicles).

Fruit: Round to subglobose, grayish white, striated drupes which persist after the leaves have fallen; by late fall only the stems or penducles remain.

Stems: New twigs light brown to tan colored, pubescent; when a climbing vine the stems are equipped with brown tendrils; short stiff lateral branchlets numerous; buds naked.

Habitat & Range: Occurs on moist to dry, well-drained sites in the sun or shade; from southern British Columbia south to southern California on the west of the Cascades and Sierra Nevada Mountains. Most common in the valleys along fence rows and in pastures, also in the woods in the surrounding foothills. In the mountains it is found on the drier ridges and south and west slopes. Where summer precipitation is sufficient to encourage the growth of competing vegetation, poisonoak disappears.

Remarks: Poisonoak is toxic to most individuals. Immunity is a relative thing, for individuals who have not been bothered by poisonoak for some years may find themselves eventually affected. Fumes from the burning plants are especially toxic.

Bees are attracted to the flowers in the spring, but none of the toxicity of the plant is transmitted through the nectar. Horses and cattle can browse the species with immunity. Household pets that have wandered through the plant are carriers of the plant irritation.

ACERACEAE   **Maple Family**

Acer **L.**

maple

Habit: Trees or shrubs with opposite, palmately lobed and veined leaves.

Leaves: Deciduous, opposite, and simple; circular in general outline; palmately lobed and veined; petiole long. (Note: One American species, *Acer negundo* L., boxelder, has pinnately compound leaves.)

Flowers: Mostly polygamous, small and borne in short or elongated clusters.

Fruit: Double samara, united at the base; wings slightly to widely divergent.

Twigs: Opposite branching; slender to stout twigs; pith round and homogeneous; leaf scar has 3 to 7 distinct bundle scars.

Remarks: There are sixteen species and varieties of maples native to the United States; four of which are indigenous to the Pacific Northwest. Of the indigenous species three are essentially shrubby in habit, though occasionally attaining small tree size.

The forage value of maple is fair. Bigleaf maple is the only western species important to the timber trade.

KEY TO THE MAPLES

1. Leaves 5″ in diameter or larger; petiole long, secretes a milky juice when squeezed.

A. macrophyllum

1. Leaves less than 5″ in diameter.   2

2. Lobes 5 to 9, mostly 7, fanlike.   *A. circinatum*

2. Lobes 3; occasionally with 2 smaller basal lobes.   *A. glabrum*

Acer circinatum Pursh

vine maple

vine maple

Habit: An erect shrub, or more commonly a helter-skelter arrangement of crooked branches that are a curse to anyone who has need of passing through them; up to 20' tall, or less commonly a small tree 30' to 40' in height.

Leaves: Circular in outline, averaging 2 to 4 inches in diameter, or sometimes slightly larger; with 5 to 9, mostly 7, shallow, fanlike lobes which are serrated along the margins; green and glabrous on the upper surface, paler beneath; base cordate; petioles 1" to 3" long, often red. If growing in the sun the leaves may take on a red color early in the summer.

Flowers: Red, borne in short terminal clusters.

Fruit: A propeller-like, double samara with the wings almost at a 180°, 1-1/4" to 2" long, brownish-red to reddish when mature.

Twigs: Slender, smooth and round, green to reddish-brown, or red if in the sun; buds 1/8" long, pointed; buds have 3 or more imbricate scales, red to reddish-brown. Buds at end of twig often paired, due to failure of terminal bud to develop.

Habitat & Range: Common understory species in the Westside forests of the Pacific Northwest, also a pioneer species on cutover and burned-over lands. Found on moist sites in the sun or shade from south-western British Columbia, southward through western Washington and Oregon, to northern California, also the Wallowa Mountains of northeastern Oregon. In Oregon, vine maple will occasionally be found on the moister slopes and along streams on the eastern slopes of the Cascade Mountains (Suttle Lake area).

Remarks: Valuable forage for deer and elk. To the woodsman vine maple is an obnoxious nuisance that frequently provokes him to strong epithets. While it satisfies no important commercial need, the wood may be used locally for fuel, and is very satisfactory for smoking fish and fowl. Larger stems have been reported to have been used to fasten wanigan logs together. Indians of the Northwest used the branches for net bows. In the fall vine maple turns various shades of red and yellow and can rival the most color-ful species of the Eastern forests.

Acer glabrum Torr.

Rocky Mountain maple

Habit: Commonly a shrub 6′ to 12′ in height, or a small tree 20′ to 30′ tall and 6″ to 12″ in diameter.

Leaves: 2″ to 5″ in diameter, palmately 3- (sometimes 5-) lobed and veined; lobe margins serrate to doubly serrate except near the base which is smooth, the base of the central lobe tends to taper inward; sinuses (indentations between lobes) usually deep and nar-rowly acute; lobe apex pointed or blunt; base broadly obtuse, truncated or indented; surfaces dark green and smooth above, and paler below; petiole slender and about the same length as the leaf blade, green to red. Trifoliate leaves may be frequently found.

Flowers: Small, greenish-yellow, borne in short terminal or axillary clusters.

Fruit: Double samara, wings about an inch long, nearly straight on the back, joined at an acute to right angle, often reddish tinted at maturity.

Twigs: Slender and smooth, at first green but becoming reddish-green to dark red, eventually becoming green to gray or reddish-brown; buds small, 1/8" to 1/4" long, ovoid, appressed, with 2 dark red valvate scales.

Habitat & Range: Found on moist, sandy and gravelly soils in open coniferous stands or brushy areas from the east slopes of the Cascades to western South Dakota and Nebraska; from Oregon through southern California, Arizona, and New Mexico. The variety *A. g. douglasii* extends north and west from eastern Oregon and eastern Washington, through parts of Alberta and British Columbia, to southwestern Alaska.

Remarks: Big game animals are reported to browse this species extensively.

Acer glabrum var. *douglasii* (**Hook.**) **Dipp.**

Douglas maple

This variety is a shrub or small tree; leaf typically with shallow, broad sinuses. Occasionally found west of the Cascades in Oregon, but usually found from southwestern Alaska, south through western British Columbia and southern Alberta, eastern Washington and Oregon, eastward to Idaho and western Montana.

Acer macrophyllum **Pursh**

bigleaf maple

Habit: A tree 40' to 100' tall and 2' to 4' in diameter; when growing in the open usually branches within the first 15 feet into several large branches, forming a dense, round, spreading crown; but in a dense stand, may be a tall, straight tree.

Leaves: 6" to 12" in diameter, palmately 5-lobed, central lobe usually wedge-shaped and narrow-waisted; margins of lobes smooth or with smaller lobes; base heartshaped; surfaces dark green above, paler below and pubescent in the axils of the larger veins; petiole long, exudes a milky sap when squeezed.

Flowers: Small, yellow, borne in long racemes just ahead of the leaves; both perfect and unisexual flowers on the same tree.

Fruit: Double (rarely triple) samara, wings 1-1/2" to 2" long, seed hairy; tan or yellowish-tan when mature; wings appressed or slightly divergent.

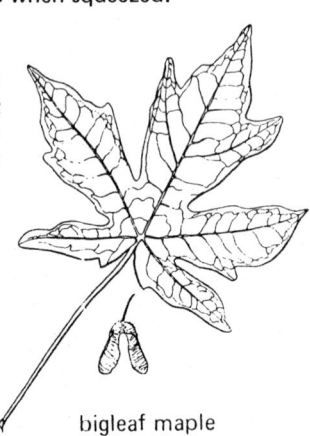

bigleaf maple

Twigs: Stout, smooth and pale green the first season, becoming bright green or dark red, eventually grayish-brown.

Bark: Smooth, grayish-brown on young trees; on old trunks grayish-brown to reddish-brown, with interlacing ridges and furrows.

Habitat & Range: Moist well-drained soils; from western British Columbia south through western Washington and Oregon to southern California. Elevational range: sea level to 5,500 feet.

Uses: Furniture and paneling; suitable for flooring. Burls weighing from a few hundred pounds to several tons are cut and shipped to France and Italy where they are sliced into veneer to be used in furniture manufacture.

Remarks: Good browse. Bigleaf maple has the largest leaves of any of the maples. It is the largest maple native to western United States, and is one of the largest species in the genus. The sap has a high sugar content, but weather conditions within the range of the species are not conducive to a high flow of sap.

RHAMNACEAE   **Buckthorn Family**

Ceanothus **L.**

ceanothus

Habit: Mostly shrubs, occasionally small trees.

Leaves: Simple; deciduous or persistent; alternate (and with 3 prominent veins from the base of the leaf), or opposite; margins entire, serrate, or almost spinose.

Flowers: Complete; individual flowers small but borne in dense clusters; white to blue. The clusters are mostly long panicles or racemes.

Fruits: Small, subglobose, 3-lobed capsule and 3-celled, smooth or sticky on the surface.

Remarks: This genus is confined to North America. There are between 50 and 60 species and most of them are limited to the Pacific Coast region. Nitrogen-fixing nodules of bacteria are found on the roots.

KEY TO THE CEANOTHUSES

1. Leaves opposite.   2

1. Leaves alternate.   3

  2. Leaves clustered at the nodes; margins mostly entire.   *C. cuneatus*

  2. Leaves not clustered at the nodes; margins with a few, almost spinose, teeth.   *C. prostratus*

3. Younger branches round.   4

3. Younger branches ribbed.   *C. thyrsiflorus*

  4. Leaves thick and leathery.   *C. velutinus*

  4. Leaves not thick and leathery.   5

5. Leaf margins smooth.   *C. integerrimus*

5. Leaf margins serrate.   *C. sanguineus*

Ceanothus cuneatus (Hook.) Nutt.

narrowleaf buckbrush   **wedgeleaf ceanothus**

Habit: An erect shrub 3' to 8' tall, or small and sprawling and growing in matlike clumps (upper elevational limits).

Leaves: Persistent, most commonly in opposite clusters; 1/4" to 3/4" long, obovate, cuneate, spatulate or oblong-elliptical; grayish-green, initially minutely hairy but soon becoming

narrowleaf buckbrush

glabrous; margins entire or occasionally with 1 or 2 teeth near the apex; apex rounded; base wedge-shaped; petiole very short.

Flowers: Small, white or yellow borne in loose clusters.

Fruit: Subglobose capsule, less than 1/4" in diameter, each lobe has a small horn near the apex.

Twigs: Lateral branchlets short, rigid and thorn-like; reddish-brown, but superficially light gray. Opposite branching.

Bark: Gray and smooth on younger stems, becoming grayish-brown.

Habitat & Range: Found on dry, gravelly or rocky soils; from the central Willamette Valley southward to southern California, locally in extreme western Nevada.

Remarks: A major component of chaparral and brush-fields. Narrowleaf buckbrush will not sprout from the roots or root crown following a fire. Heat, however, appears to stimulate the germination of dormant seeds in the soil. It is an important winter browse plant for deer in many localities.

Ceanothus integerrimus Hook. & Arn.

deerbrush

Habit: An erect, loosely branched shrub 4' to 12' tall.

Leaves: Deciduous (occasionally semi-persistent), alternate, 1" to 3" long and about half as broad, ovate to elliptical; margins smooth; green to dark green and smooth above, paler and glabrous or sparsely pubescent on the underside; 3 prominent veins from the base of the leaf; petiole about 1/2" long.

Flowers: Small, white (sometimes blue or pinkish); borne in long terminal or axillary clusters.

Fruit: Round to round-triangular, sticky capsule; each lobe has a slight crest or ridge down the side.

Twigs: Round, slender, frequently arching, green to tannish-green, often with warty areas on the older branches.

Habitat & Range: Grows on many types of soil, but does best where the soil is moderately fertile and well drained; from western Washington southward through California, and eastward into western Nevada and Arizona.

Remarks: The Range Plant Handbook reports, *Deerbrush is one of the most valuable browse plants of the West and in California it provides more forage than any other browse species. Deerbrush is so important in the Sierras and southern Cascades that management of many ranges is based on its growth requirements. It is considered a good to excellent browse for . . . deer.*

Ceanothus prostratus Benth.

squawcarpet   **mahala mat**

Habit: A low, prostrate, evergreen shrub with leathery, hollylike leaves and creeping branches which frequently take root at the nodes. Older plants may form a dense carpet-like mat up to 10' across.

Leaves: Persistent, opposite, thick and leathery; 1/4" to 1" long, spatulate, cuneate, obovate or obovate-elliptical; dark green glabrous and lustrous above, paler or grayish-green beneath; sparse, almost-spinose teeth along the upper margin, entire below; base wedge-shaped; petiole very short.

Flowers: Small, blue, borne in loose terminal clusters.

Fruit: Subglobose capsule about 1/4" broad, each lobe with a wrinkled, dorsal horn or boss.

Twigs: Lateral twigs usually not over 6" long, or commonly spurlike; new twigs reddish to reddish-brown, initially hairy but becoming smooth.

Habitat & Range: On dry sites in the sun; in the Cascade Mountains from Washington southward into northern California, eastward into Idaho and Nevada.

Remarks: Found in mixed-conifer or ponderosa pine stands. Squaw carpet provides some protection against soil erosion and may act as a nursecrop for coniferous reproduction. Forage value low.

Ceanothus thyrsiflorus Esch.

blueblossom

Habit: Erect shrubs up to 12' in height, or small trees up to 20' tall, on exposed situations it may be low-growing to prostrate.

Leaves: Persistent; alternate; simple; but smaller leaves are often clustered about the base of the principal leaf; 3/4" to 2" long, oblong-ovate to elliptical; dark glossy green above, paler and commonly smooth below; margins finely serrate and at times revolute (occasionally entire); prominently 3-veined from the base; petiole less than 1/2" long.

Flowers: Small, blue (rarely white), borne in dense clusters up to 3" long.

Fruit: Subglobose capsule about 1/6" in diameter, black and somewhat sticky.

Twigs: Slender green, distinctly ribbed for the first 2 or 3 years.

Habitat & Range: Found on dry, well-drained sites in the sun or shade; from Douglas County in western Oregon southward to southern California.

Remarks: Blueblossom is one of the largest and hardiest of the ceanothuses. It forms dense thickets following a fire; a pioneer species on cut-over lands and along new road cuts. Planted as an ornamental.

Ceanothus sanguineus Pursh

redstem ceanothus   **buckbrush**

Habit: An erect, loosely branched shrub 5′ to 10′ tall, with moderately slender, purplish-red stems.

Leaves: Deciduous, alternate; 1″ to 3-1/2″ long ovate to ovate-elliptical; thin, dark green and glabrous above, paler beneath; prominently 3-veined from the base; margins serrate; petiole up to 1″ long.

Flowers: Small, white and borne in dense cluster up to 4″ long.

Fruit: Subglobose capsule up to 3/16″ in diameter, lobes smooth except for an inconspicuous ridge.

DECIDUOUS
THIN

buckbrush

Twigs: Slender, purplish-red smooth. Buds often stalked.

Habitat & Range: Found on dry to moist, well-drained sites in the sun or partial shade; from southern British Columbia southward to northern California, eastward to Idaho and Montana.

Remarks: Fairly palatable to big game animals.

Ceanothus velutinus **Dougl.**

snowbrush

Habit: Evergreen shrub 2′ to 10′ tall with light green stems; often thicket forming.

Leaves: Persistent, alternate, thick and leathery, 1-1/2″ to 2-1/2″ long, broadly ovate to ovate-elliptical; dark glossy green (sticky during warm weather) above; underside pale green and at first slightly tomentose, but soon becoming smooth; margins finely serrate; 3 prominent veins from the base of the leaf; petiole 1/2″ to 3/4″ long. The foliage has a sickeningly sweet odor when rubbed or during very warm weather.

Flowers: Small, white, borne in dense clusters 2″ to 5″ long.

Twigs: Stout, smooth, light green, larger stems green.

Habitat & Range: Found on a wide variety of sites and exposures; from British Columbia and Saskatchewan southward through western United States. It is quite likely that snowbrush has the most extensive range of the ceanothuses.

SPICY SMELL

EVERGREEN,
LEATHERY, GREEN STEMMED

snowbrush

Remarks: Snowbrush frequently invades cutover and burned-over lands. Seeds retain their viability for several years. If root crown is not killed by fire, its crown sprouts abundantly. Fire also appears to stimulate germination of the undamaged seeds.

Snowbrush often forms extensive thickets or fields. If the plants are not too dense they may serve as an excellent nurse crop for Douglas-fir. In many cases, especially in portions of the ponderosa pine region, the brush is so dense as to preclude regeneration.

It is a poor forage for wildlife. Deer frequently bed in the thickets and may crop the foliage during all seasons. In eastern Oregon, abundant snowbrush indicates enough soil moisture to support Douglas-fir. Hitchcock and Cronquist (1973) recognize 2 varieties.

Rhamnus **L.**

buckthorn

Habit: Trees or shrubs with bitter bark.

Leaves: Deciduous or persistent; alternate, simple, prominently penniveined; petiolate.

Flowers: Monoecious or polygamo-dioecious (perfect and unisexual flowers on the same plant), clustered.

Fruits: Round or oblong, fleshy drupes.

Buds: Naked or with imbricated scales.

KEY TO THE BUCKTHORNS

Leaves 3'' to 6'' long, deciduous.   *R. purshiana*

Leaves usually less than 3'' long, persistent.
                                             R. californica

Rhamnus californica **Esch.**

California buckthorn   **California coffeeberry**

Habit: Evergreen shrubs growing in rounded clumps, 4' to 8' tall.

Leaves: Alternate, persistent, 1-1/2'' to 2-1/2'' long, oblong-elliptical to oblong-obovate; dark green and smooth above; paler and smooth or pubescent below, pubescence on lower veins rusty in color; margins finely serrate to entire, often slightly revolute; venation arcuate-pinnate; petiole 1/8" to 1/2" long, round, and rusty-pubescent.

Flowers: Small, greenish, few in a cluster.

Fruit: Round drupe, about 1/4" in diameter, reddish-black to black; usually contains two seeds.

Twigs: Slender and round, initially with a brownish pubescence, later becoming dark reddish-brown and smooth, eventually grayish-brown.

Buds: Naked, about 1/8" long, brown in color.

Habitat & Range: Usually found on dry, shallow, stony soils in the sun; from southwestern Oregon south to southern California.

Remarks: A common component of the chaparral in California. Twigs and bark have a bitter taste. Provides some cover for deer, and birds eat the fruit. It is a secondary host for the rust of velvet grass.

Rhamnus purshiana **DC.**

cascara buckthorn   **chittam**

Habit: A tree up to 50' tall and 10" to 20" in diameter, or sometimes an erect shrub up to 15 feet high.

Leaves: Alternate, deciduous, 2" to 6" long, oblong to oblong-elliptical; dark glossy green above, paler and glabrous below, often with a brownish pubescence along the veins; margins entire, wavy or serrate; prominently penniveined; petiole 1/2" to 1" long, often pubescent; thin to somewhat leathery in texture.

Flowers: Small, green-white, borne in loose clusters, axillary.

Fruit: Round drupe, 1/4" to 1/2" in diameter, black on the outside with a yellowish, sweetish pulp.

Twigs: New twigs slender to moderately stout, reddish-brown and pubescent, later becoming dark reddish-brown and smooth. Larger branches gray to grayish-brown.

Buds: Naked, about 1/2" long, rusty tomentose; usually 2 or 3 distinct segments exposed.

Bark: Thin, grayish-brown to gray-reddish brown, smooth or somewhat scaly (on large trees), often mottled with chalky-white patches. Inner bark yellow. Tastes bitter.

Habitat & Range: Grows on moist, well-drained soils. Ranges from western and southern British Columbia south on the west side of the Cascade Mountains to lower California, east through northern Idaho to western Montana.

Uses: The cured bark, one of the most important natural drugs produced in North America, is used as a laxative.

Remarks: Tolerant. Vigorous stump sprouter. Associated with Dougals-fir, grand fir, western hemlock, western redcedar, red and white alders, bigleaf maple, vine maple, and several other species.

The species seldom reaches a very large size because of the stripping of the bark. Barked trees should be felled so that the stumps will sprout.

Birds and some of the smaller mammals will eat the fruit. Deer may crop the foliage and twigs.

CELASTRACEAE

Pachistima **Raf.**

Habit: Low, evergreen shrubs, with 4-angled twigs.

Leaves: Persistent, opposite, simple; margins serrate; petiole short.

Flowers: Perfect; very small; borne in the leaf axils.

Fruit: Capsule.

Pachistima myrsinites **(Pursh) Raf.**

Oregon boxwood   **mountain lover**

Habit: Low, evergreen shrub.

Leaves: 1/2" to 1-1/2" long, ovate to ovate-elliptical or obovate; thick and leathery; dark green, glabrous and glossy above, pale below; margins finely serrate; petiole up to 1/16" long.

Fruit: 2-valved, white, ovate capsule, about 1/4" long.

Twigs: Slender, reddish-brown, ridged.

SMALL,
LEAVES
EVERGREEN

Habitat & Range: Found on dry to moist, sandy or gravelly loams, under open timber; ranges from the Cascade and Sierra-Nevada Mountains, east to the Rocky Mountains.

Oregon boxwood

Remarks: Cropped by deer and elk. Planted as an ornamental. Resembles huckleberry except for the opposite leaves.

ELEAGNACEAE   Oleaster Family

Shepherdia Nutt.

buffaloberry

Habit: Shrubs or occasionally small trees.

Leaves: Deciduous, opposite, simple (smaller leaves may be found at the base of the main leaf); margins entire; petiole short.

Flowers: Dioecious, borne in axillary spikes.

Fruit: Berry.

Remarks: This genus contains but 3 species; all are found in western North America.

KEY TO THE BUFFALOBERRIES

Branches with thorns; leaves finely pubescent.
S. argentea

Branches lack thorns; rust dots on underside of the leaf.   *S. canadensis*

Shepherdia argentea (Pursh) Nutt.

silver buffaloberry

Habit: Erect, spiny shrubs or small trees, 4' to 20' in height.

Leaves: Opposite; 3/4'' to 1-3/4'' long, 1/4'' to 3/4'' wide, oblong-lanceolate to oblong-elliptical, thick; light green and with a silvery pubescence on both surfaces; apex round; base cuneate to acute; margins entire; petiole about 1/8'' long, pubescent.

Fruit: Subglobose or ovoid berry, about 1/4'' in diameter, red in color.

Twigs: Opposite branching. New twigs slightly ribbed, grayish-white and pubescent, becoming light grayish-brown; lateral branchlets short, rigid, spinose or thorny.

Bark: Gray and shaggy.

Habitat & Range: Found on dry or moist, well-drained sites in the sun or shade; from east side of the Cascade and Sierra-Nevada Mountains, eastward through the Great Plains States to the Great Lakes.

Remarks: The fruit is edible, and it is eaten by grouse and squirrels.

Shepherdia canadensis (L.) Nels.

russet buffaloberry

Habit: A sprawling or erect shrub up to 6' in height.

Leaves: Opposite; 1'' to 2-1/2'' long, ovate to oblong-ovate; dark green above, pale green or silvery, and with rusty dots on the underside; margins entire; apex acute; base round; petiole up to 1/4'' long.

Fruit: Red or orange-red, almost translucent berry, about 1/4'' in diameter.

Twigs: Opposite branching; younger twigs with a rusty scurfiness.

Habitat & Range: Found on dry or moist, well-drained sites, in the sun or shade. Ranges from Alaska south to east central Oregon, the northern Intermountain Region, eastward to New England, and the Appalachian Mountains.

TWIGS, LEAF UNDERSIDES RUSTY-DOTTED

russet buffaloberry

Remarks: An Indian name for this species is soopolallie (soap-berry—crushed berries yield a soapy froth).

Browsed by white-tailed deer. Fruits are eaten by birds.

ARALIACEAE   Ginseng Family

Oplopanax Mig.

Habit: Shrubs with stout stems which are frequently armed with numerous prickles.

Leaves: Deciduous, alternate, simple, palmately lobed and veined; petiole long, armed with irritating prickles.

Flowers: Small, greenish-white, borne in terminal clusters (panicles).

Fruit: Drupe.

Stems: Usually armed with slender, stiff, irritating cortical-spines or prickles.

Oplopanax horridum (Sm.) Mig.

devilsclub

Habit: A semi-prostrate to erect shrub, 3' to 12' tall with large, long-stemmed, palmately lobed and veined leaves clustered near the ends of the stems. The leaves and stems are armed with irritating prickles.

Leaves: 5'' to 15'' in diameter, orbicular; margins palmately 5 to 9 lobed, lobe margins coarsely serrate to doubly serrate; bright green above and paler below, scattered prickles along the veins on both surfaces; petiole, long, thick, armed with prickles.

Flowers: Small, white, borne in a conical-shaped terminal cluster 3'' to 6'' long.

Fruit: Bright red, flattened, ellipsoidal drupes.

Stems: 1/2" or larger in diameter, tan, abundantly armed with slender, irritating, stiff prickles.

Habitat & Range: Occurs on moist, well-drained sites in the sun or shade, usually along streams or around seeps. Ranges from Alaska to northern California.

CORNACEAE   Dogwood Family

Cornus **L.**

dogwood

Habit: Tolerant, moist-site shrubs or small trees.

Leaves: Deciduous, opposite (rarely alternate), simple; margins entire (sometimes wavy); venation arcuate.

Flowers: Perfect; borne in compact heads surrounded by 4 to 6 large creamy-white or pink bracts, or small and borne in clusters.

Fruit: Drupe.

Twigs: Branching opposite (rarely alternate). Twigs slender; buds with valvate scales or naked.

KEY TO NORTHWESTERN DOGWOODS

1. Buds naked, slender, dark brown; twigs red.   2

1. Foliage buds with green, valvate scales; twigs green to gray; flower buds in naked, hemispherical head.   *C. nuttallii*

    2. Stone of fruit smooth.   *C. stolonifera*

    2. Stone a fruit grooved.
                  C. stolonifera var. *occidentalis*

Cornus nuttallii Aud.

Pacific dogwood

Habit: Trees up to 60' tall (usually much smaller), with a round to oblong-conical crown.

Leaves: 3" to 5" long, 1-1/2" to 3" wide, broadly elliptical to ovate or slightly obovate; bright green above, paler below; margins entire to wavy; apex acute; base acute to wedge-shaped; petiole 1/2" to 1" long, grooved and occasionally minutely pubescent. Leaves red in autumn. Arcuate veins.

Flowers: Very small, greenish-white, borne in a dense compact head and surrounded by 4 to 6 broad, creamy white bracts.

Fruit: Flattened, reddish drupes borne in a tight cluster.

Twigs: New twigs slender, light green, initially minutely pubescent, later becoming dark reddish-purple and somewhat glaucous, eventually grayish-brown and smooth.

Buds: About 1/3" long, slender ovate, with valvate scales. At the tip of the twig there are two sets of paired buds, one set immediately above the lower set and just below the terminal bud. As a consequence there is a whorled branch arrangement at the end of the past season's growth.

Pacific dogwood

Bark: Thin, dull gray, smooth; on larger trunks the bark sometimes breaks into thin rectangular scales or blocks.

Habitat & Range: Found on moist, well-drained loamy or gravelly soils in the sun or shade. From southwestern British Columbia southward on the west side of the Cascade and Sierra Nevada Mountains to southern California; local in central western Idaho.

Remarks: Very tolerant. Often an understory tree. While the species may flower under heavy shade, it will seldom produce fruit. Associated with bigleaf maple, red and white alders, vine maple, willow, Douglas-fir, western hemlock and redwood.

Cornus stolonifera var. *occidentalis* **(T. & G.) Hitchc.**

western dogwood　　　　　　　　　　**creek dogwood**

Habit: A large, loosely branched shrub with reddish stems, up to 15' high.

Leaves: 2" to 6" long, ovate to ovate-elliptical; dark green and lustrous above, the surface appears somewhat wrinkled because of the sunken veins; pale green and slightly pubescent below; margins entire to wavy; apex and base both acute; petiole up to 1" long. The leaves turn red in the fall. Arcuate veins.

Flowers: Small, white, borne in flat-topped, terminal clusters.

Fruit: White or ivory, berry-like drupe, about 1/4" in diameter.

Twigs: Slender; red to purplish-red in the sun, or green when shaded. Often red above, green below.

western dogwood

Buds: Naked, slender, dark brown; terminal bud about 5/16" long, lateral buds shorter and tightly appressed to the twig.

Habitat & Range: Found on moist, well-drained sites, along streams; from Alaska to southern California on the Westside.

Remarks: Foliage and new twigs browsed by deer. Little (1979) calls this *Cornus occidentalis.*

Cornus stolonifera Michx.

red-osier dogwood

A shrub very similar to *C. stolonifera* var. *occidentalis,* from which it differs chiefly in the presence of runners (stolons). Spans the US and Canada; in Oregon, chiefly found east of the Cascades.

GARRYACEAE   Silk-Tassel Family

Garrya Dougl.

silktassel   **garrya**

Habit: Evergreen shrubs or small trees.

Leaves: Persistent, opposite, simple, and leathery; petiolate.

Flowers: Dioecious; borne in pendent, narrow cylindrical clusters, often densely tomentose.

Fruit: Fleshy (later becoming dry), berrylike drupe.

KEY TO THE SILKTASSELS

Leaf margins curled or revolute; leaf densely pubescent below.   *G. elliptica*

Leaf margins not revolute; leaf smooth.   *G. fremontii*

Garrya elliptica **Dougl.**

wavyleaf silktassel   coast silktassel

Habit: Erect, bushy shrub up to 8' high, or a small tree 20' to 30' tall.

Leaves: 1-1/2" to 2-1/2" long, elliptical to oval, opposite; leathery; dark green and nearly smooth above, paler and tomentose below; margins entire to slightly wavy, prominent and irregularly revolute; petiole stout, up to 1/2" long, flattened and grooved above.

Flowers: Borne on a long, slender, pendent spike, paired, both the stalk and the flower are covered with a dense purplish-gray pubescence.

Fruit: Round drupe, up to 1/4" in diameter, covered with a purplish-gray pubescence.

Twigs: Moderately stout, round, at first yellowish-brown and pubescent, later smooth and reddish-brown, gray-reddish-brown, or dark reddish-brown. Opposite branching.

Habitat & Range: Occurs on dry, gravelly or sandy loams; in the Coast Range and near the ocean from southwestern Oregon to central California.

Garrya fremontii **Torr.**

Fremont silktassel

Habit: An erect, evergreen shrub up to 10' in height.

Leaves: Opposite. 1" to 2-1/2" long, 1/2" to 1-1/2" wide, elliptical, oval-elliptical or broadly obovate, leathery; light yellow-green and smooth above, paler and smooth or sparingly pubescent below; margins entire; petiole up to 1/2" long, light yellow-brown and glabrous.

Twigs: Slender to moderately stout, glabrous, light yellow-green, becoming reddish-green on the surface exposed to the sun; older branches gray-olive drab. Opposite branching.

Flowers: Paired flowers are borne on a long, pendent spike, with a dense purplish-gray pubescence.

Fruit: Dark blue to bluish-black drupe, about 1/4'' in diameter, glabrous or slightly pubescent.

Habitat & Range: Found on dry sites in the sun, in the Cascades from central Washington south through the Sierra Nevada Mountains to southern California.

Remarks: A desirable shrub for ornamental planting.

ERICACEAE   Heath Family

Arbutus L.

madrone

Habit: Evergreen trees or shrubs with thick, leathery leaves; bark exfoliates.

Leaves: Persistent, alternate, simple; margins entire or serrate; petiolate.

Flowers: Perfect; bell-shaped or urn-shaped; white to pink.

Fruit: Pebbly-skinned, berrylike drupe.

Bark: Exfoliates.

Arbutus menziesii Pursh

Pacific madrone

Habit: Evergreen tree 60' to 100' tall and 2' to 6' in diameter; with sloughing bark.

Leaves: 3" to 5" long, 1-1/2" to 3" wide, leathery, oblong to oblong elliptical; light green when they first unfold, becoming dark green and glabrous above, pale silvery-green and glabrous below; margins entire to very finely serrate; rounded or pointed at the apex; base round or broadly obtuse; petiole grooved, up to 1" long, light green and smooth. Dead leaves fall in spring or early summer. Leaves stay green 13 or 14 months.

Flowers: White, urn-shaped, about 1/4" long, borne in clusters up to 6" long.

Fruit: Orange-red, pebbly-skinned, berrylike drupe, about 1/3" in diameter.

Twigs: Stout, light green and smooth, becoming orange-brown and eventually reddish-brown.

Buds: Ovoid-oblong, about 1/3" long, with imbricated scales which are green, later becoming light brown, lateral buds smaller.

Bark: On young stems thin, red or orange-brown, separates into scales or short strips and exfoliates, on large trees, reddish-brown, scaly and flaking.

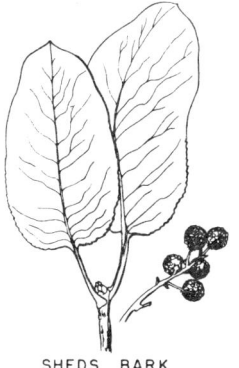

SHEDS BARK

Habitat & Range: Somewhat tolerant. Found on dry to moist and well-drained loamy, gravelly or rocky soils. From southwestern British Columbia south on the west side of the Cascade and Sierra Nevada Mountains to southern California. Elevational range: from sea level to 4,700 feet.

Pacific madrone

Uses: Little used at present. It has been used to manufacture charcoal, and can be used for furniture and
panelling and substituted for dogwood in shuttles.
The wood is difficult to dry because of its great tendency to warp and check.

Arctostaphylos Adams

manzanita

Habit: Evergreen shrubs or small trees with stiff,
crooked branches and dark reddish-brown, exfoliating bark.

Leaves: Persistent, alternate, simple, held parallel to the
twig in some species.

Flowers: Perfect; 1/4", urn-shaped, white to pinkish.

Fruit: Mealy, berrylike drupe. Looks like a tiny apple.

Bark: Smooth, reddish-brown, exfoliating in most species.

Remarks: Essentially a North American genus. The
manzanitas are the principal component of the brush
fields in California. "Manzanita" is Spanish for "little
apple".

KEY TO THE MANZANITAS

1. Prostrate or creeping shrub.   *A. uva-ursi*

1. Erect shrubs.   2

   2. Leaves and twigs hairy.   *A. columbiana*

   2. Leaves and twigs smooth.   3

3. Leaves bright green.   *A. patula*

3. Leaves whitish-green. Flower clusters sticky.
                                                  A. viscida

Arctostaphylos columbiana Piper

hairy manzanita

Habit: Bushy shrub or small tree, with stiff and somewhat gnarled branches—seldom exceeds 12' in height and 5" in diameter.

EVERGREEN
HAIRY

Leaves: Leathery, 1" to 2" long, elliptical, round or oval; dull green or pale blue-green, hairy on both surfaces; margins entire, both apex and base rounded to broadly acute; petiole stout, hairy, up to 3/4" long.

hairy manzanita

Flowers: Pinkish-white, urn-shaped, borne in small terminal clusters.

Fruit: Smooth, red, berrylike drupe, 1/4" to 1/3" in diameter, subglobose.

Twigs: Young twigs grayish and hairy, becoming smooth and dark reddish-brown.

Bark: Smooth, brown on young stems, becoming dark reddish-brown; exfoliates revealing lighter underbark.

Habitat & Range: Occurs in the sun on well-drained sandy, gravelly or rocky soils; on the west side of the Cascade and Sierra Nevada Mountains from Washington to California. This species is common along the coast as well as in the Coast Range and the Cascade Mountains.

Remarks: In the southern part of its range, it intergrades with hoary manzanita.

Arctostaphylos patula Greene

green manzanita

Habit: Evergreen shrub up to 6' in height.

Leaves: 1" to 2" long, ovate to elliptical; light green and glossy on both surfaces, or at times with a very sparse, minute pubescence; margins entire; apex and base both rounded; petiole up to 3/4" long.

Flowers: Pinkish-white, urn-shaped, borne few to a cluster.

Fruit: Round, chestnut-brown to black, berrylike drupe, about 1/4" in diameter.

Habitat & Range: Found on dry, well-drained sites in the sun, in the mountains and on the eastern slopes and foothills from Mt. Hood south to southern California, Nevada, and Arizona. Elevational range: 2,500 to 6,000 feet.

MAHOGANY BARK

green manzanita

Remarks: A good browse for mule deer.

Arctostaphylos uva-ursi (L.) Spreng.

kinnikinnick   **bearberry**

Habit: An evergreen, mat-forming shrub.

Leaves: 1/2" to 1" long, obovate, spatulate or ovate, leathery; dark green and smooth above, paler beneath; margins entire; apex round or broadly obtuse, sometimes notched; base wedge-shaped; petiole about 1/8" long. The leaves are often held in a vertical plane parallel to the twig by a twist in the petiole.

Flowers: White or pink, urn-shaped, about 1/4'' long.

Fruit: Round, red, berrylike drupe about 1/4'' in diameter; contains 1 to 5 slightly ridged seeds.

Stems: Slender, mostly trailing, frequently root at the nodes; erect branches 4'' to 8'' high.

REDDISH
FRUIT

Bark: Mostly smooth or sparsely pubescent, dark reddish-brown; on older stems the bark breaks into narrow strips and exfoliates.

Habitat & Range: Grows on a variety of soils, but does best in the sun or partial shade. Found in western and northern North America, northern Europe and northern Asia. Elevational range: in the United States from sea level to 8,000 feet.

kinnikinnick

Remarks: The mat-forming character makes the species useful for erosion control. It is the only manzanita occurring outside of North and Central America.

Arctostaphylos viscida **Parry.**

whiteleaf manzanita

Habit: Rigidly branched, evergreen shrub up to 9' tall.

Leaves: Whitish-green, stiff, leathery, persistent, 1'' to 1-1/2'' long, entire, broadly ovate to elliptical.

Flowers: White or pinkish, urn-shaped, in many-flowered, sticky-stemmed cluster.

Fruit: Light-red, flatly-globose, 1/6'' to 1/3''.

Bark: Smooth, reddish-brown.

Habitat & Range: Dry slopes and foothills in northern California, and Siskiyou Mountains in southwestern Oregon.

Gaultheria **L.**

gaultheria   **wintergreen**

Habit: Evergreen shrubs or subshrubs.

Leaves: Persistent, alternate, simple, leathery; with a short petiole.

Flowers: Perfect; urn-shaped, white to pink, borne in clusters.

Fruit: Berry.

Gaultheria shallon **Pursh**

salal

Habit: An evergreen shrub, 1' to 2-1/2' (occasionally up to 10') in height.

Leaves: 1-1/2'' to 3-1/2'' long ovate to oval, leathery; dark glossy green and smooth above, paler beneath; margins very finely serrate; base rounded or subcordate; venation arcuate; petiole up to 1/4'' long, pubescent.

Flowers: Pinkish, urn-shaped, about 1/4'' long, borne in loose clusters.

Fruit: Bluish-black, globose or ovoid berry, about 5/16'' in diameter.

salal

Twigs: New twigs green to red and pubescent, later becoming grayish-brown and smooth. Twigs conspicuously zigzag.

Habitat & Range: Found on dry to moist, well-drained sites in the sun or shade; on the west side of the Cascade and Sierra Nevada Mountains from British Columbia to southern California.

Remarks: Salal is perhaps the most common shrub in the understory of the Pacific Northwest forests. It reaches its largest size in the fog belt along the Pacific Coast where dense, extensive patches of the species often hinder the establishment of reproduction on cut-over and burned-over areas. Related species are found in northeastern Oregon and the Rocky Mountains.

Many birds and mammals feed upon the fruit. Deer and elk will browse the species occasionally.

The foliage is often used for greenery by the florists.

Ledum L.

Labrador-tea

Habit: Evergreen shrubs.

Leaves: Persistent, alternate, simple; margins entire and often revolute; pubescent, scurfy or glandular on the underside; petiole short.

Flowers: Perfect; borne in terminal clusters.

Fruit: 5-celled capsule.

Remarks: This genus has but 3 species; all are found in North America, including one which is also found in northern Europe and Asia.

Ledum glandulosum Nutt.

Pacific Labrador-tea

Habit: Evergreen shrub up to 3' tall.

Leaves: 3/4" to 2-1/4" long, elliptical to lanceolate-elliptical, leathery; dark yellow-green and glabrous above, paler and with a white scurfiness on the underside; margins entire and revolute; apex and base both acute; midrib heavy, pale yellow-green; petiole less than 1/4" long. The leaves appear to be concentrated on the upper ends of the stems.

Flowers: White to pinkish-white, small, borne in a flat-topped or saucerlike cluster.

Fruit: Subglobose capsule, oblong-ovoid, about 1/6" long.

Stems: Slender, reddish-brown and pubescent, later smooth and gray-reddish brown; bud scales imbricated, light brown or light reddish-brown, pubescent.

Habitat & Range: Found on moist sites in the sun, usually around bogs and swamps; mostly along the coastal area from Washington to southern Oregon.

Remarks: Slightly toxic to livestock. Hitchcock and Cronquist (1973) recognize 2 varieties.

Menziesia Smith

menziesia

Habit: Shrubs.

Leaves: Deciduous, alternate, simple, margins entire or finely serrate; petiolate.

Flowers: Perfect; borne few to a cluster.

Fruit: A small, 4- to 5-parted capsule.

Menziesia ferruginea **Hook.**

rusty menziesia

Habit: A straggly, erect shrub up to 12 feet high.

Leaves: Alternate, 1-1/4" to 2-1/2" long, thin, elliptical, obovate or obovate-elliptical; dark green to
bluish-green and sparsely pubescent above, paler and
sparsely and minutely pubescent below; apex and
base both acute; nipple-like tip of midrib protrudes
beyond blade; margins finely serrate; petiole up to
1/4" long, pubescent.

Flowers: Small, yellowish to greenish-purple, 2 to 8 in a
terminal cluster.

Fruit: Ovoid, 4-celled capsule, about 1/4" long, glabrous.

Twigs: New twigs slender, yellowish-tan and minutely
pubescent, later becoming gray-reddish brown and
breaking up into very fine shreds.

Habitat & Range: Found on moist, well-drained soils
along the coast and in the mountains; from Alaska to
northern California, eastward to western Montana.

Remarks: Poisonous to livestock if eaten in large quanti-
ties. Hitchcock and Cronquist (1973) recognize 2
varieties.

Rhododendron **L.**

rhododendron

Habit: Mostly shrubs, occasionally small trees. Tolerant; prefer moist, acid soils.

Leaves: Deciduous or persistent, alternate (commonly
concentrated at the ends of the stems or branches),
simple, thin or leathery; margins entire; petiolate.

Flowers: Perfect; funnel-shaped or bell-shaped; fairly large, clustered.

Fruit: A semi-woody, 5-parted capsule.

Remarks: This is a very large genus containing an abundance of species, varieties and hybrids. Many are cultivated for ornamental purposes.

KEY TO RHODODENDRON SPECIES

Leaves persistent, leathery.   *R. macrophyllum*

Leaves deciduous.   *R. occidentale*

Rhododendron macrophyllum D. Don.

Pacific rhododendron

Habit: A straggly, evergreen shrub up to 12' high.

Leaves: Persistent, 3" to 6" long, elliptical to oblong, thick and leathery; dark green and smooth above, paler or sometimes rusty below; margins entire, often slightly revolute; apex and base both acute; petiole about 1" long, stout.

Flowers: Rose-purple, occasionally white, 1" to 1-1/2" long, borne in a round, loose cluster.

Fruit: Capsule about 1/2" long, brown in color.

Stems: Moderately stout, green and glabrous, eventually gray-reddish-brown. Buds large, pointed, with many imbricate scales.

Habitat & Range: Occurs on moist, well-drained sites in the sun or shade; found on the west side of the Cascade and Sierra Nevada Mountains from British Columbia to central California. Elevational range: sea level to 4,500 feet.

Remarks: Considered poisonous to sheep.

Rhododendron occidentale (T. & G.) Gray

western azalea

Habit: Loosely branched shrub up to 10' high.

Leaves: Deciduous, 1-1/2" to 4" long, 1/2" to 1" wide, elliptical, obovate or obovate-elliptical; green and smooth above; paler and smooth, or with sparse fine hairs beneath; margins entire; apex acute; base acute or wedge-shaped; petiole usually less than 1/2" long.

Flowers: White or tinged with pink, 1-1/4" to 1-3/4" long, borne in loose clusters.

Fruit: Capsule about 1/2" long, brown, and pubescent.

Twigs: New twigs slender, light reddish-brown or orange-brown, finely pubescent, becoming grayish-brown and smooth; buds ovoid, about 1/4" long, with red, imbricated scales.

Habitat & Range: Found on moist, well-drained soils in the sun or shade; from southwestern Oregon south to southern California.

Remarks: Poisonous to livestock. Planted as an ornamental.

Vaccinium L.

huckleberry

Habit: Deciduous or evergreen shrubs.

Leaves: Deciduous or persistent, alternate, simple; margins entire or serrate; petiole short.

Flowers: Perfect; white or pinkish-white and urn-shaped, small and clustered.

Fruit: Round berry.

Twigs: New twigs ridged, smooth, or pubescent.

Remarks: Found on moist, acid soils in both the Old and New World. Besides huckleberries, this genus includes blueberries and cranberries.

KEY TO THE HUCKLEBERRIES

1. Leaves persistent, glossy, stiff, and leathery.
   V. ovatum

1. Leaves deciduous.   2

    2. Leaf margins entire.   *V. parvifolium*

    2. Leaf margins serrate.   *V. membranaceum*

Vaccinium membranaceum Dougl.

big whortleberry

Habit: Erect shrub 1' to 5' high.

Leaves: Deciduous, 1" to 2" long, 3/8" to 3/4" wide, ovate, obovate or broadly elliptical, thin, pale green on both surfaces, smooth or occasionally sparsely and minutely pubescent; margins serrate, rarely entire; apex and base both acute; petiole about 1/8" long.

THIN LEAVES, RIBBED TWIGS

big whortleberry

Flowers: Greenish-white, about 1/8" long.

Fruit: Black, round berry, about 1/4" in diameter, sweet and edible.

Twigs: Slender, green, and smooth, ridged or angled.

Habitat & Range: Found on dry to moist, sandy or gravelly loams, in the sun or shade; from Alaska southward to northern California, eastward to western Montana.

Remarks: Fruits are gathered and sold commercially. Numerous birds and mammals feed on the fruit. Foliage and younger twigs are important game browse in some localities.

Vaccinium ovatum Pursh

evergreen huckleberry

Habit: Evergreen shrub, with small, glossy, waxy leaves; up to 10' tall.

Leaves: Evergreen, 1/2" to 1-1/2" long, ovate to oblong-ovate, thick and leathery; appear to be slightly folded along the midrib; dark glossy green, waxy and smooth above, paler and smooth below; apex acute; base round; margins finely serrate; petiole up to 1/8" long, stout and pubescent.

Flowers: Pink, about 1/4" long, borne in small cluster.

Fruit: Round, bluish-black berry, up to 1/4" in diameter.

Twigs: Slender, reddish-brown and pubescent, later becoming smooth; ridged on younger growth; buds about 1/8" long, with red imbricated scales.

WAXY LEAF

Habitat & Range: Grows on moist, well-drained

evergreen huckleberry

sandy and gravelly loams, in the sun or shade; on the west side of the Cascade and Sierra Nevada Mountains from British Columbia to central California. Most abundant along the coast; locally in the Cascade Mountains in Oregon.

Remarks: Very tolerant. Found along the coast associated with salal, hairy manzanita, rhododendron, Pacific waxmyrtle, lodgepole pine, Sitka spruce, western hemlock and Douglas-fir.

Fruits are eaten by birds, mammals, and man. Foliage is used for greenery by the florists. Planted as an ornamental. An important browse for elk and deer.

Vaccinium parvifolium Smith

red huckleberry

Habit: A shrub 4′ to 10′ tall (occasionally up to 18′), closely and finely branched, with green, ribbed twigs.

Leaves: Deciduous, alternate, simple, elliptical to oblong-elliptical, 1/2″ to 1-1/2″ long (generally under 1″); dark green above and paler beneath; margins smooth; petiole about 1/8″ long.

Flowers: Small, greenish-white or sometimes reddish.

Fruit: A bright red berry with a translucent skin; about 1/4″ in diameter.

Twigs: Younger twigs green (occasionally red) and angular or ribbed.

Buds: Small, bud scales red.

Habitat & Range: Grows on all types of sites

RIDGED STEMS

RED BERRIES
VERY THIN LEAVES

red huckleberry

from Alaska to California (on the Westside in the Pacific Coast states). Elevation: sea level to 5,000 feet.

Remarks: Berries are palatable to birds, mammals, and humans. Used by florists as greenery; planted as an ornamental. Browsed by elk and deer. Occasionally the buds, leaves, and stems may all be red.

OLEACEAE   Olive Family

Fraxinus L.

ash

Habit: Large streambank trees with opposite branching and narrow-ridged bark.

Leaves: Deciduous, opposite, pinnately compound; margins entire or serrate.

Flowers: Dioecious or polygamous (both bisexual and unisexual flowers on the same tree), small, borne in dense clusters. Staminate (male) flower clusters extend only 1/2″ out from the twig. Pistillate (female) flower clusters are large, open panicles.

Fruit: Single samara with an elongated, straight, terminal wing.

Twigs: Stout, flattened at the nodes; bud scales brown to black and densely tomentose. Leaf scars contain nearly continuous line of bundle scars.

Fraxinus latifolia Benth.

Oregon ash

Habit: Tree 40′ to 80′ tall and 1′ to 2-1/2′ in diameter with a narrow or broad crown.

Leaves: 5" to 14" long, with 5 to 9 broad ovate, obovate, or elliptical leaflets; densely tomentose on both surfaces when they first appear, at maturity light green and smooth or slightly tomentose above, paler and pubescent or tomentose below; terminal leaflet petiolate, lateral leaflets sessile or with a short petiole; rachis pubescent or tomentose; leaflet margins entire to serrate.

Flowers: Dioecious, small, white, borne in dense clusters.

Fruit: Single samara with a terminal wing; 1-1/2" to 2" long.

Twigs: Stout, round (except for the nodes which are flattened); olive drab and tomentose when new, eventually becoming gray-reddish brown.

Oregon ash

Bark: Up to 1-1/2" thick, dark gray or gray brown, furrowed and with flat ridges which may be slightly scaly.

Habitat & Range: Found on moist, sandy, rocky or gravelly soils, usually near stream, on bottomlands or around the margins of swampy areas; on the west side of the Cascade and Sierra Nevada Mountains from southwestern British Columbia southward to central California. Elevational range: sea level to 2,500 feet.

Uses: Shovel, rake, and hoe handles, furniture, baseball bats, oars, baskets, boxes and crates, boat building and cooperage.

Remarks: Intermediate tolerance. Usually associated with bigleaf maple, red alder, black cottonwood, willows, Oregon white oak, Douglas-fir and grand fir. Fairly important browse for deer and elk.

CAPRIFOLIACEAE   Honeysuckle Family

Lonicera L.

honeysuckle

Habit: Shrubs or climbing vines.

Leaves: Deciduous to semi-persistent, opposite, with short petioles (in some instances the leaves may be united at their bases); margins entire, rarely lobed.

Flowers: Perfect; tubular or trumpet-shaped, borne in terminal clusters.

Fruit: Berry.

Lonicera involucrata Banks

black twinberry

Habit: Erect shrub up to 10' tall.

Leaves: Deciduous, opposite, 1-1/2" to 5" long, ovate, obovate, ovate-elliptical, or oval; dark green and smooth above; paler and pubescent, becoming smooth beneath; margins entire; apex acute; base acute to obtuse; petiole up to 1/2" long, veins arcuate.

Flowers: Paired, about 1/2" long, pubescent, surrounded at the bases by 2 bracts which eventually become reddish in color; flowers and bracts pubescent.

Fruit: Paired, dark purple or black berries, about 1/4" in diameter.

Twigs: Slender, light yellow-green, ribbed and pubescent when new, becoming light reddish-brown and smooth. Terminal bud narrow-conical, about 1/4" long; lateral buds smaller and appressed to the twig. Opposite branching.

Bark: Yellowish-gray or grayish-brown and shreddy.

black twinberry

Habitat & Range: Found on moist sites, usually near streams or bodies of water; from Alaska southward to the Southwest, eastward to the Lake States and Quebec.

Remarks: In the West associated with willows and alders. The best known, most common and widely distributed of the western honeysuckles. In the Rocky Mountains elk are reported to browse the new growth. Hitchcock and Cronquist (1973) recognize 2 varieties.

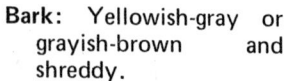

Sambucus **L.**

elder

Habit: Moist-site shrubs or trees with soft, pinnately compound leaves; pith large and spongy.

Leaves: Deciduous, opposite, pinnately compound; margins serrate; leaflet base inequilateral.

Flowers: Perfect; small, white, borne in terminal clusters.

Fruit: Small berries in dense clusters. May be toxic to humans if eaten uncooked.

Stems: Stout, with a large, spongy pith. Opposite.

KEY TO THE ELDERS

1. Flower and fruit clusters flat or saucer-shaped.
   S. cerulea

1. Flower and fruit clusters round, dome-shaped, or
   pyramidal. *S. racemosa*

Sambucus racemosa L.

red elder **red elderberry**

Habit: A shrub or small tree from 8' to 20' tall.

Leaves: Opposite, 6" to 12" long, pinnately compound
with 5 to 7 lanceolate to oblong-ovate leaflets; apex
sharply pointed; margins serrate; upper surface dark
green, smooth or slightly hairy, paler beneath.

Flowers: White, borne in dome-shaped clusters. Flowers
earlier than *S. cerulea*.

Fruit: Red (occasionally yellow, black, even white)
berries 1/16" to 1/8" in diameter. Fruit cluster
dome-shaped. May be toxic to humans unless cooked.

Stems: Soft, with large white pith. Opposite branching.
New sprouts may grow to 12' in height in one year.

Bark: Smooth, light or dark gray.

Habitat & Range: Occurs on moist, well-drained sites in
the sun; most common on the west side of the Cascade and Sierra Nevada Mountains from British
Columbia south to California.

Remarks: Red elder is normally a loosely branched
shrub which coppices freely, forming clumps. The
fruit is commonly eaten by birds, and small mammals
but may be toxic to humans unless cooked (reports
vary).

Hitchcock and Cronquist (1973) recognize 4 varieties. Little (1979) calls this *S. callicarpa.*

Sambucus cerulea Raf.

blue elder   **blue elderberry**

Habit: Usually a large shrub or small tree from 10′ to 20′ or more tall.

Leaves: Opposite, 6″ to 12″ long, pinnately compound with 5 to 9 leaflets similar in appearance to those of *S. racemosa.*

Flowers: White in terminal flat-topped clusters.

Fruit: Dark blue-black berries covered with a white powdery bloom. Fruit clusters flat-topped.

FLOWER CLUSTERS
FLATTENED

blue elder

Stems: Long, slender, often with glaucous bloom; pith large, soft, light tan or orange-brown. Opposite branching. New coppice growth makes very rapid initial growth (as much as 15′ the first season).

Bark: Rough, grayish-brown to black.

Habitat & Range: Found on moist, well-drained sites in the sun; from British Columbia south to California, east through Idaho, Utah, and Nevada. Elevations: sea level to 9,000 feet.

Remarks: The fruit is eaten by birds and mammals; but may be toxic to humans until cooked. The latter use it for jellies and wines.

Symphoricarpos L

snowberry   waxberry

Habit: Tolerant, small shrubs with fine, slender
branches.

Leaves: Deciduous, opposite, simple, small; margins
entire to lobed; petiolate.

Flowers: Perfect; white to pink, bell-, tubular-, or
funnel-shaped.

Fruit: Round to ovoid, white, waxy berry.

Twigs: Very fine or slender, pith hollow; opposite
branching.

Remarks: This genus contains about 15 species, all of
which are found in North America.

KEY TO THE SNOWBERRIES

Leaves usually smooth above; corolla densely hairy
inside.   *S. albus*

Leaves usually pubescent on both surfaces; corolla
with few hairs.   *S. mollis*

Symphoricarpos albus (L.) Blake

snowberry

Habit: Finely branched shrub up to 6' tall.

Leaves: Opposite; 3/4" to 2-1/2" long, average about
1"; ovate, elliptical or oval; green and usually glabrous
above, paler and glabrous or slightly pubescent below;
margins entire (frequently lobed on new vigorous
shoots); petiole up to 1/4" long.

Flowers: Pinkish-white, bell-shaped, up to 1/4'' long, clustered.

Fruit: Round, white, waxy berry, up to 1/2'' in diameter, usually 3 to 5 in a cluster, persist well into the winter.

Twigs: Smooth, light yellow-brown, very slender or fine; pith orange-brown, hollow; opposite branching.

WHITE BERRIES HANG ON

snowberry

Bark: Tan-gray to grayish-brown; tends to split lengthwise on the older stems.

Habitat & Range: Occurs on dry to moist, well-drained sites in the sun or under partial shade; nearly continent-wide in distribution (Mexico excepted).

Remarks: An important browse for game animals. Many birds feed on the fruits. Planted as an ornamental. Hitchcock and Cronquist (1973) recognize 2 varieties.

Symphoricarpos mollis **Nutt.**

spreading snowberry　　　　　**creeping snowberry**

Habit: A low shrub usually not more than 18'' high, or almost prostrate. Very similar to *S. albus.*

Leaves: 1/2'' to 1'' long, occasionally longer, elliptical, oval or nearly round, green above, paler below, pubescent on both surfaces (occasionally almost glabrous above); margins entire; petiole up to 1/4'' long.

Flowers: Small, pinkish, bell-shaped, often pubescent, clustered.

Fruit: Round, white, waxy berry, up to 1/4″ in diameter.

Twigs: Very slender or fine, younger twigs usually pubescent; pith hollow; opposite branching.

Habitat & Range: Found on dry to moist sites, usually in the sun; from British Columbia to southern California, including the coast ranges.

Remarks: Many birds feed on the fruit.

Viburnum L.

viburnum

Habit: Shrubs or small trees.

Leaves: Deciduous (or persistent), opposite, simple; margins entire, serrated or lobed; petiolate.

Flowers: Perfect; white or pink, clustered.

Fruit: 1- to 3-seeded drupe.

Buds: Naked or with imbricated scales.

KEY TO THE VIBURNUMS

Leaf margins dentate, not lobed; leaves glossy above.   *V. ellipticum*

Leaf margins serrate, usually 3-lobed near the tip; not glossy.   *V. edule*

Viburnum ellipticum Hook.

western wayfaring tree   **western viburnum**

Habit: Loosely branched shrub up to 12′ in height.

Leaves: Opposite, 1-1/2" to 3" long, oval to almost round, dark glossy green and glabrous above, pale green below and finely pubescent; margins coarsely dentate, except for the lower portion which is entire or slightly wavy; apex round; base round to sub-cordate; venation arcuate; petiole 3/4" to 1" long, grooved above, reddish, pubescent.

Flowers: White, about 1/3" across, borne in terminal clusters.

Fruit: Purplish-black to black, subglobose drupe, about 1/3" in diameter.

Twigs: Gray-reddish brown, becoming grayish-brown; bud scales reddish-brown, imbricated, hairy along the margins. Opposite branching.

Habitat & Range: Found on dry to moist, well-drained sites in the sun or shade; from Washington to California on the west side of the Cascade and Sierra Nevada Mountains.

Viburnum edule (Michx.) Raf.

moosewood viburnum   **highbush-cranberry**

Habit: Opposite-branched shrub up to 10' high.

Leaves: Opposite, thin, 1-1/2" to 3" long, round to oval, broadly elliptical or obovate; green and glabrous above, paler and finely pubescent below; margins serrate, 3-lobed above the middle; apex of lobes acute; base round to cordate; petiole up to 1" long.

Flowers: White, borne in terminal clusters.

Fruit: Red drupe, globose to oblong, about 1/2" in diameter.

Habitat & Range: Found in moist, cool areas, in the sun or shade; from Alaska to Oregon, eastward to New England.

Linnaea L.

NOTE: There is only one species of *Linnaea;* so no generic description will be given.

Linnaea borealis L.

twin-flower

Habit: Very low, trailing evergreen shrub with small, round lustrous, opposite leaves. Very tolerant. Usually less than 8" tall. The trailing stems take root at the nodes.

Leaves: Opposite, persistent, round, 1/2" in diameter or slightly larger; lustrous green on upper surface; paler and prominently netted-veined on underside; margins sparsely and irregularly toothed.

Flowers: Pink, tubular-bell-shaped, in pairs at tips of slender flower stalks.

Fruit: Paired, ovoid, yellowish capsules.

Habitat & Range: Prefers cool, moist, densely-forested sites with deep soil. In northeastern Oregon, twin-flower is an indicator of a site moist enough for grand fir (*Abies grandis*). Widely distributed on good sites in northern United States, Canada, northern Europe, and northern Asia.

COMPOSITAE   Sunflower Family

Artemisia L.

sagebrush

Habit: Dry-site herbs, shrubs, or occasionally small trees, with aromatic foliage.

Leaves: Deciduous or persistent, alternate, simple but often clustered; aromatic; bitter to the taste; often pubescent.

Flowers: Small, inconspicuous, white to yellow, borne in terminal spikes or clusters.

Fruit: Achene.

Remarks: Several species are important browse plants on the western ranges.

Artemisia tridentata **Nutt.**

big sagebrush

Habit: Small to large silvery-green shrub up to 15′ high, occasionally arborescent and much branched; bark shreddy.

Leaves: Persistent, alternate, simple, but usually several leaves at a node, sessile, 1/2″ to 1-1/2″ long, long-cuneate; silvery-green on both surfaces; margins smooth, except for the apex which is 3-lobed; base wedge-shaped. Strong-scented.

Flowers: Small, yellowish, tubular, borne on long spikes.

Fruit: Very small achene, 4- to 5-sided.

Twigs: New twigs slender, silvery-gray and pubescent, becoming grayish-brown.

Bark: Grayish-brown, splits lengthwise, shreddy.

Habitat & Range: Found on a variety of soils from the Cascades and Sierra-Nevada Mountains eastward to the Dakotas and Nebraska, from British Columbia south to the Southwest, also northern Lower California.

TANGY
ODOR

big sagebrush

Remarks: Big sagebrush is perhaps the most abundant shrub in the semi-arid portions of western United States, and certainly the most common and widely distributed sagebrush.

An important browse for game animals and sheep. It is the state flower of Nevada.

The Range Plant Handbook states *Tall, dense stands of the plant are indicative of fertile soil suitable for small grains and adapted for irrigated farming.*

Baccharis L.

Habit: Shrubs or herbaceous plants.

Leaves: Deciduous or persistent, alternate, simple, usually serrate.

Flowers: Dioecious, white or yellow in color.

Fruit: Compressed, ribbed achenes.

Remarks: This genus is indigenous to the Americas.

Baccharis pilularis DC.

kidneywort baccharis

Habit: An evergreen, mat-forming, almost prostrate shrub, or up to 12" high.

Leaves: Persistent, somewhat leathery, 1/2" to 1-1/4" long, oblanceolate to obovate, dark green or yellow-green and glabrous above, paler beneath; margins entire near the base, sparsely serrate above, revolute; apex acute to narrowly rounded; base wedge-shaped; sessile.

Flowers: Pistillate flowers whitish, staminate flowers yellowish.

Fruit: Achene about 3/8" long, ribbed.

Stems: Slender, new twigs light brown to brown, minutely pubescent, finely ribbed; later grayish-brown, ribbed and roughened by small, offset leaf scars.

Habitat & Range: On dry, well-drained sites in the sun; along the coast from northern Oregon to southern California.

Remarks: Recommended for sand-dune fixation.

Chrysothamnus **Nutt.**

rabbitbrush

Habit: Small, dry-site shrubs with grass-like leaves.

Leaves: Persistent, alternate, simple, entire; sessile.

Flowers: Perfect; yellow, borne on small heads in terminal clusters.

Fruit: Slender, achenes, round and ribbed in cross-section.

Remarks: This genus contains about 12 species; all are found in the arid or semi-arid regions of western North America. All have a latex sap.

KEY TO THE RABBITBRUSHES

Foliage gray-green; branchlets fuzzy.   *C. nauseosus*

Foliage yellow-green; branchlets glandular, occasionally slightly pubescent.   *C. viscidiflorus*

Chrysothamnus nauseosus (Pall.) Britt.

gray rabbitbrush

Habit: Erect shrubs with slender stems, up to 7' tall.

Leaves: Persistent, 1/2" to 2-1/2" long, about 1/16" wide, linear; grayish-green and tomentose or pubescent on both surfaces; sessile.

Flowers: Small heads of yellow flowers, borne in terminal, saucerlike clusters.

Fruit: Achene, 5-ribbed, smooth or minutely hairy.

Twigs: New twigs slender, round, grayish to light yellow in color.

Habitat & Range: Grown on dry sandy or gravelly soils in the sun; found in the Intermountain Region between the Cascade and Sierra Nevada Mountains and the Rocky Mountains.

GRASS-LIKE LEAVES

gray rabbitbrush

Remarks: Has several subspecies and varieties. Commonly associated with big sagebrush. In the northern parts of its range, it is an important winter browse for elk, moose, and mule deer. Sap contains latex.

Chrysothamnus viscidiflorus (Hook.) Nutt.

green rabbitbrush

Habit: Shrub, 1' to 8' in height.

Leaves: Persistent; 1/2" to 2" long, linear or linear-oblanceolate, nearly grasslike; light green, smooth or slightly pubescent; sticky; sessile.

Flowers: Small yellow flowers borne in a round terminal cluster. Bloom in late summer.

Fruit: Achene; 5-ribbed, more or less pubescent.

Twigs: Slender, new twigs green, glandular and minutely hairy, later becoming ashy-gray or grayish-yellow, roughed by raised, offset leaf scars.

Habitat & Range: Found on dry sites in the sun; in the Intermountain Region from Washington and Montana south to the Southwest.

Remarks: This is a polymorphic species with many subspecies and varieties. Stems have a latex sap, the highest content is found in the forms growing on alkali soils.

REFERENCES

1. Gilkey, Helen M. and Patricia L. Packard - WINTER TWIGS - NORTHWESTERN OREGON AND WESTERN WASHINGTON. Oregon State University Press, Corvallis, Oregon. 1962.

2. Gilkey, Helen M. and LaRea J. Dennis - HANDBOOK OF NORTHWESTERN PLANTS. Oregon State University Book Stores, Inc., Corvallis, Oregon. 1967.

3. Hayes, Doris W. and George A. Garrison - KEY TO IMPORTANT WOODY PLANTS OF EASTERN OREGON AND WASHINGTON. Ag. Handbook No. 148, U.S.D.A. 1960.

4. Hitchcock, C. Leo and Arthur Cronquist - FLORA OF THE PACIFIC NORTHWEST. University of Washington Press. 1973.

5. Little, E.L., Jr. - ATLAS OF UNITED STATES TREES. Vol. 1. U.S.D.A. Misc. Pub. #1146. 1976.

6. Little, E.L., Jr. - ATLAS OF UNITED STATES TREES. Vol. 3. U.S.D.A. Misc. Pub. #1314. 1976.

7. Little, E.L., Jr. - CHECKLIST OF UNITED STATES TREES. U.S.D.A. Ag. Handbook #541, Government Printing Office. 1979.

8. Peck, Morton E. - A MANUAL OF HIGHER PLANTS IN OREGON. Binfords and Mort, Portland. 1961.

9. Sudworth, G.B. - FOREST TREES OF THE PACIFIC SLOPE. U.S.D.A. Forest Service Bulletin (unnumbered), Government Printing Office. 1908.

10. U.S. Forest Service - RANGE PLANT HANDBOOK. U.S.D.A. Government Printing Office. 1937.

RECOMMENDED READING

1. Benson, Lyman - PLANT CLASSIFICATION. D.C. Heath and Co., Boston. 1959.

2. Brockman, C.F. - TREES OF NORTH AMERICA. Golden Press, New York. 1968.

3. Dallimore, W. and A.B. Jackson - HANDBOOK OF CONIFERAE. Edward Arnold & Co., London. 1948.

4. Fowels, Harry A. et al. - SILVICS OF FOREST TREES OF THE UNITED STATES. Ag. Handbook No. 271. Forest Service, U.S.D.A. 1965.

5. Harlow, Harrar and White - TEXTBOOK OF DENDROLOGY. 6th ed. McGraw-Hill, New York. 1978.

6. Johnson, Hugh - THE INTERNATIONAL BOOK OF TREES. Simon and Schuster, Inc. New York. 1973.

7. Lyons, C.P. - TREES, SHRUBS AND FLOWERS KNOWN IN WASHINGTON. J.M. Dent & Sons (Canada) Ltd., Vancouver, B.C. 1956.

8. McMinn, H. and E. Maino - AN ILLUSTRATED MANUAL OF PACIFIC COAST TREES. University of California Press, Berkeley. 1959.

9. Pacific Northwest Section, American Society of Range Management, in Cooperation with U.S. Forest Service - NORTHWEST RANGE PLANT MANUAL: SHRUBS (Part 3 of 3).

10. Preston, R.J. - NORTH AMERICAN TREES. Iowa State College Press, Ames. 3rd ed. 1976.

SUMMARY OF SIMILAR AND DISTINCTIVE
FEATURES OF NATIVE BROADLEAF SPECIES

LEAVES

Opposite Leaves
Acer spp.
Ceanothus cuneatus
Ceanothus prostratus
Cornus spp.
Fraxinus latifolia
Garrya spp.
Lonicera involucrata
Pachystima myrsinites
Philadelphus spp.
Sambucus spp.
Shepherdia spp.
Symphoricarpos spp.
Viburnum spp.

Compound Leaves
Cytisus scoparius
Fraxinus latifolia
Berberis spp.
Rhus spp.
Robinia pseudoacacia
Rosa spp.
Rubus spp. (not R. parviflorus)
Sambucus spp.
Sorbus spp.

Persistent Leaves
Arbutus menziesii
Arctostaphylos spp.
Artemisia tridentata
Baccharis pilularis
Berberis spp.
Castanopsis chrysophylla
Ceanothus spp. (not
    C. sanguineus)
Cercocarpus spp.
Chrysothamnus spp.
Garrya spp.
Gaultheria shallon
Ledum glandulosum
Lithocarpus densiflorus

Persistent Leaves (Continued)
Myrica californica
Pachystima myrsinites
Purshia tridentata
Quercus chrysolepis
Rhododendron macrophyllum
Rubus discolor
Rubus laciniatus
Rubus ursinus
Umbellularia californica
Vaccinium ovatum

**Genera with Both Simple and
    Compound Leaves**
Cytisus   Rubus

**Genera with Both Persistent
    and Deciduous Leaves**
Artemisia   Quercus
Baccharis   Rhamnus
Ceanothus   Rhododendron
Cercocarpus   Rubus
Myrica   Vaccinium

**Palmately Lobed and Veined
    Leaves**
Acer spp.
Oplopanax horridum
Physocarpus spp.
Ribes sanguineum
Rubus parviflorus

**Leaves Prominently
    Penniveined**
Alnus spp.
Amelanchier spp.
Betula spp.
Cercocarpus betuloides
Lithocarpus densiflorus
Rhamnus purshiana

Revolute Leaf Margins
Alnus rubra
Castanopsis chrysophylla
Ceanothus thyrsiflorus
Cercocarpus ledifolius
Garrya elliptica
Ledum glandulosum
Lithocarpus densiflorus
Purshia tridentata
Rhododendron macrophyllum

Glands on Leaf Margins or Petiole
Alnus rhombifolia
Philadelphus lewisii
Prunus spp.

Aromatic Leaves
Artemisia tridentata
Ceanothus velutinus
Myrica californica
Rosa eglanteria
Umbellularia californica

FLOWERS

Dioecious Species
Fraxinus latifolia
Garrya spp.
Oemleria cerasiformis
Populus spp.
Salix spp.
Shepherdia spp.

Monoecious Species
Alnus spp.
Betula spp.
Castanopsis spp.
Corylus spp.
Lithocarpus densiflorus
Myrica californica
Quercus spp.

Flowers Borne in Aments
Alnus spp.
Betula spp.
Castanopsis chrysophylla
Corylus cornuta var. californica
Lithocarpus densiflorus
Myrica spp.
Populus spp.
Quercus spp.
Salix spp.

FRUITS

Achenes
Artemisia tridentata
Baccharis pilularis
Cercocarpus spp.
Chrysothamnus spp.
Purshia tridentata
Rosa spp. (borne in a fleshy hip)

Samaras
Acer spp.
Fraxinus latifolia

Berries
Gaultheria shallon
Lonicera involucrata
Berberis spp.
Ribes sanguineum
Sambucus spp.
Shepherdia spp.
Symphoricarpos spp.
Vaccinium spp.

Capsule
Ceanothus spp.
Ledum glandulosum
Menziesia ferruginea
Pachystima myrsinites
Philadelphus spp.
Populus spp.
Rhododendron spp.
Salix spp.

Legume
Cytisus scoparius
Robinia pseudoacacia
Ulex europaeus

Follicle
Holodiscus spp.
Physocarpus spp.
Spiraea spp.

Nuts or Nutlets
Alnus spp.
Betula spp.
Castanopsis chrysophylla
Corylus cornuta var. californica
Lithocarpus densiflorus
Quercus spp.

Drupes or Druplets
Arbutus menziesii
Arctostaphylos spp.
Celtis reticulata
Cornus spp.
Garrya spp.
Myrica spp.
Oplopanax horridum
Oemleria cerasiformis
Prunus spp.
Rhamnus spp.
Rhus spp.
Rubus spp.
Umbellularia californica
Viburnum spp.

Pome (Apple)
Amelanchier spp.
Crataegus spp.
Pyrus spp.
Sorbus spp.

Compound Fruits
Cornus nuttallii--multiple of
  drupelets
Rubus spp.--aggregate of
  drupelets

TWIGS AND BRANCHES

Armed with Spines or Thorns or Prickles
Crataegus spp.
Ribes spp.
Robinia pseudoacacia
Rosa spp.
Rubus spp. (not
  R. parviflorus)
Ulex europaeus

Lammas Shoots
Rhamnus purshiana
Alnus rubra

New Twigs Distinctly Ribbed or Angular
Alnus rubra
Castanopsis chrysophylla
Ceanothus thyrsiflorus
Cytisus scoparius
Holodiscus discolor
Lonicera involucrata
Populus trichocarpa
Quercus garryana
Quercus kelloggii
Robinia pseudoacacia
Ulex europaeus
Vaccinium spp.

EXFOLIATING BARK

Arbutus menziesii

Arctostaphylos spp.

Physocarpus spp.

Rubus spectabilis

PITH

Triangular—Alnus spp. Betula spp. occasionally remotely triangular

Stellate—Castanopsis chrysophylla   Populus spp.
            Lithocarpus densiflorus   Quercus spp.

Chambered—Oemleria cerasiformis. Celtis reticulata chambered at the nodes only.

Hollow—Symphoricarpos spp.

Large and Spongy—Sambucus spp.

BUDS

Naked—Cornus stolonifera var. occidentalis
        Rhamnus spp.
        Rhus spp.
        Robinia pseudoacacia (also submerged)

Stalked—most Alnus spp.; Ceanothus sanguineus

Clustered at Tip of Twig—Quercus spp. Also less frequently in Castanopsis chrysophylla, Lithocarpus densiflorus and Prunus species.

ROOTS

Nitrogen-Fixing Bacteria on the Roots
Alnus spp.   Robinia pseudoacacia
Cytisus scoparius   Ulex europaeus
Ceanothus spp.

WINTER TWIG KEY

By George W. York[1]

1a - Leaf scars alternate.

  2a - Buds naked.

    3a - Leaf scars broadly V- to U-shaped. . . . . .
. . . . *Rhus diversiloba*

    3b - Leaf scars rounded; bundle scars 3 . . . . .
. . . . *Rhamnus purshiana*

  2b - Buds scaly.

    4a - At least the flower buds short-stalked, or
if buds not stalked, the pith continuous,
very minute, dense, and 3-angled in cross
section.

      5a - Pith round in cross section. . . . .
. . . . *Ceanothus sanguineus*

      5b - Pith 3-armed or 3-angled in cross section.

        6a - Fruiting structures woody, cone-
like, persisting through the winter.
Buds conspicuously stalked . . . *Alnus*

        6b - Fruiting structures not woody or
conelike and not persisting through
the winter; buds not conspicuously
stalked; buds usually on spur shoots
after first season . . . . *Betula*

    4b - Buds not stalked; or if stalked, pith
coarsely spongy on drying, and neither
very minute nor 3-angled in cross section.

      7a - Lowermost (or the single) bud scale
directly over the leaf scar.

        8a - Bud scale single, saclike. . . . . . . *Salix*

---

[1] Adapted from a key in **WINTER TWIGS-NORTHWESTERN OREGON AND WESTERN WASHINGTON** by Helen M. Gilkey and Patricia L. Packard. 1962. Oregon State University Press, Corvallis. This key printed here by permission of these authors and the OSU Press.

8b - Bud scales several, not saclike. . . . . . . *Populus*

7b - Lowermost bud scale lateral over leaf scar.

9a - Buds globose, sessile, often appearing 2-ranked on horizontal branches. Scales papery, brown. . *Corylus cornuta* var. *californica*

9b - Buds not as above and never appearing 2-ranked.

10a - Bundle scars more than 7.

11a - Shrub; densely spiny; bundle scars in a single series . . . . *Oplopanax horridum*

11b - Tree or rarely shrubby; bundle scars obscure, grouped. 12

12a - Bud scales smooth (glabrate) . . . .
. . . . *Quercus kelloggii*

12b - Bud scales downy . . *Quercus garryana*

10b - Bundle scars 7 or fewer, sometimes indistinguishable or shriveled leaf scars.

13a - Bundle scar 1.

14a - Leaf scars not sharply triangular, slightly raised . . . . *Vaccinium*

14b - Leaf scars sharply triangular, not raised . . . . *Spiraea*

13b - Bundle scars more than 1.

15a - Pith solid or chambered, not coarsely spongy.

16a - Bundle scars 5.

17a - Leaf scars ragged; bark shreddy . . . . *Physocarpus*

17b - Leaf scars not ragged; bark not shreddy . . . . *Sorbus*

16b - Bundle scars 3, though sometimes obscure.

18a - Leaf scars shriveled, on greatly raised, persistent petiole bases. . . . . *Rubus*

18b - Leaf scars clean and visible; petiole bases deciduous, but sometimes leaving a slight ridge.

19a - Leaf scars linear; bundle scars sometimes obscure . . . . *Rosa*

19b - Leaf scars broader than linear; bundle scars obvious.

20a - Bud scales densely pubescent. *Holodiscus*

20b - Bud scales smooth.

21a - Lowermost bud scales distinctly swollen, fleshy at the base.

22a - Bud scales not keeled; buds globose or nearly so . . . . *Crataegus*

22b - Bud scales, at least the lower, keeled; buds not globose.

23a - Stipule scars present, linear, sometimes inconspicuous . . . . *Prunus*

24a - Buds ovoid, 1/4" to 3/8" long; twigs of moderate thickness . . *Prunus virginiana*

24b - Buds narrow, conical, averaging 3/16" long; twigs slender . . . . *Prunus emarginata*

23b - Stipule scars absent . . . . *Pyrus fusca*

21b - Lowermost scales not swollen at base.

25a - Pith chambered. . . . . *Oemleria cerasiformis*

25b - Pith continuous. . . . . *Amelanchier*

15b - Pith with spongelike cavities, at least when dry . . . . *Ribes*

1b - Leaf scars opposite.

26a - Leaf scars covered by a membrane.

27a - Bundle scars 3. . . . . *Philadelphus*

27b - Bundle scars many in a U line . . . . . *Fraxinus*

26b - Leaf scars not covered by a membrane.

28a - Scars raised on persistent petiole bases and obscured by corky growths . . *Symphoricarpos*

28b - Scars not greatly raised; petiole bases not persistent, though a ridge sometimes remains.

29a - Pair of leaf scars meeting around stem in an ascending curve or point . . . . *Acer*

30a - Exposed bud scales 2 . . . . *Acer glabrum*

30b - Exposed bud scales more than 2.

31a - Terminal buds usually absent; buds subtended by long white hairs . . . . *Acer circinatum*

31b - Terminal buds usually present; buds not subtended by hairs . . . .
. . . . *Acer macrophyllum*

29b - Pair of leaf scars meeting around stem in a straight line, or a descending curve or point, or rarely not meeting.

32a - Bundle scars generally 5 or 7 (rarely 3); twigs stout, with large leaf scars . .
. . . . *Sambucus*

33a - Buds diverging; upper margin of leaf scar notched . . *Sambucus cerulea*

33b - Buds appressed; upper margin of leaf scar entire . . *Sambucus racemosa*

32b - Bundle scars 3; twigs slender; leaf scars narrow.

34a - Twigs dull reddish, with predominantly gray overcoating; buds valvate. . . . . *Cornus nuttallii*

34b - Twigs deep lustrous red; buds naked . . . .
. . *Cornus stolonifera* var. *occidentalis*

PALEODENDROLOGY OF OREGON

by R.F. Keniston

The first forests of Oregon must have developed about 400 million years ago during the Devonian geologic period. At that time, there were no vertebrate animals on land or in the air. In fact, the only vertebrate animals were some of the primitive fishes found chiefly in the rivers and in parts of the ocean near the mouths of rivers. These primitive fishes included Ostracoderms, which were fish with heads and parts of the body covered with bony plates. Later in that period, came sharks and other types of fishes. At that time on the land were the first plants with stems. They must have occurred chiefly in marshy places, near rivers or lakes; and they were apparently fernlike plants and giant horse-tails. But there were also a few Cordaites, which were early conifers, although quite fernlike in appearance.

Following the Devonian Period, from 345 to 280 million years ago, was the great Carboniferous Period—the Great Coal Age, consisting of the Mississippian and Pennsylvanian geologic periods. During this time, much of the land of the earth was occupied by humid, tropical forests of large tree-ferns and so-called seed-ferns which were really primitive gymnosperms. But trees with annual rings, such as we now know, did not become common until much later—during the Mesozoic Era. During this Carboniferous Period, however, amphibians and insects became common. The Paleozoic Era, or the great period of ancient life, ended with the folding of the Appalachian Mountains about 230 million years ago. At that time most of Oregon was covered by warm seas; volcanoes were active in the northeastern part of the state and later in southwestern Oregon.

During the succeeding great geologic era, called the Mesozoic or Middle-Life Era, which lasted from 230 million to 70 million years ago, the first forests with trees resembling any we know today became common. Early conifers, like those in the Petrified Forests of Arizona, lived during this great age of reptiles.

During the first 50 million years of the Mesozoic Era, during a period called the Triassic, most of Oregon was still covered by warm seas, the climate was humid, and the land plants were apparently still trees with fernlike leaves or giant ferns or giant horse-tails. Evidences of plants living at that time were much limited because only plants living near margins of lakes or in swamps have much chance of leaving fossil remains. Plant fossils usually consist of imprints of leaves or sometimes fruits, or petrified wood. If a plant fell into water and was covered by mud, or by volcanic ash, there was some chance of its remains being preserved in the fossil record.

During the Jurassic period in Oregon, which was from 180 to 135 million years ago, ferns, cycads, ginkgos, and conifers were common. These were of kinds no longer living, but were abundantly represented in the fossil record and bore sufficient resemblance to living forms so that their relationship could be recognized. The ginkgos were like modern ginkgos, except the leaves were divided by deep sinuses.

It was during the following period, the Cretaceous Period, which lasted from 135 to 70 million years ago, that the fossil record in Oregon became rather complete. During Cretaceous time, an inland sea evidently covered much or most of the state—including much of the John Day and Crooked River basins of Central Oregon—and extended northward into Washington and British Columbia and southward into California. The land plants must have lived on large islands or peninsulas extending into this body of water. During the Cretaceous Period a great variety of flowering plants, grasses, and deciduous trees spread over the earth. Trees like oak, maple, and elm became common, but not, apparently, in Oregon.

The end of the Cretaceous Period came with the Rocky Mountain Uplift at which time the oceans or seas withdrew from the continents and a large mountain chain was formed throughout the length of the western hemisphere. The dinosaurs died out completely and the mammals became the dominant land animals. The rise of the mammals coincided with the rise of the flowering plants—that is angiosperms. It was on these plants that the mammals depended for food.

During the Eocene Epoch in Oregon which lasted from 63 million until about 36 million years ago, the forests of this state apparently still consisted of lush tropical vegetation. In Oregon, the Eocene rocks are largely of volcanic origin; and it was the volcanic ash falling in lakes and swamps which helped preserve most of the plant fossils that we find today. The vegetation of the dry, upland sites is scarcely known because conditions for formation of fossils did not exist. In Oregon, the Eocene plant fossils do not include any of our common present-day trees, such as alder, oak, and maple. There were, however, in what is now the John Day Basin, members of the laurel family and other families which are now largely restricted to the warmer parts of the earth. These included in Oregon the palm, fig, cinnamon, avacado, and nectandra. Most of these plants are now found only in the subtropical portions of eastern U.S. and in the Caribbean and Central American regions. Cycads and giant ferns were also common. In portions of Oregon during the Eocene were found in some abundance leaves of a yewlike tree which we now know to have been *Metasequoia*. Also there were a few oaks as evidenced particularly by occasional acorns or acorn cups. Some of the principal Eocene fossils in Oregon are found near Clarno, in central Oregon. Clarno is on the John Day River between Antelope and Fossil. The plants of the Eocene period in western Oregon were quite similar to those in central Oregon indicating that there was then no major climatic or physiographic barrier between these two parts of the state.

During the Oligocene Epoch in Oregon which lasted from 36 to 25 million years ago, there was still a general uniformity in vegetation in Oregon from the Pacific Ocean to the eastern interior of the state. The Willamette Valley and parts of the Coast Range were then covered by warm seas. In the land areas a warm-temperature type of vegetation covered both eastern and western Oregon. By Oligocene time, the trees were more nearly like those that we know today. Some of the trees common in Central Oregon were dawn-redwood *(Metasequoia)*, maple, oaks, elm, basswood, sycamore, ginkgo, and Katsura. Katsura is an Asiatic tree which is now found only in China and Japan. Also there were birch, beech, chestnut and *Liquidambar*. With the exception of the dawn-redwood and the Katsura, both of which are confined to Asia, all the other trees still live in the U.S., although many of them only in the eastern U.S.

During the Oligocene, land mammals were also becoming of somewhat more familiar types. Instead of the giant, ungainly mammals, many of which died out at the end of the Eocene, we now had such semi-familiar mammals as three-toed horses, camels, giant pigs, sabertoothed cats, Oreodonts, and tapirs. The more tropical kinds of plants had disappeared. In their place were typically temperate trees, many of which have relatives still living in the U.S., but not necessarily now in Oregon. Temperate forests had developed in high latitudes in North America and in Eurasia during the previous Eocene Epoch, notably in Alaska and Greenland. The climate of Oregon evidently had become drier and warmer so that much of this vegetation had migrated from Alaska or Greenland southward.

During the vast time required for the migration of this temperate Arcto-Tertiary flora from Alaska southward, several species which had started out from Alaska failed to survive. Other species were added to this forest along the way so that when it arrived in Oregon, it was somewhat different from the forest which had existed in Alaska previously. This forest which existed in Oregon during Oligocene time much more closely resembles the modern forest of eastern U.S. or of eastern Asia than it does the present forest of Oregon. There was also some resemblance to the present forests of western Oregon because parts of the Oligocene forest have survived in western Oregon where the climate is relatively humid as compared to the dry climate found now in central Oregon.

There have been many fossil findings representing the Oligocene Epoch and the following Miocene Epoch, which lasted from 25 to 13 million years ago. One of the reasons for the abundance of plant fossils of the Oligocene and Miocene in Oregon is the great volcanic activity. The volcanic ash falling on the plants and plant remains in margins of lakes and in swamps helped preserve them; then following these ash deposits, great flows of basalt were poured out of the volcanoes at that time, and these layers of basalt helped preserve the underlying layers of softer material from erosion.

The fossil record of western Oregon is less well known than that of eastern Oregon largely because of the forest cover that hides the rock outcrops so that not so many fossils have been discovered. But during the Oligocene many of the same species were found in western Oregon as in eastern. These included basswood, elm, avocado, catalpa, lancewood, and palm. Many of these latter species now occur only in the warm-temperate and tropical regions of North America. In Oligocene time, along the western parts of Oregon, occurred the first clearly defined representation of the genus *Sequoia* rather than the *Metasequoia*.

During the Miocene Period most of the trees in Oregon had leaves which resembled those of living species; so the vegetation would have had something of a familiar look to a modern man. There were many similarities between the forests of the Oligocene and Miocene Epochs. By Miocene time in what is now the valley of the East Fork of the John Day River near Dayville, Oregon, were found leafy twigs of a swamp cypress, a species of *Taxodium,* which genus is now found only in southeastern U.S. There was also a black oak, *Quercus pseudolyrata,* which remotely resembled *Quercus borealis* and various other modern red oaks. There were also species of *Carya* and *Platanus,* neither of which is now represented in the modern flora of Oregon. There was another black oak, *Quercus meriamiae,* with more slender leaves, somewhat resembling those of southern red oak of eastern U.S. There was a *Metasquoia,* a ginkgo, an elm, and three species of maple, including one with pinnately compound leaves resembling those of modern box-elder. There was a poplar whose leaves closely resemble those of the modern swamp cottonwood, *Populus heterophylla;* a birch resembling paper birch; a hop hornbeam, resembling *Ostrya virginiana;* a beech resembling *Fagus grandifolia;* and a chestnut-oak similar to *Quercus michauxii;* also a species of *Leitneria.*

Also included in the Miocene flora found near Dayville were several Gymnosperms and Angiosperms which are now restricted to Asia. These included *Ginkgo, Metasequoia, Celphalotaxus, Keteleeria, Pterocarya, Zelkova, Cercidiphyllum,* and *Mathilus.* These representatives found only in the modern Asiatic floras are called the Asian element of the Miocene forests of Oregon. Twenty-four of the species, many of which have already been referred to, have their close living equivalents in eastern North America, and these are known as the East-American element. There are a few living species, only 24 in number, which have modern equivalents in western North America. These are called the Western-American element. Only nine species of this Western-American element are not also found in eastern North America or in eastern Asia.

It was during the Pliocene Epoch, which lasted from 13 million to 1 million years ago, that the rise of the Cascades and of the Coast Range had proceeded to the extent that there was formed a significant barrier between eastern and western Oregon. By that time the climate and topography of Oregon had become much as we know them today. The climate of western Oregon is now much moister than that of eastern Oregon because the moisture-bearing winds from the ocean lose much of their moisture in passing over the Coast Range and the Cascade Range. Also the drier land masses of interior Oregon tend to increase rather than diminish the moisture-carrying capacity of the air; so we now have a sharp difference in the precipitation and evaporation; and hence, the flora of western Oregon and of eastern Oregon. This difference existed both during the Pliocene and the most recent or Pleistocene Epochs, the Pleistocene Epoch being only the last one million years.

During the Pliocene there were eruptions of lava cones at the crest of the Cascade Range and extensive out-pouring of lava in south-central Oregon. Horses, rhinoceroses, camels, antelopes, bears, and mastodons lived in the John Day country. There were large areas of grasslands because of the drier climate east of the high Cascade Range and there was a warm-temperature climate west of the Cascades. The forest and forest trees had a strong resemblance to the modern forests and trees.

Fossils from The Dalles area show that during the Pliocene Epoch there were four or five kinds of oaks, an acacia with thorns, a birch, a box elder, a willow, an elm, and a sycamore. In the Warm Springs area, there was a great deal of aspen, with willow, cottonwood, cherry, and box elder. In the Dayville area in central Oregon, there was an elm, a sycamore, and a willow. These latter were common along streams in central Oregon. It was notable that during the Pliocene the leaves were of relatively small size and of thick texture as compared to those of the previous epochs. In the Alvord Creek area along the east flank of the Steens Mt. in southeastern Oregon were fir, spruce, pine, willow, poplar, cherry, and maple. These apparently lived along the borders of a small lake. It would appear that the amount of rainfall occurring in eastern Oregon must have been at least twice as much as it is today.

Near Troutdale, Oregon, (west of the Cascades) there were found Pliocene oaks, willows, elms, sweetgum, and persimmon and a *Sequoia* closely resembling *Sequoia sempervirens.* So, although the Oregon forests of the Pliocene bore considerable resemblance to the modern forests, there was still the difference that there must have been more abundant moisture in both eastern and western Oregon at that time.

Much of the woody vegetation of Oregon as we have seen is derived from the temperate vegetation of the Eocene Period in Alaska. This we have already referred to as the Arcto-Tertiary vegetation because it existed in the Arctic regions during the beginning of the Tertiary or Cenozoic Era. This Arcto-Tertiary Flora had migrated to Oregon by the Oligocene Epoch. Most of the trees now living in Oregon originated from the Arcto-Tertiary vegetation. There was, however, another significant element or source of woody vegetation in Oregon. This is the so-called Sierra-Madrean Flora which originated in Northwestern Mexico.

The Sierra-Madrean flora consists of trees and shrubs suited to a drier climate than the Arcto-Tertiary flora. In the Sierra-Madrean flora we have open, parklike woodland with small, rounded trees or xerophytic brush-lands—brushlands consisting of species adapted to dry conditions. This oak woodland prototype which was found in the Sierra Madre Occidentale in Northwestern Mexico, migrated northward during the Oligocene Epoch. During the Miocene, the Sierra-Madrean vegetation dominated the plain then occupying the area of much of California and of the Great Basin from the latitude of San Francisco and Salt Lake City southward.

In Pliocene time, the uplift of the Cascades and the Sierra-Nevada had formed a major climatic barrier. Summer rain ceased in California and became scant in Oregon and in Washington. As the mountains continued to rise, during the Pliocene and more rapidly during the Pleistocene, the Cascades and the Sierras became the dividing line between the relatively moist western forest and a dry interior forest and desert region to the eastward. This Sierra-Madrean flora, during the Pliocene invaded Oregon in several ways: A northward extension of California oak woodland is represented in southwestern Oregon in the vicinity of the Rogue River Valley. The sagebrush desert occupies much of the southeastern part of Oregon. Some species of the Juniper-Piñon woodland now occupy significant areas in Oregon, and some species related to those typical of the California Chaparral occur in drier portions of Oregon. So these Sierra-Madrean species moved into Oregon in the areas that became too dry for the Arcto-Tertiary forest species.

Some of the species of the California oak woodland which are also found in southwestern Oregon in the vicinity of Rogue River Valley include *Arctostaphylos viscida* (white manzanita), *Arctostaphylos manzanita* or *A. patula* (green manzanita); *Pinus sabiniana* (Digger pine) which apparently did occur recently in small quantity in southwestern Oregon; *Ceanothus integerrimus* (deer brush); *Rhamnus californica* (coffeeberry); *Arbutus menziesii* (madrone); *Alnus rhombifolia* (white alder); *Quercus chrysolepis* (canyon live oak); and a species of *Cercocarpus,* mountain mahogany.

The sagebrush desert of the southeastern border of Oregon includes *Artemisia tridentata* (big sagebrush); several other species of sage; and *Purshia tridentata* (antelope brush or bitterbrush). Rather widespread in eastern Oregon are *Chrysothamnus nauseosus,* and other species of rabbitbrush; also *Juniperus occidentalis* (western Juniper). These are considered by some botanists to be typical species of the *Juniper-Piñon* woodland which occupies many scattered small mountain ranges in the Great Basin and in the high plateau country of southwestern United States.

The Siskiyou Mountains of southwestern Oregon and northwestern California form part of a group of mountain chains known geologically as the Klamath Mountains. Their rocks are older and harder than those of the Coast Ranges and similar to those of the Sierra Nevada. During the Miocene Epoch the Coast Ranges were submerged, and during the Pleistocene there was a downward movement of 1,500 feet of the whole coast of northern California and southern Oregon. There were numerous other changes in sea level related to the several advances and retreats of glaciers during the Pleistocene Epoch. This succession of movements, subsidence, and uplift helps explain the fact that in the Klamath Mountains in general, and in the Siskiyous in particular, we have a number of species restricted to that area, such as *Picea brewerana* (weeping spruce); *Quercus sadleriana* (Sadler oak); and *Quercus garryana* variety *brewerii*, (Brewer oak); and various other species. These species apparently survived in the Siskiyou-Klamath area when advances of the ocean or unfavorable climate in other parts of California exterminated the species in most other localities. Most modern species of *Cupressus* in the United States seem to occur only in small, scattered, widely separated localities where the surviving *Cupressus* has developed in each case into a separate species. This is apparently true of Baker cypress *(Cupressus bakeri),* which is found in Josephine County, Oregon, and in Siskiyou and Shasta Counties in California, in the Siskiyou-Klamath mountain region.

Along the coast of California there are several areas of relict forest or woodland where trees that at one time were of one species, became isolated over considerable geologic time and in each locality developed into a separate species. This is true notably of Monterey Cypress *(Cupressus macrocarpa)* and Monterey Pine *(Pinus radiata),* which have very limited natural ranges. It is true of many other species of *Cupressus* and of closed-cone pines remotely related to *Pinus radiata.*

From the standpoint of origin and moisture and temperature limitations, plant geographers and ecologists have divided the modern forests of Oregon and the other

Pacific states into several broad groups. The first group is called the **Pacific Forest**. This occupies the lowlands of the Pacific slope from Kodiak, Alaska, south to and including the Redwood belt of extreme southwestern Oregon and northwestern California, and inland north of the Cascade Mountains across British Columbia to northwestern Montana and southward to parts of northern Idaho. This includes most of the west-side forests of Washington and Oregon and the coastal forest of northern California.

The second category is the **Sierran Sub-alpine Forest** which occupies the higher elevations in the Cascade Mountains and the Sierra-Nevada, but is represented also in the high neighboring ranges immediately to the east and west. In Washington this occurs at elevations of 3,000 to 5,500 ft.; in Oregon at about 4,000 to 7,000 ft. and in California mainly at 7,000 to about 10,000 ft.

The third category is the **Sierran Montane Forest** which occupies the eastern slopes of the Cascade Mts. and adjacent ranges from Kamloops, British Columbia, to Klamath Lake, Oregon, and the higher levels in eastern Washington, the mountains of eastern Oregon, the mountains in California at about 2,000 to 5,000 ft. elevation in the northern part of California, and 5,000 to 7,500 ft. in the southern part of the Sierras. Also it includes mountain ranges of western Nevada and the high mountains of northern Baja California.

The Wallowa Mountains of northeastern Oregon appear to be more closely related geologically to the Rocky Mountains than to the Cascade-Sierra complex. The Wallowas are granitic mountains like the Rockies and were formed from a giant subterranean intrusion of igneous rock known as the Wallowa Batholith, which is believed to be related to the Idaho Batholith which formed during the early Cretaceous Epoch. The main part of the Rocky Mountain uplift apparently occurred at the close of the Cretaceous. The Wallowa Mts. may have been formed as part of the same general uplift that formed the Rockies and the Andes.

The vegetation of the Wallowa Mountains has more in common with vegetation of the northern Rockies than it does with the vegetation of the remainder of Oregon. This Rocky Mountain relationship is most evident in the subalpine forest of the Wallowas which occurs at elevations from about 6,000 to 7,800 ft. and includes a great deal of alpine fir *(Abies lasiocarpa)* and some Engelmann spruce *(Picea engelmannii)* which are typical Rocky Mountain species. However, mountain hemlock and whitebark pine, more typical of the Pacific Forest than of the Rocky Mt. Forest, occur fairly commonly in parts of the Wallowas. Mountain hemlock *(Tsuga mertensiana)* is not particularly abundant in the Wallowa Mts.; but whitebark pine, *(Pinus albicaulis)* is rather common at altitudes above 7,000 ft., where it is associated with alpine fir and is a common timberline tree. At lower elevations in the Wallowas, the Rocky Mountain Montane Forest blends with elements of the Pacific Forest and the Sierran Montane Forest. Douglas-fir and ponderosa pine are fairly common. True firs include representations of both *Abies concolor* (white fir) and *Abies grandis* (grand fir). The most common alder is Rocky Mountain or thinleaf alder *(Alnus tenuifolia)*. In the drier areas adjacent to the Wallowas, the Rocky Mountain juniper *(Juniperus scopulorum)* is apparently more common than western juniper, *(Juniperus occidentalis)*. Some of the cottonwoods of the Wallowas appear to be intermediate between black cottonwood and narrowleaf cottonwood. Narrowleaf cottonwood *(Populus angustifolia)* is considered a Rocky Mountain species but occurs in Oregon in the Steens Mountain area. The cottonwood of the Wallowa area is classed as black cottonwood *(Populus trichocarpa)*.

REFERENCES

Baldwin, Ewart M., 1964. GEOLOGY OF OREGON. 2nd Edition. U. of O. Coop. Bookstore, Eugene. 165 pp.

Benson, Lyman, 1957. PLANT CLASSIFICATION. 688 pp. Heath. Boston.

Cain, Stanley A., 1944. FOUNDATIONS OF PLANT GEOGRAPHY. 556 pp. Harper. New York.

Chaney, Ralph W., 1933. STUDIES OF THE PLIOCENE PALEOBOTANY OF CALIFORNIA. 144 pp. Carnegie Institution of Washington. Publication No. 412.

Chaney, Ralph W., 1934. STUDIES OF THE PLEISTOCENE PALEOBOTANY OF CALIFORNIA. 192 pp. Carnegie Institution of Washington. Publication No. 415.

Chaney, Ralph W., 1948. THE ANCIENT FORESTS OF OREGON. 56 pp. Condon Lectures. U. of Oregon Press. Eugene.

Chaney, Ralph W., 1944. PLIOCENE FLORAS OF CALIFORNIA AND OREGON. 407 pp. Carnegie Institution of Washington. Publication No. 553.

Dansereau, Pierre, 1957. BIOGEOGRAPHY: AN ECOLOGICAL PERSPECTIVE. 394 pp. Ronald Press, New York.

Dunbar, Carl O., 1960. HISTORICAL GEOLOGY. 2nd Edition. 500 pp. Wiley, New York.

Kummel, Berhnard, 1961. HISTORY OF THE EARTH. 610 pp. Freeman. San Francisco & London.

Polunin, Nicholas, 1960. INTRODUCTION TO PLANT
GEOGRAPHY. 640 pp. McGraw-Hill. New York.

Wulff, E.V., 1950. AN INTRODUCTION TO HISTORI-
CAL PLANT GEOGRAPHY. 223 pp. Authorized
translation (from Russian) by Elizabeth Brissenden.
Chronica Botanica Company. Waltham. Mass.

DISTINGUISHING CHARACTERISTICS OF
FAMILIES OF SOME COMMON NORTHWEST
TREES AND SHRUBS

Aceraceae (Maple family)
Fl.:   small, clustered, polypetalous; in racemes, corymbs, panicles, or fascicles
Fr.:   double (rarely triple) samara
Wood: diffuse-porous
T. & B.: opposite branching; twigs rounded at nodes
Leaves: opposite; simple, palmately lobed (except in *A. negundo:* pinnately compound)

Anacardiaceae (Sumac family)
Fl.:   perfect or imperfect
Fr.:   a drupe, or nutlike
Leaves: deciduous or persistent, alternate or rarely opposite, pinnately compound or simple, rarely stipulate

Araliaceae (Ginseng family)
F.:   panicled or racemed umbels. Ovary inferior. Petals & stamens 5.
Fr.:   ovary 2- or more loculed. Fruit berrylike, containing nutlets.
Leaves: Alternate or whorled

Berberidaceae (Barberry family)
Fl.:   both stamens & pistils, sepals 6 or absent, petals 6 or absent, anthers opening by an uplifted valve.
Fr.:   dry or fleshy
Leaves: alternate compound (Oregon)

Betulaceae (Birch family)
Fl.:   monoecious, mostly anemophilous; both sexes in aments; staminate **preformed** (except in *Carpinus)*

Betulaceae (continued)

Fr.: (1) a nut subtended by a papery or woody involucre or (2) nutlets in a conelike cluster

Wood: diffuse-porous

T. & B.: phyllotaxy 1/2 or 1/3 (in most genera); twigs slender or medium

Leaves: prominently penniveined in herringbone pattern; margins often serrate.

Caprifoliaceae (Honeysuckle family)

Fl.: corolla regular or irregular, generally 5 lobed with equal no. of stamens

Fr.: ovary inferior, 2 to 5 lobed, fruit fleshy or dry

Leaves: opposite

Compositae (Sunflower family)

Fl.: small in close heads, subtended at base by a whorl of bracts forming an involucre. Corollas generally 5 toothed

Fr.: achene, ovary wholly inferior

Cornaceae (Dogwood family)

Fl.: usually perfect; usually small, in terminal clusters or heads

Fr.: drupe

T. & B.: branching usually opposite; twigs usually slender, upcurving (in *Cornus*)

Leaves: deciduous; opposite (rarely alternate)

Cupressaceae (Cypress or Cedar family)

Fl.: monoecious, except in *Juniperus* (which is dioecious)

Fr.: cones with decussate (or ternate) scales; conescales valvate or peltate (coaleasced in *Juniperus*)

Wood: durable; usually colored

Cupressaceae (continued)

Leaves: decussate (or ternate); decurrent, scalelike or awl-like leaves in **flat** sprays or sprays square or hexagonal in cross section; dead leaves fall in **sprays** (small twig and leaves)

Ericaceae (Heath family)

Fl.: sympetalous; perfect; often showy

Fr.: berry, capsule, or drupe

Leaves: evergreen in many genera; usually alternate, simple

Bark: in manzanita and madrone, inner layer reddish and smooth, often exposed.

Fagaceae (Beech family)

— the most valuable group of hardwood timber trees of Europe and North America Except for genus *Nothofagus,* family confined to Northern Hemisphere

Fl.: monoecious; staminate in aments, except in *Fagus* (which has round clusters); pistillate either (1) solitary or in few-flowered spikes—in *Quercus* and *Fagus,* or (2) in bisexual aments—in *Castanea, Castanopsis,* and *Lithocarpus*

Fr.: nut with scaly or spiny involucre; in many spp. fruit requires 2 growing seasons to mature.

Wood: ring-porous (or semi-ring-porous) in all U.S. genera except *Fagus,* which is diffuse-porous

T. & B.: phyllotaxy 2/5 or 1/2

Leaves: evergreen or deciduous (in the latter case, **dead** leaves tend to persist)

Grossulariaceae (Currant or Gooseberry Family)

Fl.: in racemes, small axillary clusters or solitary, perfect and regular.

Fr.: ovary 1-chambered with parietal placentation, berry.

Grossulariaceae (continued)

    Leaves: alternate, palmately veined.

Lauraceae (Laurel family)

—	noted for aromatic or medicinal properties
Fl.:	polypetalous; perfect in *Umbellularia;* dioecious in *Sassafras*
Fr.:	drupe (in 2 major U.S. genera)
Wood:	diffuse-porous in *Umbellularia;* ring-porous in *Sassafras*
Roots:	roots of *Sassafras* strongly aromatic
Leaves:	evergreen and strongly aromatic in *Umbellularia;* deciduous in *Sassafras*

Leguminosae (Pea Family)

Fl.:	polygamous or perfect in most tree genera; zygomorphic to nearly actinomorphic
Fr.:	a legume
Wood:	ring-porous; durable, colorful
Leaves:	pinnately or bi-pinnately compound, in most genera (rarely simple)
Roots:	roots have nodules containing nitrogen-fixing bacteria

Myricaceae (Sweet Gale family)

Fl.:	imperfect, both sexes in aments; species monoecious or dioecious
Fr.:	drupe
Leaves:	deciduous, alternate, simple

Oleaceae (Olive family)

Fl.:	actinomorphic; 4-merous; sympetalous (petals absent in most U.S. spp. of *Fraxinus*)
Fr.:	various; (samara in *Fraxinus*)
Wood:	in *Fraxinus,* ring-porous, resilient
T. & B.:	branching usually opposite
Leaves:	simple or compound (usually pinnately compound in *Fraxinus*); usually opposite

Pinaceae (Pine family)

Fl.: monoecious

Fr.: cone with spirally arranged, imbricate scales; bracts present (longer or shorter than cone scales)

Wood: resin-ducts always present in most genera; only occasionally in *Tsuga*

Leaves: needlelike or linear; appear (1) scattered singly around twig, or (2) two-ranked, or (3) in clusters (secondary needles of *Pinus, Larix,* and *Cedrus*)

Rhamnaceae (Buckthorn family)

Fl.: small, usually in simple or racemously or paniculately arranged umbels, regular and perfect, polygamous or dioecious

Fr.: capsule or berrylike drupe

Leaves: simple, deciduous or evergreen

Rosaceae (Rose family)

Fl.: actinomorphic, perfect, polypetalous, 5-merous

Fr.: often a drupe or pome

Leaves: simple or compound; often serrate; sometimes evergreen

Salicaceae (Willow family)

Fl.: dioecious; both sexes in aments

Fr.: capsule containing seeds tufted with silklike (or cottonlike) hairs; capsules in catkins

Wood: diffuse-porous; soft

T. & B.: phyllotaxy 2/5

Leaves: simple, deciduous

Taxaceae (Yew family)

Fl.: dioecious (rarely monoecious)

Fr.: fleshy; one-seeded, drupelike

Wood: hard (for a conifer); colorful (reddish or yellow) very durable

Taxaceae (continued)

Leaves: flat, linear, pointed; bases spirally arranged but twisted near base to form 2 ranks (usually)

Taxodiaceae (Redwood family)

Fl.: monoecious

Fr.: cone has spirally arranged peltate scales (usually woody)

Wood: very durable; usually red or brown

Leaves: spirally arranged (often twisted to form two ranks); linear or awl-like; deciduous in some genera; dead leaves fall in **sprays** (small twig and leaves)

— These trees tend to be very long-lived

SHADE TOLERANCE OF SOME COMMON
AMERICAN FOREST TREES
WESTERN CONIFERS

Very Tolerant:

Tsuga heterophylla	western hemlock
Abies lasiocarpa	subalpine fir
Thuja plicata	western redcedar
Taxus brevifolia	Pacific yew

Tolerant:

Picea sitchensis	Sitka spruce
Picea engelmannii	Engelmann spruce
Tsuga mertensiana	mountain hemlock
Abies amabilis	Pacific silver fir
Abies grandis	grand fir
Abies concolor	white fir
Sequoia sempervirens	redwood
Calocedrus decurrens	incense-cedar
Chamaecyparis lawsoniana	Port-Orford-cedar
Chamaecyparis nootkatensis	Alaska-cedar

Intermediate:

Pinus monticola	western white pine
Pinus lambertiana	sugar pine
Pinus radiata	Monterey pine
Picea pungens	blue spruce
Pseudotsuga menziesii	Douglas-fir
Abies magnifica	California red fir
Sequoiadendron giganteum	bigtree

Intolerant:

Pinus edulis	pinyon
Pinus ponderosa	ponderosa pine
Pinus jeffreyi	Jeffrey pine
Pinus contorta	lodgepole pine
Pinus attenuata	knobcone pine
Pseudotsuga macrocarpa	bigcone Douglas-fir
Abies procera	noble fir
Juniperus spp	juniper

Very Intolerant:

Larix occidentalis	western larch

WESTERN HARDWOODS

Very Tolerant:
    Acer circinatum . . . . vine maple

Tolerant:
    Lithocarpus densiflorus . . . . . tanoak
    Acer macrophyllum . . . . bigleaf maple
    Umbellularia californica . . . . . California-laurel

Intermediate:
    Castanopsis chrysophylla . . . . golden chinkapin
    Fraxinus latifolia . . . . Oregon ash
    Arbutus menziesii . . . . madrone

Intolerant:
    Alnus rubra . . . . red alder
    Quercus garryana . . . . Oregon white oak

Very Intolerant:
    Populus tremuloides . . . . quaking aspen
    Populus spp . . . . cottonwoods
    Salix spp . . . . willows

EASTERN CONIFERS

Tolerant:
    Thuja occidentalis . . . . northern white-cedar

Intermediate:
    Pinus strobus . . . . eastern white pine
    Pinus elliottii . . . . slash pine
    Taxodium distichum . . . . baldcypress

Intolerant:
    Juniperus virginiana . . . . eastern redcedar
    Pinus resinosa . . . . red pine
    Pinus echinata . . . . shortleaf pine
    Pinus taeda . . . . loblolly pine
    Pinus virginiana . . . . Virginia pine

Very Intolerant:
    Pinus banksiana . . . . jack pine
    Pinus palustris . . . . longleaf pine

EASTERN HARDWOODS

Very Tolerant:
Fagus grandifolia . . . . American beech
Ilex spp . . . . holly
Diospyros spp . . . . persimmon
Acer saccharum . . . . sugar maple
Cornus florida . . . . flowering dogwood

Tolerant:
Acer rubrum . . . . red maple
Acer saccharinum . . . . silver maple
Tilia spp . . . . basswood
Nyssa spp . . . . tupelos
Aesculus spp . . . . buckeyes

Intermediate:
Castanea dentata . . . . American chestnut
Quercus alba . . . . white oak
Quercus rubra . . . . northern red oak
Ulmus americana . . . . American elm
Celtis spp . . . . hackberry
Magnolia spp . . . . magnolias
Fraxinus americana . . . . white ash
Platanus occidentalis . . . . American sycamore

Intolerant:
Juglans nigra . . . . black walnut
Juglans cinerea . . . . butternut
Carya spp . . . . hickories
Betula papyrifera . . . . paper birch
Liriodendron tulipifera . . . . . yellow-poplar
Sassafras spp . . . . sassafras
Liquidambar styraciflua . . . . . sweetgum
Prunus serotina . . . . black cherry
Gleditsia triacanthos . . . . honeylocust
Catalpa spp . . . . catalpas

Very Intolerant:
Salix spp . . . . willows
Populus tremuloides . . . . quaking aspen
Populus spp . . . . cottonwoods
Robinia pseudoacacia . . . . . . black locust

U.S. FOREST REGIONS*

The more abundant and/or more commercially valuable trees are listed for each region or division of a region in approximate order of importance.

PACIFIC COAST FOREST TREES

Northern portion (western Washington and western Oregon)
  Douglas-fir
  western hemlock
  grand, noble, & silver firs
  western redcedar
  Sitka and Engelmann spruces
  western white pine
  Port-Orford and Alaska-cedars
  western and subalpine larches
  lodgepole pine
  mountain hemlock
  oaks, ash, maples, birches, alders, cottonwood, madrone

Southern portion (California)
  ponderosa and Jeffrey pines
  sugar pine
  coast redwood and bigtree
  white, red, and grand firs
  incense-cedar
  Douglas-fir
  lodgepole pine
  knobcone, digger, and Monterey pines**
  bigcone Douglas-fir
  Monterey and Gowen cypresses
  western and California junipers
  oaks, buckeye, laurel, alder, madrone

---

  * From Forest Trees & Forest Regions of the U.S., USDA Misc. Publ. No. 217 (1936).
 ** Monterey pine is now widely planted in the southern hemisphere.

FOREST TREES OF ALASKA

Coast forest
  western hemlock
  Sitka spruce
  western redcedar
  Alaska-cedar
  mountain hemlock
  lodgepole pine
  black cottonwood
  red and Sitka alders
  willows

Interior forest
  white and black spruces
  Alaska white and Kenai birches
  black cottonwood
  balsam poplar
  aspen
  willows
  tamarack

ROCKY MOUNTAIN FOREST TREES

Northern portion—Northern Idaho and western Montana
  lodgepole pine
  Douglas-fir
  western larch
  Engelmann spruce
  ponderosa pine
  western white pine
  western redcedar
  subalpine and grand firs
  western and mountain hemlocks
  whitebark pine
  balsam poplar

Central Montana, Wyoming, and South Dakota
  lodgepole pine
  Douglas-fir
  ponderosa pine
  Engelmann spruce
  subalpine fir

limber pine
aspen and cottonwood
Rocky Mountain juniper
white spruce

Eastern Oregon, central Idaho, and eastern Washington
ponderosa pine
Douglas-fir
lodgepole pine
western larch
Engelmann spruce
western redcedar
western hemlock
white, grand, and alpine firs
western white pine
oaks (in Oregon)
junipers (in Oregon)

Central portion (Colorado, Utah, and Nevada)
lodgepole pine
Engelmann and Colorado blue spruces
subalpine and white firs
Douglas-fir
ponderosa pine
aspens and cottonwoods
pinyon and singleleaf pinyon
Rocky Mountain juniper and Utah juniper
bristlecone and limber pines
mountain-mahogany

Southern portion (New Mexico and Arizona)
ponderosa pine
Douglas-fir
white, subalpine, and corkbark firs
Engelmann and blue spruces
pinon and Mexican piñon
one-seeded, alligator, and Rocky Mountain junipers
aspen and cottonwoods
limber, Mexican-white, and Arizona pines
oaks, walnut, sycamore, alder, boxelder
Arizona and smooth cypresses

HAWAIIAN FOREST TREES

ohia lehus (Metrosideros polymorpha)
koa (Acacia koa)
mamane (Sorphora chrysophylla)
kukui (Candlenut) (Aleurites triloba)
naio (false sandalwood) (Myoporum sandwicensi)
pua (Osmanthus sandwicensis)
a'e (Xanthoxylum kauaiense)
lama (Maba sandwicensis)
alaa (Sideroxylon auahiense)
koaia (Acacia koaia)
kopico (Straussia oncocarpa)
kolea (Suttonia spathulata)
iliahi (sandalwood) (Santalum freyconetianum)
algaraba (mesquite) (Prosopis juliflora)—native of
    S.W. U.S.

CENTRAL HARDWOOD FOREST TREES

Northern portion
white, black, northern red, scarlet, bur, chestnut, and
    chinquapin oaks
shagbark, mockernut, pignut, and bitternut hickories
white, blue, green, and red ashes
American, rock, and slippery elms
red and silver maples
beech
pitch, shortleaf, and Virginia pines
yellow-poplar (tulip poplar)
sycamore
chestnut
black walnut
cottonwood
black locust
roughleaf hackberry
black cherry
basswood
Ohio buckeye
eastern redcedar

Southern portion
  white, post, southern red, blackjack, Shumard red,
    chestnut, swamp chestnut, and pin oaks
  red (sweet) and black gums
  mockernut, pignut, southern shagbark and bigleaf
    shagbark hickories
  shortleaf and Virginia pines
  green, white, and blue ashes
  yellow-poplar (tulip poplar)
  winged, American, and red elms
  sycamore
  black walnut
  beech
  dogwood
  persimmon
  swamp and eastern cottonwoods
  willows
  eastern redcedar
  osage-orange
  holly

Texas portion
  post, southern red, and blackjack oaks
  Ashe and other junipers
  mesquite

NORTHERN FORESTS TREES (northeastern U.S.)

Northern portion
  red, black, and white spruces
  balsam fir
  white, red (Norway), jack, and pitch pines
  hemlock
  quaking aspen & bigtooth aspen
  basswoods
  black cherry
  American, rock, & slippery elms
  white and black ashes
  sugar and red maples
  beech
  northern red, white, black, and scarlet oaks
  yellow, paper, black, and gray birches

shagbark and pignut hickories
butternut
northern white-cedar
tamarack

Southern portion (Appalachian region)
white, northern red, chestnut, black, and scarlet oaks
chestnut
hemlock
white, shortleaf, pitch, and Virginia pines
black, yellow, and river birches
basswood
sugar and red maples
beech
red spruce
southern balsam fir
yellow-poplar (tulip poplar)
cucumber magnolia
black walnut and butternut
black cherry
pignut, mockernut, and red hickories
black locust
tupelo
buckeye

SOUTHERN FOREST TREES

Pinelands
longleaf, shortleaf, loblolly, and slash pines
southern red, black, post, turkey, laurel, & willow
oaks
redgum (sweetgum)
winged, American, and cedar elms
black, red, sand, and pignut hickories
eastern and southern redcedars
pond and sand pines

Hardwood bottoms and swamps
red (sweet) gum, swamp and black tupelos
water, laurel, live, overcup, Texas, and swamp
chestnut oaks
baldcypress

pecan, water, swamp, and pignut hickories
American beech
river birch
water, green, pumpkin, and white ashes
red and silver maples
cottonwood and willows
sycamore
sugarberry (southern hackberry)
honeylocust
holly
red, white, and sweet bays
southern magnolia
pond pine

TROPICAL FOREST TREES

mangrove
royal and thatch palms
Florida yew
wild fig
pigeon-plum
blolly
wild tamarind
gumbo limbo
poisonwood
inkwood
mastic ("wild olive")
Jamaica dogwood

STATE TREES

State	Common Name	Scientific Name
Alabama	southern pine	Pinus spp.
Alaska	Sitka spruce	Picea sitchensis
Arizona	palo verde	Cercidium spp.
Arkansas	pine	Pinus spp.
California	redwood	Sequoia sempervirens
	giant sequoia	Sequoiadendron giganteum
Colorado	blue spruce	Picea pungens
Connecticut	white oak	Quercus alba
Delaware	American holly	Ilex opaca var. opaca
Dist. of Columbia	scarlet oak	Quercus coccinea
Florida	cabbage palmetto	Sabal palmetto
Georgia	live oak	Quercus virginiana
Hawaii	candlenut	Aleurites moluccana
Idaho	western white pine	Pinus monticola
Illinois	oak	Quercus spp.
Indiana	yellow-poplar	Liriodendron tulipifera
Iowa	oak	Quercus spp.
Kansas	cottonwood	Populus spp.
Kentucky	yellow-poplar	Liriodendron tulipifera
Louisiana	southern magnolia	Magnolia grandiflora
Maine	eastern white pine	Pinus strobus
Maryland	white oak	Quercus alba
Massachusetts	American elm	Ulmus americana
Michigan	eastern white pine	Pinus strobus
Minnesota	red pine	Pinus resinosa
Mississippi	southern magnolia	Magnolia grandiflora
Missouri	flowering dogwood	Cornus florida
Montana	ponderosa pine	Pinus ponderosa
Nebraska	American elm	Ulmus americana
Nevada	singleleaf pinyon	Pinus monophylla
New Hampshire	paper birch	Betula papyrifera
New Jersey	northern red oak	Quercus rubra
New Mexico	pinyon	Pinus edulis
New York	sugar maple	Acer saccharum
North Carolina	flowering dogwood	Cornus florida
North Dakota	American elm	Ulmus americana

State	Common Name	Scientific Name
Ohio	Ohio buckeye	Aesculus glabra
Oklahoma	eastern redbud	Cercis canadensis
Oregon	Douglas-fir	Pseudotsuga menziesii
Pennsylvania	eastern hemlock	Tsuga canadensis
Rhode Island	red maple	Acer rubrum
South Carolina	cabbage palmetto	Sabal palmetto
South Dakota	white spruce	Picea glauca
Tennessee	yellow-poplar	Liriodendron tulipifera
Texas	pecan	Carya illinoensis
Utah	blue spruce	Picea pungens
Vermont	sugar maple	Acer saccharum
Virginia	flowering dogwood	Cornus florida
Washington	western hemlock	Tsuga heterophylla
West Virginia	sugar maple	Acer saccharum
Wisconsin	sugar maple	Acer saccharum
Wyoming	cottonwood	Populus balsamifera

INDEX